Women reading Shakespeare, 1660–1900

*This book is dedicated to Sasha's mother, Penny Roberts,
and to the memory of Ann's mother, Ada Beatrice Harris*

Women reading Shakespeare 1660–1900

An anthology of criticism

Edited by Ann Thompson and Sasha Roberts

MANCHESTER UNIVERSITY PRESS
Manchester and New York

distributed exclusively in the USA by St. Martin's Press

Copyright © Ann Thompson and Sasha Roberts, 1997

Published by Manchester University Press
Oxford Road, Manchester M13 9NR, UK
and Room 400, 175 Fifth Avenue, New York, NY10010, USA

Distributed exclusively in the USA by
St. Martin's Press, Inc., 175 Fifth Avenue, New York, NY10010, USA

British Library Cataloguing-in-Publication Data
A catalogue record for this book is available from the British Library

Library of Congress Cataloging-in-Publication Data
Women reading Shakespeare, 1660–1900: an anthology of criticism / edited
by Ann Thompson and Sasha Roberts.
    p.   cm.
Includes bibliographical references and index
  ISBN 0-7190-4703-x hardback—ISBN 0-7190-4704-8 pbk.
  1. Shakespeare, William, 1564–1616—Criticism and interpretation.
2. Shakespeare, William, 1564–1616—Characters – Women. 3. Feminism
and literature—United States. 4. Feminism and literature—Great Britain.
5. Literature and society—Great Britain. 6. Women and literature—
United States. 7. Women and literature—Great Britain. 8. Women—
England—Social conditions. 9. Women in literature. I. Thompson, Ann,
1947–. II. Roberts, Sasha. Title
PR2975.W68 1997
822.3'3—dc20   96–26247
                                                        CIP

ISBN 0-7190-4703-x *hardback*
ISBN 0-7190-4704-8 *paperback*

First published 1997

01 00 99 98 97   10 9 8 7 6 5 4 3 2 1

Typeset by Carnegie Publishing, Preston
Printed in Great Britain by Redwood Books, Trowbridge

Contents

Entries are in chronological order, prefaced by a biographical note. Extracts from more than one work by the same author are grouped together under the date of her earliest publication. Principal topics, plays and characters only are listed here for ease of reference: see index for full details.

Figures

Quick reference topics

See pp. 270–2 for individual works and pp. 273–83 for full index of subjects and characters.

Wives and husbands

Daughters and fathers

Social relations and class distinctions

Cross-dressing and boy actors

Writing for children

Acknowledgements

Our work on this book has been made possible by our regular access to the British Library (and its Inter-library Loan Service), the University of London (Senate House) Library and the Library of Roehampton Institute London. In addition we have used the specialist resources of the Birmingham Shakespeare Library, the Brotherton Library (University of Leeds), the Library of Congress, the Fawcett Library (London), the Folger Shakespeare Library, the Shakespeare Centre and the Shakespeare Institute (Stratford-upon-Avon) and the Stratford-upon-Avon Records Office. We would like to express our gratitude to Niky Rathbone at the Birmingham Shakespeare Library, Evelyn Timberlake and Sheridan Harvey at the Library of Congress, and Georgianna Ziegler at the Folger Shakespeare Library.

Ann gave a paper consisting of a preliminary survey of some of this material at the 'Elizabethan Theatre' conference in Waterloo, Ontario, Canada in July 1991; this has subsequently been published as 'Pre-Feminism or Proto-Feminism?: Early Women Readers of Shakespeare' in *Elizabethan Theatre* 14 (1996), 195–211. The audience on that occasion and later audiences in London, Sheffield and Chichester were generous with their comments and suggestions.

We are also grateful to the British Academy and to Roehampton Institute London for research grants towards travel, photocopying and typing expenses, and to Judy Cobb and Sue Lambsden for their work on the final typescript. Finally we would like to thank Anita Roy (formerly of Manchester University Press) for commissioning and encouraging the project.

Introduction

Women have been reading Shakespeare for four centuries. Many have left written records of their responses to, impressions and opinions of Shakespeare's works, forming a rich history of women's criticism of Shakespeare; a history that is often forgotten today. The period covered by this anthology, 1660–1900, marked many changes for women as readers of Shakespeare. Different genres became available to women as vehicles for Shakespeare criticism, and women were increasingly involved in the popular dissemination of Shakespeare, whether as story-tellers for children or as editors of plays. Women used their reading of Shakespeare to raise a wide range of contemporary concerns – marital relations, repression in the family, the improvement of women's education, the ideal of Womanhood, ethnic difference, the experience of civil war (to name but a few) – and expressed different, often opposing views on how to read a Shakespeare play. As early as 1834 the *Edinburgh Review* reported a distinctively '*female* criticism' of Shakespeare (John Wilson, review of Anna Jameson, *Characteristics of Women*: 181), yet the voices of women readers of Shakespeare before 1900 have, in the twentieth century, largely been ignored. The vast majority of writers included in this anthology are out of print and their work is available only in specialist libraries; even there, it is rarely read. We hope this selection will demonstrate that this neglect is undeserved.

The Shakespearian texts that women read in the seventeenth, eighteenth and nineteenth centuries took many different forms. In 1664, when Margaret Cavendish wrote her account of Shakespeare, only a limited number of Shakespeare folios and quartos were in circulation; by 1726, Lewis Theobald was able to remark that 'this Author is grown so universal a Book, that there are very few Studies, or Collections of Books, tho' small, amongst which [Shakespeare] does not hold a Place: And there is scarce a Poet, that our *English* tongue boasts of, who is more the Subject of the Ladies Reading' (*Shakespeare Restored*: v–vi). In the course of the eighteenth century women had more opportunities to attend performances of plays and adaptations of Shakespeare, and to read Shakespeare in abridged acting editions or copies of the Complete Works – indeed women could be counted amongst the subscribers to or direct financial backers of the numerous eighteenth-century editions of the Complete Works. By the early nineteenth century women were encouraged to read expurgated editions, such as Henrietta Bowdler's *The Family Shakespeare* (1807, mistakenly attributed to her brother Thomas), to protect them from Shakespeare's profanity and obscenity – or forbidden to read Shakespeare altogether. By contrast boys, as Mary Lamb explained in 1807, 'are generally permitted the use of their fathers' libraries at a much earlier age than girls are; they frequently have the best scenes of Shakespeare by heart, before their sisters are permitted to look into this manly book' (*Tales from Shakespear*: vi–vii). For most of the period in question women were denied the education thought suitable for men: it was only in the 1860s that English and American women were allowed to pursue a rigorous course of higher education on a par with men. Similarly, women's access to academic, professional and literary networks was limited; even the formidable Mary Cowden Clarke expresses with poignant frequency her gratitude at being accepted into what she always calls the 'fraternity' of Shakespearean scholarship.

Following Margaret Cavendish's 'Sociable Letter' of 1664 – the first critical essay ever to be published on Shakespeare – women's contributions to Shakespeare studies in the eighteenth century took a variety of approaches. In 1753, for instance, Charlotte Lennox attacked Shakespeare's 'defective' use of sources (*Shakespear Illustrated*: 36), while in 1769 Elizabeth Montagu sought to defend Shakespeare's 'genius' against the charge of 'want of delicacy and politeness in his pieces' (*Essay on the Writings and Genius of Shakespear*: 5); six years later, Elizabeth Griffith set out to champion the morality of Shakespeare's plays. In the 1730s, the Shakespeare Ladies Club was influential in supporting the project to erect a monument to Shakespeare in Westminster Abbey (completed in 1741) and in petitioning theatre managements to revive Shakespeare's plays on stage – helping to pave the way for Garrick's revival of Shakespeare in the 1740s. By the late nineteenth century increasing numbers of women were using the theatre review as a vehicle for literary criticism – as in the comments we have included by Emma Lazarus and Charlotte Porter on Salvini's performance of *King Lear*. In 1815 Sarah Siddons was an early contributor to a long tradition of performers publishing their reminiscences; Fanny Kemble, Helena Faucit, Adelaide Ristori and Mary Anderson are notable nineteenth-century examples included in this anthology.

Women's writing on Shakespeare flourished in the nineteenth century. Anna Jameson's *Characteristics of Women: Moral, Poetical and Historical* (London, 1832) went through a remarkable thirty editions in England and America by 1920, and became a model for character-based criticism, such as Henrietta Lee Palmer's *The Stratford Gallery: or the Shakspeare Sisterhood* (Philadelphia, 1859) and M. Leigh-Noel's *Shakspeare's Garden of Girls* (London, 1885). Since the early nineteenth century women had produced editions of Shakespeare's plays: Elizabeth Inchbald selected and commented on Shakespeare's plays for the *British Drama* collection (1806–9), and Henrietta Bowdler 'corrected' them for *The Family Shakespeare* (London, 1807). In 1860, with the publication of an unabridged edition of Shakespeare's Complete Works, Mary Cowden Clarke claimed herself to be 'the first of his female subjects who has been selected to edit his works' (*Shakespeare's Works*: vi); by the end of the century several women were editing single editions of Shakespeare's plays as textbooks. Women also edited popular volumes of collected quotations from Shakespeare on different topics, such as Chloe Blakeman Jones's *The Lovers' Shakspere* (Chicago, 1897), and contributed biographies of Shakespeare and histories of Stratford-upon-Avon. Both in England and America, women were to play a large part in the growing 'youth market' for Shakespeare in the nineteenth century, preparing juvenile editions and numerous adaptations of Shakespeare's 'tales', with the aim of introducing and popularising Shakespeare's plays. Mary Cowden Clarke's *The Girlhood of Shakespeare's Heroines* (London, 1850–2) has become infamous among these; it was frequently reprinted in the course of the century and narrates the imaginary childhoods of Shakespeare's female characters (a poignant moment in the preparation of this collection was the discovery of all five volumes of the first edition uncut and unread in the open stacks at the Folger Shakespeare Library). Cowden Clarke was respected by her contemporaries as the author of the first Concordance of the plays, co-author of *The Shakespeare Key* (London, 1879), co-editor of two editions of the Complete Works and author of numerous essays and periodical articles; earning a living by her work, she must be one of the earliest professional women writers on Shakespeare.

From the mid nineteenth century Shakespeare study groups and societies proliferated in both England and America, with clubs as far afield as the St Andrew's Club for Women (Scotland) and the Coterie – a black women's club founded in Kansas in 1889 with the purpose of studying Shakespeare. The women's club provided its members with an informal and supportive forum to read and discuss Shakespeare's works (on women's clubs and Shakespeare societies see the entries for Elizabeth Wormeley Latimer, Kate Richmond-West, Grace Latham, Julia Wedgwood and Jessie O'Donnell). Several papers given by women at clubs were later published, such as Elizabeth Wormeley Latimer's 'parlor lectures' given to 'ladies' in Baltimore (1886: v), Kate Richmond-West's 'interpretations' delivered to a 'class of fifty colored men and women'

(1890: 3), and Grace Latham's reading of *Julius Caesar* (1891) – all included in this anthology. Latham was also a regular contributor to the New Shakspere Society (founded in 1873) and its *Transactions*, while the emergence of specialist journals in the final decades of the nineteenth century, particularly in the United States – *Shakespeariana, Poet-Lore* and *The American Shakespeare Magazine* – increased the opportunities for women to publish their work. Indeed, the nineteenth century periodical press provided women with an unprecedented vehicle for Shakespeare criticism. Women contributed articles on Shakespeare to a wide range of titles reaching different audiences: these included literary journals such as *The Contemporary Review* and *Blackwood's Edinburgh Magazine*; special interest magazines like *The Girl's Own Paper*; specialist journals such as *Shakespeariana* and *The American Shakespeare Magazine*, both edited by women; regional publications, and periodicals of a general nature, such as *The Century* in America and *The Gentleman's Magazine* in England.

In what sense might this writing be said to constitute a pre-history of modern feminist criticism of Shakespeare? In 1834, when comparing Sarah Siddons's views on *Macbeth* with those of 'the best female critic of the age', Anna Jameson, John Wilson remarked that 'the woman's heart, in both cases alike, revealed to them truths which seem to have escaped the perception of us male critics' (Mrs Siddons: 365). For Wilson, 'female criticism' entailed special pleading for female characters combined with a woman's insight into female nature. Character criticism of Shakespeare's heroines indeed became the dominant model for women's criticism of Shakespeare in the nineteenth century – but its applications were various and often surprising. Some writers develop intimate accounts of women's behaviour, and while Mary Cowden Clarke explored the childhood traumas of Shakespeare's heroines Helena Faucit 'lived into their future' (*On Some of Shakespeare's Female Characters*, 1885: 48). Most of our authors agree that Shakespeare had a special insight into female psychology and sometimes comment on how remarkable this is, given the absence of female performers on his stage: 'how mistaken', writes Helena Faucit, 'is the opinion of those who maintain that Shakespeare was governed, in drawing his heroines, by the fact that they were acted by boys … As if Imogen, Viola, and Rosalind were not "pure women" to the very core' (329).

While several writers argue for the 'essential' qualities of womanhood in Shakespeare's heroines, and articulate conventional gender stereotypes in so doing, Shakespeare himself is claimed to defy those stereotypes by entering into the consciousness of a woman as easily as a man: 'nay, one would think he had been Metamorphosed from a man to a woman,' remarked Margaret Cavendish, 'for who could Describe *Cleopatra* Better than he hath done?' (*Sociable Letters*, 1664: 246). This can serve as a way of feminising Shakespeare: as Mary Cowden Clarke explains, Shakespeare, 'the most manly thinker and most virile writer that ever put pen to paper, had likewise something essentially feminine in his nature, which enabled him to discern and sympathize with the innermost core of woman's heart' ('Shakespeare as the Girl's Friend', 1887: 356). Women writers are often encouraged by Shakespeare's relative lack of formal education (having been deprived of this themselves), and they are ready to applaud behaviour in his heroines that challenges social norms. Particular heroines are repeatedly championed as role models for women, forming a hierarchy of female characters within the Shakespeare canon that might surprise modern critics. Portia, 'the most wonderful of all Shakspeare's feminine creations' (Leigh-Noel, *Shakspeare's Garden of Girls*, 1885: 118) is praised for her intellect, independence and affection; Imogen for her 'infinite' love for her husband (Faucit, 1885: 277); Constance in *King John* and Katherine of Aragon in *Henry VIII* are admired for their spirited defiance, and are accepted as two of the major starring roles for actresses; while ingenious defences are offered of female characters 'warped and weakened by circumstance' (Mary Cowden Clarke, 1887: 355): Ophelia, Desdemona, Cleopatra and, perhaps above all, Lady Macbeth.

But many of the authors included here also use their writing on Shakespeare to raise issues of particular concern to women. They address subjects such as women's education, women's role in public life, and power relations between the sexes in society and in marriage. The general title, *Characteristics of Women, Moral, Poetical, and Historical* (1832), under which Anna Jameson's book first appeared is indicative of her interest in wider issues: 'it appears to me', she writes in the introduction, 'that the condition of women in society, as at present constituted is false in itself, and injurious to them'. Instead of offering conventional 'essays on morality and treatises on education', Jameson chose 'to illustrate certain positions by examples': the example set by Shakespeare's heroines of intellectual and affectionate women (5). Jameson's confidence that in writing about Shakespeare she is also analysing the position of women in society is shared by many of the women represented here. They find it natural to turn from a discussion of *Othello* to questioning how far the rule of father over daughter can be justified, or from a discussion of *The Merchant of Venice* to regretting the lack of professional opportunities for women. Several authors offer subtle readings of women's experience of repression and exclusion in a society dominated by men; writers such as Dorothea Beale and Katharine Lee Bates played an active role in improving women's education, while many of those writing towards the end of the nineteenth century were known to support women's suffrage.

Writing about her role as a critic of Shakespeare in 1859, Henrietta Lee Palmer disclaimed 'the intention of presumptuously identifying herself' with well-known 'scholars and expounders'; men with access to a university education. 'Yet does she confidently claim the right to speak of these, his Sisterhood, as one woman may justly speak of another' (*The Stratford Gallery*, preface). Many women writers in this anthology share Palmer's self-consciousness about her gender; we find, particularly in the eighteenth century, modest disclaimers and apologies for ignorance and incompetence – some of them clearly tongue in cheek. Some writers seek to contrast their own writing with traditional academic discourse, the preserve of 'University men' (Elizabeth Wormeley Latimer, 1886: vi): Constance O'Brien, for instance, disapproved of those 'burdening themselves with a quantity of theories, criticism and information about their play ... letting the real substance of it go unheeded' ('Julius Caesar', 1886: 353), while Mary Cowden Clarke attacked editorial footnotes as 'mere vehicles for abuse, spite and arrogance' (*Shakespeare's Works*: vii). Several women draw confidence from their female predecessors in Shakespeare criticism: Elizabeth Griffith, for instance, cites the example of Elizabeth Montagu; Elizabeth Inchbald refers to work by Charlotte Lennox; M. Leigh-Noel speaks of Anna Jameson as the authoritative writer on Shakespeare's heroines; Elizabeth Wormeley Latimer recommends the work of Helena Faucit and Constance O'Brien, while Mary Cowden Clarke had the idea of producing her *Concordance* in Mary Lamb's garden. Some writers address their work to their women friends – Anna Jameson, for example, dedicated her *Characteristics of Women* to Fanny Kemble – while others share a sense of writing for a community of female readers: Helena Faucit, for instance, addresses her readership as 'my sister-women' (viii). By the end of the nineteenth century there were diverse groups of female (as well as male) readers for women's Shakespeare criticism, among them academics, educationalists, suffragettes, housewives and schoolgirls.

The canon of Shakespeare criticism inherited by readers of Shakespeare in the late twentieth century has been one dominated by men. Yet by the late nineteenth century women had made a significant contribution to Shakespeare criticism that was acknowledged, by men, to be important. In 1884 Professor William Taylor Thom of the Hollins Institute, Virginia, took issue with the 'thoroughly Philistine view' that few women 'understand' Shakespeare voiced by the *New York Tribune*: Thom retorts that

the brilliant and solid work in recent years on Shakespeare [by women] –
both as writers and as interpreters of his gracious heroines – gives a curious
inappropriateness to the *Tribune's* censure, and constitutes of itself a very
patent answer thereto. Mrs. Cowden Clarke, Mrs. Furness, Lady Helen
Faucit Martin, Mrs. Siddons, Mrs. Jameson, and many others, can be most
worthily cited and compared with the best workers among the men.
('Shakespeare Study for American Women', 1884: 99)

In part the neglect of women's Shakespeare criticism has been a question
of the hierarchy of recognised genres of criticism within the academy.
The scholarly edition, monograph, essay and article in a learned journal
have long been established as the legitimate forums for critical debate.
Because few women published in these genres before 1900, the enormous
output of women's writing on Shakespeare – discovered in autobiog-
raphies, theatre criticism, books for a general readership, club records,
popularisations, adaptations and, perhaps above all, in periodicals –
has been overlooked in histories of Shakespeare criticism. But by re-
examining our notion of the genres of Shakespeare criticism we can
rediscover the work of women reading Shakespeare; what Elizabeth
Wormeley Latimer describes as 'fugitive Shakspearian criticism' (1886:
vi). That history of women reading, writing, discussing, presenting and
popularising Shakespeare is one of diversity. While this anthology reveals
several recurring themes and shared opinions amongst women readers,
it also demonstrates that women's Shakespeare criticism before 1900 was
far from homogeneous. Women used their writing on Shakespeare in
many different ways according to their interests: the women represented
here both encourage conventional gender stereotypes and challenge contemporary attitudes towards women; they number both suffragists and
anti-suffragists, while some contribute to debate without seeking to make
any explicit reference to gender. Our authors differ and disagree with
one another, as well as mark out the common ground between them;
and there are many more women's voices to be heard which we were
unable to include in this anthology. The history of Shakespeare criticism
is one in which women played a significant role before 1900: we hope
this anthology will demonstrate that their work should not be forgotten.

Editorial policy

This collection is neither complete nor definitive. There is an enormous
amount of women's writing about Shakespeare from this period which
we have not been able to include. For a start, we have limited ourselves to
printed (as opposed to manuscript) sources and to British and American

authors. We have focused on what could broadly be called 'criticism', though this can include such things as prefaces to other works like editions, and reminiscences of performers. We have excluded entire categories of women's writing on Shakespeare, such as collections of quotations, contributions to Shakespearean biography and creative writing – partly because this last is covered in the two collections of essays edited by Marianne Novy (*Engaging with Shakespeare* and *Women's Re-Visions of Shakespeare*), and because our interest is as much in women's critical reception and appropriation of Shakespeare as in adaptations or 'offshoots'.

Even so we have had to leave out many women altogether, and be rigorously selective in the extracts we have decided to include. We have collected enough material for ten volumes of this size (including a whole book on Mary Cowden Clarke), and it has been painful both to exclude some authors, and to cut and fillet those who got in. In cutting, our policy has been to give priority to analytical and reflective passages over plot-summaries or straightforward descriptions. Some extracts, especially those from nineteenth-century writers, can stand alone without editorial intervention. In other cases, such as with some of the eighteenth-century writers, we have made use of summary and paraphrase as well as direct quotation.

We have attempted to represent the variety of women's writing on Shakespeare across the whole period and to cover a wide range of genres. We have arranged the material chronologically by author, and tried to facilitate cross-checking by providing indices by play, character and topic. In some ways our selection inevitably mirrors the material we have found: there is, for example, very little on the Sonnets and Poems here simply because women do not seem to have written about them very much; equally there is less on the Histories as compared with the Comedies and Tragedies – a discrepancy still apparent in modern feminist criticism. We have tried not to let our own late twentieth-century concerns wholly predict our decisions about what material to include, but naturally we have selected what we have personally found most interesting, and we know other people would have made other choices. We hope reviewers and readers will inform us of favourite authors, passages or topics we should have included: we are aware they must be legion.

Introductions provide biographical details in so far as we have been able to discover them, publication histories and information on periodical readerships, and, where relevant, short accounts of women's involvement in Shakespeare clubs, editing and education. We have concentrated on the literary, theatrical and professional contexts of our authors and observed their contacts with or references to other women writers; we are sure there are more connections between women writers to be discovered. We were pleased at how easy it was to find appropriate illustrations by women from Angelica Kauffmann in 1783 to Pamela Coleman Smith in 1898: this is another tradition of women's reception and reproduction of Shakespeare which would repay proper investigation.

We very much hope that some of our readers will investigate particular authors further for themselves, make more of their work available and add more names to this very preliminary survey of women readers of Shakespeare.

Quotations, references and dates

Quotations from Shakespeare within the extracts are given in the form in which they appear in the original, except that we have emended double hyphens to single hyphens and double quotation marks to single quotation marks (excluding quotes within quotes), and we have deleted quotation marks for indented quotes. For the convenience of modern readers we have added act, scene and line references to *The Riverside Shakespeare* edited by G. Blakemore Evans (Boston: Houghton Mifflin, 1974). Thus in the case of Elizabeth Griffith's chapter on *Othello* for example (pp. 33–9), the lines from the play are given exactly as she gives them, as are her references to say 'Act II, Scene XIV', but they are followed by the Riverside references in square brackets: [II. iii. 260–5]. Readers should be warned that some of our authors seem to be using rather eccentric or inaccurate editions – or perhaps they are quoting from memory. Brief explanatory notes to the text, where necessary, are also in square brackets.

Many of the authors represented here are working with contemporary assumptions about the chronology of Shakespeare's plays which are very different from those familiar to modern readers; we can find *Othello* discussed as a late play, *The Tempest* as an early one, *Henry VIII* as an Elizabethan composition. Our own assumptions about dates are based on 'The Canon and Chronology of Shakespeare's Plays' in *William Shakespeare: A Textual Companion* by Stanley Wells and Gary Taylor with John Jowett and William Montgomery (Oxford: Oxford University Press, 1987), pp. 69–144.

Margaret Cavendish (née Lucas), Duchess of Newcastle, 1623–1673

Margaret Cavendish became the second wife of the Duke of Newcastle (who was thirty years her senior) in 1645 and shared his continental exile during the Commonwealth period. Encouraged by her husband, himself an amateur writer and patron of the arts, she published extensively, and in a wide range of genres: poetry, essays, fiction, plays, letters, a biography of her husband, and 'A True Relation of My Birth, Breeding, and Life', the first autobiography to be published by a woman in England. Regarded by many of her contemporaries as eccentric, she is being rediscovered today as an outspoken feminist and an engaging if idiosyncratic writer. In the dedication to the universities of Oxford and Cambridge of her *Philosophical and Physical Opinions* (1655) she objected to the limitations placed on women: 'we are kept like Birds in Cages, to Hop up and down in our Homes, not Suffer'd to fly abroad, to see the several Changes of Fortune and the Various Humors, Ordained and Created by Nature, and wanting the Experience of Nature, we must needs want the Understanding and Knowledge' (sig. B2v). The section on 'Female Orations' in her *Orations of Divers Sorts* (1662) similarly provides a feminist polemic against the restrictions and prejudices which had reduced women to inferiority and powerlessness.

Margaret Cavendish's nineteen plays (plus some fragments) were closet dramas, written while the English theatres were closed, for reading or performance by family members; recent revivals vindicate the author's ability to manipulate what were to become Restoration clichés with wit and freshness while providing strong roles for the central female characters. Her opinions on literature and on women writers are frequently expressed in her prefaces and introductions.

Margaret Cavendish, Duchess of Newcastle, 'Letter CXXIII' in *CCXI Sociable Letters*. London: William Wilson, 1664

The *Sociable Letters* are more like essays on a wide variety of topics, addressed to female correspondents many of whom seem to be fictional inventions. Cavendish's Letter CXXIII was the first critical essay ever to be published on Shakespeare and as such merits inclusion here, even though it has been reprinted in recent times, notably in G. Blakemore Evans (ed.), *The Riverside Shakespeare*. Cavendish undertakes to defend Shakespeare from the 'dispraise' of a neoclassical criticism, asserting the realism of his characters in the face of the implied charge of offences against decorum and praising his wit and eloquence. Although she was an enthusiastic attender of plays during her years in Europe, as well as a playwright, her repeated references to Shakespeare's 'readers' and his 'book' reflect the fact that she had inevitably, during the Commonwealth period, become acquainted with his works in print rather than on the stage.

Madam,

I Wonder how that Person you mention in your Letter, could either have the Conscience, or Confidence to Dispraise *Shakespear*'s Playes, as to say they were made up onely with Clowns, Fools, Watchmen, and the like; But to Answer that Person, though *Shakespear*'s Wit will Answer for himself, I say, that it seems by his Judging, or Censuring, he Understands not Playes, or Wit; for to Express Properly, Rightly, Usually, and Naturally, a Clown's, or Fool's Humour, Expressions, Phrases, Garbs, Manners, Actions, Words, and Course of Life, is as Witty, Wise, Judicious, Ingenious, and Observing, as to Write and Express the Expressions, Phrases, Garbs, Manners, Actions, Words, and Course of Life, of Kings and Princes; and to Express Naturally, to the Life, a Mean Country Wench, as a Great Lady, a Courtesan, as a Chast Woman, a Mad man, as a Man in his right Reason and Senses, a Drunkard, as a Sober man, a Knave, as an Honest man, and so a Clown, as a Well-bred man, and a Fool, as a Wise man; nay, it Expresses and Declares a Greater Wit, to Express, and Deliver to Posterity, the Extravagancies of Madness, the Subtilty of Knaves, the Ignorance of Clowns, and the Simplicity of Naturals, or the Craft of Feigned Fools, than to Express Regularities, Plain Honesty, Courtly Garbs, or Sensible Discourses, for 'tis harder to Express Nonsense than Sense, and ordinary Conversations, than that which is Unusual; and 'tis Harder, and Requires more Wit to Express a Jester, than a Grave Statesman; yet *Shakespear* did not want Wit, to Express to the Life all Sorts of Persons, of what Quality, Profession, Degree, Breeding, or Birth soever; nor did he want Wit to Express the Divers, and Different Humours, or Natures, or Several Passions in Mankind; and so Well he hath Express'd in his Playes all Sorts of Persons, as one would think he had been Transformed into every one of those Persons he hath Described; and as sometimes one would think he was Really himself the Clown or Jester he Feigns, so one would think, he was also the King, and Privy

Counsellor; also as one would think he were Really the Coward he Feigns, so one would think he were the most Valiant, and Experienced Souldier; Who would not think he had been such a man as his Sir *John Falstaff*? and who would not think he had been *Harry* the Fifth? and certainly *Julius Caesar, Augustus Caesar*, and *Antonius*, did never Really Act their parts Better, if so Well, as he hath Described them, and I believe that *Antonius* and *Brutus* did not Speak Better to the People, than he hath Feign'd them; nay, one would think that he had been Metamorphosed from a Man to a Woman, for who could Describe *Cleopatra* Better than he hath done, and many other Females of his own Creating, as *Nan Page*, Mrs. *Page*, Mrs. *Ford*, the Doctors Maid, *Bettrice* [Beatrice], Mrs. *Quickly*, *Doll Tearsheet*, and others, too many to Relate? and in his Tragick Vein, he Presents Passions so Naturally, and Misfortunes so Probably, as he Pierces the Souls of his Readers with such a True Sense and Feeling thereof, that it Forces Tears through their Eyes, and almost Perswades them, they are Really Actors, or at least Present at those Tragedies. Who would not Swear he had been a Noble Lover, that could Woo so well? and there is not any person he hath Described in his Book, but his Readers might think they were Well acquainted with them; indeed *Shakespear* had a Clear Judgment, a Quick Wit, a Spreading Fancy, a Subtil Observation, a Deep Apprehension, and a most Eloquent Elocution; truly he was a Natural Orator, as well as a Natural Poet, and he was not an Orator to Speak Well only on some Subjects, as Lawyers, who can make Eloquent Orations at the Bar, and Plead Subtilly and Wittily in Law-Cases, or Divines, that can Preach Eloquent Sermons, or Dispute Subtilly and Wittily in Theology, but take them from that, and put them to other Subjects, and they will be to seek; but *Shakespear*'s Wit and Eloquence was General, for, and upon all Subjects, he rather wanted Subjects for his Wit and Eloquence to Work on, for which he was Forced to take some of his Plots out of History, where he only took the Bare Designs, the Wit and Language being all his Own; and so much he had above others, that those, who Writ after him, were Forced to Borrow of him, or rather to Steal from him; I could mention Divers Places, that others of our Famous Poets have Borrow'd or Stol'n, but lest I should Discover the Persons, I will not Mention the Places, or Parts, but leave it to those that Read his Playes, and others, to find them out. I should not have needed to Write this to you, for his Works would have Declared the same truth: But I believe, those that Dispraised his Playes, Dispraised them more out of Envy, than Simplicity or Ignorance, for those that could Read his Playes, could not be so Foolish as to Condemn them, only the Excellency of them caused an Envy to them. By this we may perceive, Envy doth not Leave a man in the Grave, it Follows him after Death, unless a man be Buried in Oblivion, but if he Leave any thing to be Remembred, Envy and Malice will be still throwing Aspersions upon it, or striving to Pull it down by Detraction. But leaving *Shakespear*'s Works to their own Defence, and his Detractors to their Envy, and you to your better Imployments, than Reading my Letter, I rest, *Madam*,

Your faithful Friend
and humble Servant.

Charlotte Lennox (née Ramsay), 1729(?)–1804

Charlotte Lennox was probably born in Gibraltar but spent some of her early years in what was then New York province, to which the family moved in 1739 when her father, an army officer, was appointed to a New York post; they apparently moved to England after he died in 1743. Charlotte Lennox's life included an unhappy marriage and a brief unsuccessful career as an actress, but she published her first book of poems in 1747 and continued to support herself and her family by writing as a poet, dramatist, novelist, translator and magazine editor. She sustained a monthly periodical, *The Lady's Museum*, for a year in 1760–1, and she learned Italian in order to write *Shakespear Illustrated*.

She was admired by her contemporaries, most notably by Samuel Johnson who said after dining with the writers Fanny Burney, Elizabeth Carter and Hannah More on 14 March 1784, 'Three such women are not to be found: I know not where I could find a fourth, except Mrs. Lennox, who is superior to them all' (*Boswell's Life of Johnson*: II. 275). He was her friend and mentor for over thirty years. She was – and is – best known for her novels, the first of which, *The Life of Harriot Stuart*, seems to be partly autobiographical. The best known is *The Female Quixote* (1752) on which she received advice from Johnson and from Samuel Richardson, who helped her to publish it. Henry Fielding praised it highly for its combination of romance and satire. Despite her constant and generally well received writing, she experienced chronic financial problems.

Shakespear Illustrated: or the Novels and Histories on which the Plays of Shakespear are Founded, Collected and Translated from the Original Authors: With Critical Remarks: In two volumes: By the Author of the Female Quixote. London: A. Millar, 1753 (despite the announcement on the title-page, *Shakespear Illustrated* actually appeared in three volumes, two in 1753 followed by a third in 1754)

In her Dedication to the Earl of Orrery, Lennox apologises that 'My *Sex*, my *Age*, have not given me many opportunities of mingling in the World'. She stresses the importance of 'Invention' or originality in a

writer and argues that 'a very small Part of the Reputation of this mighty
Genius depends upon the naked Plot, or Story of his plays'. Commending
Shakespeare's realism in characterisation, she writes, '[His] Excellence is
not the Fiction of a Tale, but the Representation of a Life; and his
Reputation is therefore safe, till Human Nature shall be changed'. Volume
I contains material on the sources of *Measure for Measure, Romeo and
Juliet, Othello, Cymbeline, All's Well That Ends Well, Twelfth Night* and
Macbeth. Volume 2 is on *The Winter's Tale, The Comedy of Errors* and
Hamlet. Volume 3 is on *The Two Gentlemen of Verona, Troilus and
Cressida, Richard II, 1 Henry IV, Henry V, 1, 2 and 3 Henry VI, Richard
III, Henry VIII, Much Ado About Nothing* and *King Lear*. As one might
expect in this period, Lennox operates on the assumption that the par-
ticular 'Novel' or 'History' she is presenting is the main or principal
source for each play, as compared with the modern acceptance of multiple
sources.

Lennox's method of treating *Measure for Measure* is typical of her
approach. She provides a translation of Novella 5 of Decade 8 of Cinthio's
Hecatommithi (which she usually refers to as 'The Story of Juriste and
Epitia'), followed by a plot-summary of Shakespeare's play. She then has
about twelve pages of 'Critical Remarks' in which she compares the two,
from which the following is a fairly full selection.

> There are a greater Diversity of Characters and more Intrigues in the fable
> of the Play, than the Novel of *Cinthio*; yet I think, wherever *Shakespear*
> has invented, he is greatly below the Novelist; since the Incidents he has
> added, are neither necessary nor probable. The Story of *Juriste* and *Epitia*,
> of itself, afforded a very affecting Fable for a Play; it is only faulty in the
> Catastrophe. The Reader, who cannot but be extremely enraged at the
> Deceit and Cruelty of *Juriste*, and very desirous of his meeting with a
> Punishment due to his Crime, is greatly disappointed to find him in the
> End, not only pardoned, but made happy in the Possession of the beautiful
> Epitia. *Shakespear*, though he has altered and added a good deal, yet has
> not mended the Moral; for he also shews Vice not only pardoned, but
> left in Tranquility [*sic*]. The cruel, the vicious and hypocritical *Angelo*,
> marries a fair and virtuous Woman, who tenderly loved him, and is
> restored to the Favour of his Prince …
>
> Since the Fable in *Cinthio* is so much better contrived than that of
> *Measure for Measure*, on which it is founded, the Poet sure cannot be
> defended, for having altered it so much for the worse; and it would be
> but a poor Excuse, for his want of Judgment, to say, that had he followed
> the Novelist closer, his Play would have been a Tragedy, and to make a
> Comedy, he was under Necessity of winding up the Catastrophe as he
> has done. The comic Part of *Measure for Measure* is all Episode, and has

no Dependance on the principal Subject, which even as *Shakespear* has managed it, has none of the Requisites of Comedy, great and flagrant Crimes, such as those of *Angelo*, are properly the Subject of Tragedy, the Design of which is to shew the fatal Consequences of those Crimes and the Punishment that never fails to attend them. The light Follies of a *Lucio*, may be exposed, ridiculed and corrected in Comedy. That *Shakespear* made a wrong Choice of his Subject, since he was resolved to torture it into a Comedy, appears by the low Contrivance, absurd Intrigue, and Improbable Incidents, he was obliged to introduce, in order to bring about three or four Weddings, instead of one good Beheading, which was the Consequence naturally expected ...

If it is granted, that the Duke could not know *Mariana's* Affair before his Disguise; what Opportunities had he of learning it afterwards? For, notwithstanding what *Mariana* says, which intimates a long Acquaintance, it is certain it could have been but a very short one; some extraordinary Accident therefore must have brought her Story to his Knowledge, which we find was known to no one else; for *Angelo's* Reputation for Sanctity was very high, and that could not have been, if his Wrongs to *Mariana* were publickly known. But why does not the Poet acquaint us with this extraordinary Accident, which happens so conveniently for his Purpose? If he is accountable to our Eyes for what he makes us see, is he not also accountable to our Judgment for what he would have us believe? ...

As the Character of the Duke is absurd and ridiculous, that of *Angelo* is inconsistent to the last Degree; his baseness to *Mariana*, his wicked Attempts on the Chastity of *Isabella*, his villainous Breach of Promise, and Cruelty to *Claudio*, prove him to be a very bad Man, long practised in Wickedness; yet when he finds himself struck with the Beauty of *Isabella*, he starts at the Temptation; reasons on his Frailty; asks assistance from Heaven to overcome it; resolves against it, and seems carried away by the Violence of his Passion, to commit what his better Judgment abhors. Are these the Manners of a sanctified Hypocrite, such as Angelo is represented to be? Are they not rather those of a good Man, overcome by a powerful Temptation? ...

It must be confessed indeed, that *Angelo* is a very extraordinary Hypocrite, and thinks in a Manner quite contrary from all others of his Order; for they, as it is natural, are more concerned for the Consequences of their Crimes, than the Crimes themselves, whereas he is only troubled about the Crime, and wholly regardless of the Consequences.

The Character of *Isabella* in the Play seems to be an Improvement upon that of *Epitia* in the Novel; for *Isabella* absolutely refuses, and persists in her refusal, to give up her Honour to save her Brother's Life; whereas *Epitia*, overcome by her own Tenderness of Nature, and the affecting Prayers of the unhappy Youth, yields to what her Soul abhors, to redeem him from a shameful Death. It is certain, however, that *Isabella* is a mere vixen in her Virtue; how she rates her wretched Brother, who gently urges her to save him! [Lennox quotes Isabella's speeches, from 'O you beast!' to "Tis best thou diest quickly' [III. i. 135–50].] Is this the Language of a modest tender Maid; one who had devoted herself to a religious Life, and was remarkable for an exalted Understanding, and unaffected Piety in the earliest Bloom of Life?

From her Character, her Profession, and Degree of Relation to the unhappy Youth, one might have expected mild Expostulations, wise Reasonings, and gentle rebukes; his Desire of Life, though purchased by Methods he could not approve, was a natural Frailty, which a Sister might have pitied and excused, and have made use of her superior Understanding to reason down his Fears, recall noble Ideas to his Mind, teach him what was due to her Honour and his own, and reconcile him to his approaching Death, by Arguments drawn from that Religion and Virtue of which she made so high a Profession; but that Torrent of abusive Language, those coarse and unwomanly Reflexions on the Virtue of her Mother, her exulting Cruelty to the dying Youth, are the Manners of an affected Prude, outrageous in her seeming Virtue; not of a pious, innocent and tender Maid ...

This Play therefore being absolutely defective in a due Distribution of Rewards and Punishments; *Measure for Measure* ought not to be in the Title, since Justice is not the Virtue it inculcates; nor can *Shakespear's* Invention in the fable be praised; for what he has altered from *Cinthio*, is altered for the worse.

Lennox is not always so negative. She finds the story of *Othello* to be altered by Shakespeare 'generally for the better' and her discussion of the play is interesting both for her defence of Shakespeare against the hostile criticisms of Thomas Rymer, published in his *A Short View of Tragedy* (1693), and for her remarks on questions of ethnicity:

The Character of Iago, says this Critic [Rymer], is against common Sense and Nature. '*Shakespear* would pass upon us a close, dissembling, false, insinuating rascal, instead of an open-hearted, frank, plain dealing Soldier; a Character constantly worn by them for some Thousands of Years in the World.' The Soldiers are indeed greatly obliged to Mr. *Rymer* for this Assertion, but though it may in general be true, yet surely it is not absurd to suppose that some few Individuals amongst them may be close dissembling Villains. *Iago* was a Soldier, it is true, but he was also an *Italian*; he was born in a Country remarkable for the deep Art, Cruelty, and revengeful Temper of its Inhabitants. To have painted an *Italian* injured, or under a Suspicion of being injured, and not to have shewn him revengeful, would have been mistaking his Character ...

The Character of *Desdemona* fares no better in Mr. *Rymer's* Hands, than that of Iago; her Love for the Moor, he says, is out of Nature. Such Affections are not very common indeed; but a very few Instances of them prove that they are not impossible; and even in *England* we see some very handsome Women married to Blacks, where their Colour is less familiar than at *Venice*; besides the *Italian* Ladies are remarkable for such Sallies of irregular Passions.

The Outlines of *Iago, Desdemona,* and *Cassio's* Characters are taken from the Novel; but that of *Othello* is entirely the Poet's own. In *Cinthio* we have a Moor, valiant indeed, as we are told, but suspicious, sullen, cunning, obstinate and cruel. Such a Character married to the fair *Desdemona* must have given Disgust on the Stage; the Audience would have been his Enemies, and *Desdemona* herself would have sunk into contempt for chusing him. With what Judgment then has *Shakespear* changed the horrid Moor of *Cinthio* into the amiable *Othello,* and made the same Actions which we detest in one, excite our Compassion in the other! The Virtues of *Shakespeare's* Moor are no less characteristic than the Vices of *Cinthio's*; they are the wild Growth of an uncultivated Mind, barbarous and rude as the Clime he is born in; thus, his Love is almost Phrensy, his Friendship Simplicity; his Justice cruel; and his Remorse Self-Murder.

When Lennox comes to *Cymbeline,* which she discusses in relation to Novel 9 of Day 2 of Boccaccio's *Decameron,* she finds that many of the incidents which are plausible in Boccaccio's mercantile setting become absurd when transposed into the ancient British court. Her hostile remarks anticipate those of Samuel Johnson, published in 1756 in his *General Observations on the Plays of Shakespeare.* Lennox is also, unlike later women writers, highly critical of Shakespeare's handling of the character of Imogen (her use of the phrase 'the injured Princess' may show acquaintance with Thomas D'Urfey's late seventeenth-century adaptation of the play under this title).

Shakespear makes the Lady in Question, not the Wife of a Merchant, but the Heiress of a great Kingdom. The Husband, who lays so indiscreet a Wager, not a simple Trader intoxicated with Liquor, but a young, noble, though unfortunate Hero, whom, for the extraordinary Qualities of his Mind and Person, the Princess has secretly married. And the Scenes, instead of a Tavern in *Paris,* are the House of a private Family in the Court of *Britain,* and the Chamber of a Princess. To this injudicious Change of the Characters is owing all the Absurdities of this part of *Shakespear's* Plot; he has given the Manners of a Tradesman's Wife, and two Merchants intoxicated with Liquor, to a great Princess, and *English* Hero, and a noble Roman ...

To pass by the Absurdity of supposing a great Princess, guarded by an incensed Father, and the jealous Vigilance of a designing Step-Mother, should be able to leave the Court, and ride like a Market-Woman with a single attendant to meet [Posthumus]; what Reason had he to expect such dangerous Proof of Affection from a Woman, who had so easily been prevailed upon to violate the Faith she had lately given him? ... The injured Princess however is impatient to be on Horseback, whips out of the Palace in a Minute, and passes invisibly, we cannot help supposing, though there is no Inchantment in the Case, through the midst of her attendants and Guards, and gallops away to meet her Husband ...

The rest of the Play is equally inconsistent, and if *Shakespear* invented here for himself, his Imagination is in this one full as bad as his Judgment. His Princess forgetting that she had put on Boy's Cloaths to be a Spy upon the Actions of her Husband, commences Cook to two young Forresters and their Father, who live in a Cave; and we are told how nicely she sauced the Broths ... Certainly this Princess had a most oeconomical Education; however she is to change her Situation, seem dead, be buried, and come to Life again, and hire herself to a new Master.

Writing on Imogen's discovery of the headless body of Cloten which she takes for Posthumus, Lennox remarks 'This is indeed a very pathetic Distress; but what does the unhappy Heiress of *Britain* do, now she thinks her Husband is killed? Why she accepts the Post of Page to the Enemy of her Father and Country; who, with a hostile Army, is wasting the Kingdom, over which, by Right of Birth, she is to reign.' She is disapproving of the heroine of *All's Well That Ends Well* whom she calls 'cruel, artful and insolent, and ready to make Use of the King's Authority to force her Husband to do her Justice ... except her extreme Cunning, she has nothing striking in her Character; and except her Perseverance, nothing amiable'. She pours scorn on Viola's actions in *Twelfth Night*: 'A very natural Scheme this for a beautiful and virtuous young Lady to throw off all at once the Modesty and Reservedness of her Sex, mix among Men, herself disguised like one; and prest by no Necessity, influenced by no Passion, expose herself to all the dangerous Consequences of so unworthy and shameful a Situation. We find this Incident managed with much more Decency in the Novel.' Olivia's love for Viola/Cesario is 'highly improbable and ridiculous ... suddenly declared, without any of those Emotions that Bashfulness, Delicacy, and a Desire of preserving the Decorum her Sex and Birth oblige her to observe'. Lennox questions whether Shakespeare, 'by mixing so much Levity in the Character of *Olivia*, designed a Satire on the Sex'.

Volume 2 contains remarks on the implausibilities of the plot of *The Winter's Tale*, where the preservation of Hermione is by 'a mean and absurd Contrivance ... How ridiculous also in a great Queen ... to submit to such Buffoonery as standing on a Pedestal, motionless, her Eyes fixed'. In the case of *Hamlet* she is critical of the madness and death of Ophelia which is

all [Shakespeare's] own Invention, and would have made a very affecting Episode if the Lady had been more modest in her Frenzy, and the Lover more uniformly afflicted for her Death; for at his first hearing it he expresses only a slight Emotion; presently he jumps into her Grave, fiercely demands to be buried with her, fights with her Brother for professing Love to her, then grows calm, and never thinks of her any more.

In volume 3 Lennox argues, unusually for this period, for the close dependence of Shakespeare's *Troilus and Cressida* on Chaucer's *Troilus and Criseyde*. She regrets that Cressida, 'too scandalous a Character to draw our Pity, does not satisfie that Detestation her Crimes raise in us by her Death, but escaping Punishment, leaves the Play without a Moral, and absolutely deficient in poetical Justice'. Cressida is however 'much more consistent in *Shakespear* than in *Chaucer*', since the latter gives her some attractive qualities; in Shakespeare she is immediately revealed as 'a compleat Jilt'. Discussing *Henry V*, she notes 'the absurdity of making the Princess the only Person in the French Court, who does not understand English', and criticises the impropriety of the final wooing scene in which 'we lose all Idea of the Dignity of the Persons who manage it, and, are readier to imagine we hear a common Soldier making love to an awkward Country Girl, than a King of *England* courting a Princess of *France*'. Similarly, she deplores the scene in *3 Henry VI* (I. iv) in which Queen Margaret and her supporters taunt the Duke of York, putting a paper crown on his head: 'With this more than fiendlike Cruelty, has *Shakespear* represented a Queen, whose Motives for taking Arms were far from being unjust, the Recovery of her Husband's Liberty and Crown, and the Restoring of her Son to the Rights and Privileges of his Birth' – but Shakespeare has altered history 'for the Sake of this shocking Absurdity in the Manners of a Female Character, in so high a Rank'.

Elizabeth Montagu (née Robinson), 1720–1800

Dubbed 'the Queen of the Blue Stockings' by Samuel Johnson, Elizabeth Montagu was a wealthy woman (both by birth and by marriage) who held literary salons in her classical-style house in Portman Square, London, which was unfortunately destroyed in World War II. Some of the interior decoration was by Angelica Kauffmann, who was a painter of murals as well as a portraitist and illustrator of Shakespeare (see Figure 1, p. 34). Montagu acted as a patron to writers including Hannah More and Fanny Burney; her younger sister was Sarah Scott, the novelist and historian. She planned with Sarah to set up a home for unmarried gentlewomen in 1767, and she proposed to found and endow a college for women in 1775 – a project which was dropped after Mrs Barbauld (a best-selling novelist) refused the post of superintendent.

In addition to the *Essay on the Writings and Genius of Shakespear* (1769), Montagu published during her lifetime three of the eighteen *Dialogues of the Dead* in 1760. These were criticisms of modern society, presented as dialogues with figures from classical history and myth; the other fifteen were written by Lord Lyttelton. Her extensive correspondence was published after her death. She began working on her *Essay* in 1765 and published it anonymously in 1769, though by December of that year she wrote to Lord Lyttelton that her identity was no longer a secret: 'I had better have employed the town crier to proclaim me as an author' (Doran: 150). The book was translated into German in 1771, French in 1777 and Italian in 1779.

Montagu's efforts on behalf of Shakespeare were appreciated by David Garrick who recommended his readers to peruse the *Essay* in the printed introduction to the 'Ode to Shakespeare' he recited at the Stratford Jubilee in 1769, and who wrote a poem called 'The Dream' in her praise which was published in *St. James's Chronicle* for 24–6 January 1771:

> Warm from the *Iliad*, when with Lightning's Speed,
> *Pallas* disguis'd saves Gallant *Diomede*,
> And wounds the God of War – my heated brain
> In Sleep rais'd Phantoms on th'embattled Plain:
> I saw arm'd all in brass with haughty air,
> Stalk forth a mighty Chief, the bold *Voltaire*,

The Gallic God of literary War!
A Giant He, among the Sons of France
And at our Shakespear pois'd his glitt'ring Lance.
Out rush'd a Female to protect the Bard,
Snatch'd up her Spear, and for the fight prepar'd:
Attack'd the Vet'ran, pierc'd his Sev'n-fold Shield,
And drove him wounded, fainting from the field.
With Laurel crown'd, away the Goddess flew,
Pallas confest then open'd to our view,
Quitting her fav'rite form of Montagu.

The manuscript in the scrapbook collection of Garrick's *Verses, Prologues and Epilogues* at the Folger Shakespeare Library contains the following alternative version of the last three lines:

Quitting her mortal Shape, away she flew
Twas Pallas, all cry'd out, the Giant slew,
Under her fav'rite form of Montagu.

Garrick also referred to Montagu in his 'Epitaph on Voltaire' published in *St. James's Chronicle* for 19–21 February 1771: 'Beneath her Arm the mighty Giant dy'd'.

An Essay on the Writings and Genius of Shakespear, Compared with the Greek and French Dramatic Poets: With Some Remarks upon the Misrepresentations of Mons. de Voltaire. London: J. Dodsley, 1769 [published anonymously]

The *Essay* is a nationalistic defence of Shakespeare and his English admirers which attempts to refute Voltaire's criticisms by arguing positively for Shakespeare's originality, by excusing some weaknesses on the grounds of the standards of his age and the poor quality of his source-materials, and by denigrating the French drama by comparison. In the Introduction, Montagu places herself with respect to the tradition of eighteenth-century scholarship:

Mr. Pope, in the preface to his edition of Shakespear, sets out by declaring, that, of all English poets, this tragedian offers the fullest and fairest subject for criticism. Animated by an opinion of such authority, some of the most learned and ingenious of our critics have made correct editions of his works, and enriched them with notes. The superiority of talents and learning, which I acknowledge in these editors, leaves me no room to entertain the vain presumption of attempting to correct any passages of this celebrated author; but the whole, as corrected and elucidated by them, lies open to a thorough enquiry into the genius of our great English classic. Unprejudiced and candid judgment will be the surest basis of his fame. He is now in danger of incurring the fate of the heroes of the fabulous ages, on whom the vanity of their country, and the superstitions of the times, bestowed an apotheosis founded on pretensions to achievements beyond human capacity, by which they lost in a more sceptical and critical age, the glory that was due to them for what they had really done; and all the veneration they had obtained, was ascribed to ignorant credulity, and national prepossession. – Our Shakespear, whose very faults pass here unquestioned, or are perhaps consecrated through the enthusiasm of his admirers, and the veneration paid to long-established fame, is by a great wit, a great critic, and a great poet of a neighbouring nation [Voltaire], treated as the writer of monstrous farces, called by him tragedies; and barbarism and ignorance are attributed to the nation by which he is admired. Yet if wits, poets, critics, could ever be charged with presumption, one might say there was some degree of it in pronouncing, that, in a country where Sophocles and Euripedes are as well understood as in any in Europe, the perfections of dramatic poetry should be as little comprehended as among the Chinese.

Montagu undertakes to defend Shakespeare from the charges of 'want of delicacy and politeness' and 'barbarism', inspired to her task by 'great admiration of his genius, and still greater indignation at the treatment he had received from a French wit'. Voltaire's criticisms and translations show that he simply does not understand Shakespeare. Montagu will examine 'First, if his fables answer the noblest end of fable, moral instruction; next, whether his dramatic imitation has its proper dramatic excellence'.

She bases her argument partly on Shakespeare's originality:

Great indulgence is due to the errors of original writers, who, quitting the beaten track which others have travelled, make daring incursions into unexplored regions of invention, and boldly strike into the pathless sublime: it is no wonder if they are often bewildered, sometimes benighted; yet surely it is more eligible to partake the pleasure and the toil of their adventures, than still to follow the cautious steps of timid imitators through trite and common roads.

She further excuses him on the grounds of his commitment to a popular theatre:

If the severer muses, whose sphere is the library and the senate, are obliged in complaisance to this degeneracy, to trick themselves out with meretricious and frivolous ornaments, as is too apparent from the compositions of the historians and orators in declining empires, can we wonder that a dramatic poet, whose chief interest it is to please the people, should, more than any other writer, conform himself to their humour, and appear most strongly infected with the faults of the times, whether they be such as belong to unpolished, or corrupted taste.

The comparison with Greek dramatists is a false one: 'Shakespear's plays were to be acted in a paltry tavern, to an unlettered audience, just emerging from barbarity: the Greek tragedies were to be exhibited at the public charge, under the care and auspices of the magistrates at Athens; where the populace were critics in wit, and connoisseurs in public spectacles'. This leads into a defence on the grounds of Shakespeare's superior realism: by 'copying nature' he

drew from an original with which the literati are seldom well acquainted. They perceive his portraits are not of the Grecian or of the Roman school: after finding them unlike to the celebrated forms preserved in learned museums they do not deign to enquire whether they resemble the living persons they were intended to represent. Among those connoisseurs, whose acquaintance with the characters of men is formed in the library, not in the street, the camp, or village, whatever is unpolished and uncouth passes for fantastic and absurd, though, in fact, it is a faithful representation of a really existing character.

And our hero triumphed over the shortcomings of his age:

Shakespear wrote at a time when learning was tinctured with pedantry; wit was unpolished, and mirth ill-bred. The court of Elizabeth spoke a scientific jargon, and a certain obscurity of style was universally affected. James brought an addition of pedantry, accompanied by indecent and indelicate manners and language ... Shakespear sometimes falls into the fashionable mode of writing: but this is only by fits; for many parts of all his plays are written with the most noble, elegant, and uncorrupted simplicity.

He simply 'by the force of his genius rose so much above the age and circumstances in which he was born'. Above all, 'In delineating characters he must be allowed far to surpass all dramatic writers, and even Homer himself; he gives an air of reality to everything'. Yet Montagu ends her Introduction on an equivocal note: 'Nature and sentiment will pronounce our Shakespear a mighty genius; judgment and taste will confess that as a writer he is far from being faultless'.

In her next chapter, 'On the Drama, or, on Dramatic Poetry', Montagu counter-attacks, calling French plays 'rather conversations, than representations of an action' which describe emotions rather than present

them directly. She gives three examples of Shakespeare's skill in expressing suffering – King Lear's reaction to the behaviour of Goneril in I. iv
('How sharper than a serpent's tooth it is / To have a thankless child'),
Constance's rejection of comfort in *King John*, III. iv ('He talks to me
that never had a son') and Macbeth's horror at his inability to say 'Amen'
after murdering Duncan (II. ii) – and comments:

> Shakespear seems to have had the art of the Dervise, in the Arabian tales,
> who could throw his soul into the body of another man, and be at once
> possessed of his sentiments, adopt his passions, and rise to all the functions
> and feelings of his situation. Shakespear was born in a rank of life, in
> which men indulge themselves in a free expression of their passions, with
> little regard to exterior appearance. This perhaps made him more ac-
> quainted with the movements of the heart, and less knowing or observant
> of outward forms: against the one he often offends, he very rarely mis-
> represents the other.

Rejecting rhyme as one of the 'false refinements of the modern stage',
she admires the Elizabethan and Jacobean use of blank verse – 'a diction
which united the harmony of verse to the easy and natural air of prose'.
Contemporary drama suffers from a 'false delicacy' causing tragedy to
'melt away in the strains of elegy and eclogue'. Corneille is criticised for
introducing love-scenes into classical tragedy, reducing the heroes to the
status of contemporary lovers, as compared with Shakespeare's *Julius
Caesar* which preserves 'Roman character and sentiments'.

Proceeding to a chapter 'On the Historical Drama', Montagu praises
Shakespeare for his use of English subject-matter despite his poor sources:

> The tragedians who took their subjects from Homer, had all the advantages
> a painter would have, who was to draw a picture from a statue of Phidias
> or Praxiteles. Poor Shakespear from the wooden images in our mean
> chronicles was to form his portraits. What judgment was there in discov-
> ering, that by moulding them to an exact resemblance he should engage
> and please! And what discernment and penetration into characters, and
> what amazing skill in moral painting, to be able, from such uncouth
> models, to bring forth not only a perfect, but, when occasion required, a
> graceful likeness! The patterns from whence he drew, were not only void
> of poetical spirit and ornament, but also of all historical dignity. The
> histories of these times were a mere heap of rude, undigested annals, coarse
> in their style, and crowded with trivial anecdotes. No Tacitus had inves-
> tigated the obliquities of our statesmen, or by diving into the profound
> secrets of policy had dragged into light the latent motives, the secret
> machinations of our politicians: yet how does he enter into the deepest
> mysteries of state!

His plays may still contain too much 'hurley-burley', but this is preferable to Corneille's 'effeminacy'. Compositions which are 'far from regular' (*King Lear* is included in this category) are redeemed by excellent passages. The realism of Shakespeare's characters is again stressed, as well as the range of their passions – much wider than the French obsession with love and ambition. These claims are substantiated by the next two chapters on the two parts of *Henry IV*. Montagu thoroughly enjoys Falstaff though his 'admirable speech upon honour would have been indecent and dangerous from any other person'. She is less enthusiastic about some of the female characters:

> Mine hostess Quickly is of a species not extinct. It may be said, the author there sinks from comedy to farce, but she helps to compleat the character of Falstaffe, and some of the dialogues in which she is engaged are diverting. Every scene in which Doll Tearsheet appears is indecent, and therefore not only indefensible but inexcusable. There are delicacies of decorum in one age unknown to another age, but whatever is immoral is equally blamable in all ages, and every approach to obscenity is an offence for which wit cannot atone, nor the barbarity or the corruption of the times excuse.

A chapter 'On the Praeternatural Beings' argues for Shakespeare's superiority to the Greek dramatists in his use of ghosts and fairies, partly on the grounds that the native tradition on which he draws is 'more solemn, gloomy and mysterious'. He is 'as judicious as bold' in his use of it, as is illustrated by an extended comparison of *Hamlet* with *The Persians* of Aeschylus. This leads on to a chapter on 'The Tragedy of Macbeth' where Montagu justifies Shakespeare's addition of the classical Hecate to the 'English' witches by a comparison with Milton. (This addition is now thought to be the responsibility of Thomas Middleton.) She argues that the absence of a Chorus makes the emotions more powerful despite some speeches suffering from 'obscure bombast'. She argues for a careful distinction between Macbeth and Lady Macbeth:

> The difference between a mind naturally prone to evil, and a frail one warped by force of temptations, is delicately distinguished in Macbeth and his wife. There are also some touches of the pencil that mark the male and female character. When they deliberate on the murder of the king, the duties of host and subject strongly plead with him against the deed. She passes over these considerations; goes to Duncan's chamber resolved to kill him, but could not do it, because, she says, he resembled her father while he slept. There is something feminine in this, and perfectly agreeable to the nature of the sex; who, even when void of principle, are seldom entirely divested of sentiment; and thus the poet, who, to use his own

phrase, had overstepped the modesty of nature in the exaggerated fierceness of her character, returns back to the line and limits of humanity, and that very judiciously, by a sudden impression, which has only an instantaneous effect. Thus she may relapse into her former wickedness, and, from the same susceptibility, by the force of other impressions, be afterwards driven to distraction. As her character was not composed of those gentle elements out of which regular repentance could be formed, it was well judged to throw her mind into the chaos of madness; and, as she had exhibited wickedness in its highest degree of ferocity and atrociousness, she should be an example of the wildest agonies of remorse. As Shakespear could most exactly delineate the human mind in its regular state of reason, so no one ever so happily caught its varying forms in the wanderings of delirium.

The last two chapters, 'Upon the Cinna of Corneille' and 'Upon the Death of Julius Caesar', attack the former and champion the latter. The use of rhyme is again deplored, and Dryden is criticised for introducing it to the English stage. Among Corneille's faults is his tendency in many plays to write a major role for a 'haughty princess' who is described by Montagu as a 'termagant lady [who] even to her lover is insolent and fierce. Were such a person to be produced on our theatre, she would be taken for a mad poetess escaped from her keepers in Bedlam, who, fancying herself a queen, was ranting, and delivering her mandates in rhyme upon the stage'. She ends her book as follows:

The genius of Shakespear is so extensive and profound, I have reason to fear a greater number of excellencies have escaped my discernment, than I have suffered faults to pass without my animadversion: but I hope this weak attempt to vindicate our great dramatic poet, will excite some critic able to do him more ample justice. In that confidence I have left untouched many of his pieces, which deserve the protection of more judicious zeal and care.

Elizabeth Griffith, 1727–1793

Elizabeth Griffith was the daughter of Thomas Griffith, comic actor and manager of the Theatre Royal in Dublin. She worked for a time as an actress, performing with the Smock Alley Theatre Company in Dublin (1749–51) and at Covent Garden (1753–5); she specialised in tragic roles such as Juliet and Jane Shore. Her career was interrupted by a romance and secret marriage with Richard Griffith which the couple turned to profit by publishing *A Series of Genuine Letters between Henry and Frances* in 1757. The success of this book lead to two further volumes of letters in 1767 and two more in 1770.

Griffith also published a number of translations from French, including volumes of a 1779–81 edition of Voltaire, and three epistolary novels, but she was mainly occupied as a playwright from 1764 to 1779, scoring successes with *The Double Mistake* (Covent Garden, 1766) and *The School for Rakes*, an adaptation of Beaumarchais' *Eugenie*, (Drury Lane, 1769); she also adapted plays by Marmontel and Goldoni. In later life she wrote her two moral works, *The Morality of Shakespeare's Drama Illustrated*, and *Essays Addressed to Young Married Women* (1782). She succeeded in supporting herself and her family by her writing.

The Morality of Shakespeare's Drama Illustrated. By Mrs Griffith. London: Cadell, 1775

Griffith dedicates her book to David Garrick, who had assisted her with the Beaumarchais adaptation. Her Preface celebrates Shakespeare in a slightly defensive mode as one who 'is a *model*, not a *copy*; he looked into nature, not into books, both for men and works'. As a woman, she can implicitly identify with the supposedly uneducated author, and throughout her book she mentions points that 'the commentators' (meaning the eighteenth-century editors) and 'the critics' have missed. She includes an adulatory reference to her predecessor Elizabeth Montagu:

> To the further honour of our Author be it said, that a Lady of distinguished merit has lately appeared a champion in his cause against this *minor critic*,

this *minute philospher*, this *fly upon a pillar of St. Paul's* [Voltaire]. It was
her example which has stirred up my emulation to this attempt; for I own
that I am ambitious of the honour of appearing to think, at least, though
I despair of the success of writing, like her.

She explains that her own purpose is to elucidate the morality of the
plays in a broad sense:

> In these remarks and observations I have not restricted myself to morals
> purely ethic, but have extended my observations and reflections to what-
> ever has reference to the general oeconomy of life and manners, respecting
> prudence, polity, decency, and decorum; or relative to the tender affections
> and fond endearments of human nature; more especially regarding those
> moral duties which are the truest source of mortal bliss – domestic ties,
> offices, and obligations.

There are chapters on thirty-six plays (i.e. all of the modern canon
except *Pericles* and *The Two Noble Kinsmen*) in the following order:
*The Tempest, A Midsummer Night's Dream, The Two Gentlemen of
Verona, Measure for Measure, The Merchant of Venice, As You Like It,
Love's Labour's Lost, The Winter's Tale, Twelfth Night, The Merry Wives
of Windsor, The Taming of the Shrew, The Comedy of Errors, Much
Ado About Nothing, All's Well That Ends Well, King John, Richard II,
1 Henry IV, 2 Henry IV, Henry V, I Henry VI, 2 Henry VI, 3 Henry
VI, Richard III, Henry VIII, King Lear, Timon of Athens, Titus Androni-
cus, Macbeth, Coriolanus, Julius Caesar, Antony and Cleopatra,
Cymbeline, Troilus and Cressida, Romeo and Juliet, Hamlet, Othello.*
In our selection we include brief extracts from a number of chapters
followed by the complete chapter on *Othello*.

Griffith's initial method is to summarise each play, point out a 'general
Moral', and quote passages illustrating 'particular maxims and sentences',
making liberal use of italics in her quotations to emphasise key lines. She
has to admit at the outset that some plays seem not to have a very obvious
general moral – *A Midsummer Night's Dream* and *The Two Gentlemen
of Verona*, for example, – and she expresses doubt that the latter is
Shakespeare's at all on account of

> the unnatural inconsistency of character, in the person of Protheus: ...
> however [Shakespeare] may sport, as he often does, with the three *unities*
> of Aristotle, *time, place*, and *action*, he seldom sins against a fourth, which
> I am surprised the Critics have not added, as being worth them all –
> namely, that of *character*; the tenor of which is generally preserved, from
> first to last, in all his works.

She is clearly interested at least as much in character as in morals, and begins to abandon her original plan with her fourth play, *Measure for Measure*:

> I cannot see what moral can be extracted from the fable of this Piece; but as the author of it seems to have thought otherwise, I shall present the reader with his idea on this subject, in his own words; where the Duke passes sentence on Angelo, his deputy, for his double villainy;
>
> > Haste still pays haste, and leisure answers leisure;
> > Like doth quit like, and *measure still for measure.*
> >   Act V, Scene vii [V. i. 410–11]

She continues:

> But as there is not matter enough here, for further expatiating upon, I shall proceed to collect together the dispersed maxims, sentiments, or morals, which may be gathered from the field at large; and which I shall arrange under their several heads, without regard to the order of the drama; as this method may best serve to give them an *united force*, and enable them to act more strongly on the minds of my readers.

With her next play, *The Merchant of Venice*, she declares, 'I shall take no further notice of the want of a moral fable, in the rest of these Plays; but shall proceed to observe upon the characters and dialogue, without interruption, for the future'. But she seizes on *As You Like it* with some relief: 'This Play begins with a reflection on the *first* and I may add the *principal*, concern in life, the education of children. Men are often more sedulous in training the brutes of their kennels, their mews and their stables, than they seem to be about the heirs of their blood, their fortunes, or their honours.'

She is interested in making generalisations about women. For example, commenting on Rosalind's remark 'O how full of briars is this working-day world!' and Celia's reply 'They are but burs, cousin, thrown upon thee in holiday foolery; if we walk not in the trodden paths, our very petticoats will catch them' [I. iii. 11–15], she says 'There is a very proper hint given here to women, not to deviate from the prescribed rules and decorums of their sex. Whenever they venture to step the least out of *their walk*, in life, they are too generally apt to *wander astray*'. In *The Winter's Tale* she commends Hermione's concern in III.ii for 'honour' on account of the challenge to her children's legitimacy rather than the slander of herself, finds Paulina 'vindictive', and praises Perdita's speech on 'bastard' gillyflowers in IV.iv as 'one of the most refined sentiments of a chaste and delicate mind'.

In *The Taming of the Shrew* Griffith draws attention to the moment in IV. iii when Petruchio deprives Katherina of her proffered new clothes, 'which satirists of our sex will be apt to say was a severe test of female temper'. She quotes approvingly Katherina's 'admirable speech' in the final scene 'wherein the description of a wayward wife, with the duty and submission which ought to be shewn to a husband, are finely set forth'. Nevertheless she wonders if the last four lines, in which Katherina offers to place her hand below her husband's foot, 'might have marred the whole beauty of the speech; the doctrine of *passive obedience and non-resistance* in the state of marriage, being there carried, perhaps, rather a little too far'. She proceeds immediately, however, to quote Luciana's speech against 'headstrong liberty' for women in *The Comedy of Errors* II.ii and the Abbess's criticism of Adriana at the end of the same play for disturbing her husband's peace with her (justifiable) jealousy as 'some excellent documents for wives'. In *Much Ado About Nothing* she appreciates Beatrice ('this lively girl'), and applauds her 'generous warmth of indignation' in support of Hero which she says disproves the common belief that women are 'prone to slander [each other]'.

She has an ingenious defence of Lady Macbeth, seizing on the line 'That which hath made them drunk hath made me bold' [II.ii.1]:

> Our sex is obliged to Shakespeare, for this passage. He seems to think that a woman could not be rendered compleatly wicked, without some degree of intoxication. It required two vices in her; one to intend, and another to perpetrate the crime. He does not give *wine and wassail* to Macbeth; leaving him in his natural state, to be activated by the temptation of ambition alone.

She also praises Lady Macbeth for expressing 'the true spirit of hospitality' when telling Macbeth not to neglect his guests. She is not so keen to excuse Cleopatra, remarking rather that her vices *'demonised* such distinguished talents, and transcendant beauty, as hers'.

When discussing *Cymbeline*, Griffith is particularly enthusiastic about Imogen's shocked response ('False to his bed?' III.iv.40ff.) when Pisanio tells her that Posthumus believes she has been unfaithful to him:

> Nothing, in situation of circumstance, in thought, or expression, can exceed the beauty or tender effect of [this] passage ... What a power of natural sentiment must a man have been possessed of, who could so adequately express that kind of ingenuous surprize upon such a challenge, which none but a woman can possibly feel! Shakespeare could not only assume all the characters, but even their sexes too ... The Commentators are all dumb upon this fine passage – not silent in admiration, but frozen into scholastic apathy.

In *Troilus and Cressida*, she finds a contrast between the content of the heroine's 'Yet hold I off' soliloquy at the end of I. ii and her character, remarking that the speech

> contains very just reflections and prudent maxims for the conduct of women, in the dangerous circumstance of love. What she says, would become the utterance of the most virtuous matron, though her own character in this piece is unluckily a bad one. But our Author's genius teemed so fertile in document, that he was unable to restrain its impulse, and coolly wait for a fit opportunity of adapting the speaker to the speech.

She quotes the subsequent Greek council scene (I. iii) at some length and challenges comparison with Homer: 'But, as I said before, on a comparison between Shakespeare and Sophocles, 'tis enough to determine the literary critics against me, that *one had written in English, and the other in Greek*'.

Her reading of *Romeo and Juliet* marks a return to the original plan: 'the catastrophe of the unhappy lovers seems intended as a kind of moral, as well as poetical justice, for their having ventured upon an unweighed engagement together, without the concurrence and consent of their parents', and it is not surprising that she thinks 'Laertes gives most excellent advice and *matronly* caution to his sister' in *Hamlet* I.iii. The Ghost's forgiveness of Gertrude 'even after her crimes' is admired, but Griffith is reluctant to discuss the substance of *Hamlet*'s 'To be or not to be' soliloquy in III.i: 'the subject is a hazardous one, and therefore had better not be meddled with. It might, perhaps, bear a discussion in philosophy, but religion forbids any manner of debate upon it'.

Final praise is reserved for *Othello*, for which Griffith's complete chapter reads as follows.

> Shakespeare has written three pieces on the subject of jealousy; the Winter's Tale, Cymbeline, and this one, besides the character of Ford, in the Merry Wives. But such was the richness of his genius, that he has not borrowed a single thought, image, or expression, from any one of them, to assist him in any of the others. The subject seems rather to have grown progressively out of itself, to have inspired its own sentiments, and have dictated its own language. This Play, in my opinion, is very justly considered as the last and greatest effort of our Author's genius, and may, therefore, be looked upon as the *chef d'oeuvre* of dramatic composition. How perfectly does *Othello*'s conduct throughout, correspond with Iago's description of it in the latter end of the First Act!
>
>> The Moor is of a free and open nature,
>> That thinks men honest, who but seem to be so.
>
> [I.iii.399–400]

FIGURE I. Angelica Kauffmann, *Othello*, V.ii.3: 'Yet I'll not shed her blood'
(1783). Kauffmann (1741–1807) was one of the original thirty-six members
when the Royal Academy was founded in 1768. She undertook interior
decoration as well as portraits and illustrations for Boydell's Shakespeare
Gallery (see also under Elizabeth Montagu, p. 22).

Such a character is not uncommon in life; whose virtues, arising more from an excellence of nature, than an exertion of philosophy, is led to judge of others by itself, and of course become the dupe of art and villainy.

Act I, Scene IV [I.ii]

Othello here expresses a very just and liberal sense of a matrimonial connection.

> But that I love the gentle Desdemona,
> I would not my unhoused free condition
> Put into circumscription, and confine,
> For the sea's worth.

[I.ii.25–8]

Scene IX [I.iii]

The argument between philosophy and feeling, in cases of misfortune or grief, is well debated here. The Duke, preaching patience to the father, upon his daughter's elopement with the Moor, says,

> Good Brabantio,
>   Take up this mangled matter at the best;
>   Men do their broken weapons rather use
>   Than their bare hands.
>   When remedies are past, the griefs are ended,
>   By seeing the worst, which late on hopes depended;
>   To mourn a mischief that is lost and gone,
>   Is the next way to draw new mischief on.
>   What cannot be preserved, when fortune takes,
>   Patience her injury a mockery makes;
>   The robbed that smiles steals something from the thief;
>   He robs himself who spends a bootless grief.

> *Brabantio.* So let the Turk of Cyprus us beguile,
>   *We lose it not so long as we can smile.*
>   He bears the sentence well, who nothing bears,
>   But the free comfort which from thence he hears;
>   But he bears both the sentence and the sorrow,
>   That to pay grief must of poor patience borrow.

> These sentences, to sugar or to gall,
>   Being strong on both sides, are equivocal.
>   But words are words. I never yet did hear,
>   That the bruised heart was healed through the ear.

[I.iii.172–5, 202–19]

I may possibly be reprehended, by some severe moralists, for noting the equipoise of such an argument as this. In this instance, indeed, I confess that I act contrary to the usual tenor of document, which always takes part on the *wise* side of a question. But, as I have said before, I do not think that ethic philosophy can ever be a gainer, by overstraining the sinews of the human mind. We ought neither to be votaries to the Cynic nor the Stoic sects. We should not, with Diogenes, *follow Nature* in the mere animal sense of the expression, nor with Zeno fly beyond it, in the metaphysical one. True virtue has no extremes. Its sphere extends not beyond the *Temperate* Zones. It sleeps in the Frozen, and but raves in the Torrid ones.

Scene X [I.iii]

I have before observed upon the exuberance of Shakespeare's document and moral. He so much abounds in maxim and reflection, that he appears frequently at a loss to find proper characters, throughout even his own extensive drama, sufficient to parcel them out to; so that he is frequently obliged to make his fools talk sense, and set his knaves a-preaching. An instance of the latter impropriety may be seen in the following passage, which contains both sound philosophy, and useful admonition. But that it may have the better effect on my readers, I wish that whenever they remember the speech, they could contrive to forget the speaker.

> *Roderigo.* What should I do? I confess it is my shame to be so fond; but it is not in my *virtue* to amend it.

> *Iago.* Virtue? A fig. *'Tis in ourselves that we are thus, or thus.* Our bodies are our gardens, to the which our wills are gardeners. So that if we will plant nettles, or sow lettuce; set hyssop, and weed up thyme; supply it with one gender of herbs, or distract it with many; either have it sterile with idleness, or manured with industry; why, the power and corrigible authority of this lies in our will. If the ballance of our lives had not one scale of reason, to poise another of sensuality, the blood and baseness of our natures would conduct us to most preposterous conclusions. [I.iii.317–29]

The plea that Roderigo offers above, for remaining still under the dominion of a lawless passion, is framed upon a fatal error, too prevalent in the world, that *virtue* is a peculiar gift from Heaven, granted *speciali gratia*, as it were, to particular and chosen persons. Hence indolent minds are apt to conclude it a vain task to restrain their passions, or resist their temptations, without the supernatural aid of such an innate endowment. Iago in his reply, reasons very justly against this dangerous and discouraging doctrine of *partial grace*; in support of which argument I shall here add a passage from a modern writer, who, when speaking on this subject, says,

The difficulties we apprehend, more than those we find, in the strife with all our passions, is the only thing that prevents philosophy or virtue from being commonly attainable in general life. What makes the difference between a chaste woman, and a frail one? *The one had struggled, and the other not.* Between a brave man and a coward? *The one had struggled, and the other not.* An honest man and a knave? *One had struggled, the other not.*[1]

Act II, Scene XIV [II.iii]

There is a great deal of after-wit reflection here, which, however, may serve as a forewarning, perhaps, to some of my Readers. Iago seeing Cassio desponding, on being cashiered by *Othello*, asks if he be hurt? To which he replies,

> *Cassio.* Past all surgery. – Reputation, reputation, reputation! *Oh, I have lost the immortal part of me, and what remains is bestial.* Oh, thou invisible spirit of wine! if thou hast no name to be known by, let us call thee Devil. – I will ask him for my post again, and he shall tell me I am a drunkard! Had I as many mouths as Hydra, such an answer would stop them all. To be now a sensible man, by and by a fool, and presently a beast! Every inordinate cup is unblessed, and the ingredient is a devil. [II.iii.260–5, 281–3, 303–8]

Act III, Scene V [III.iii]

The following passage will speak for itself:

> *Iago.* Good name, in man or woman, dear my lord,
>   Is the immediate jewel of their souls.
>   Who steals my purse steals trash, 'tis something, nothing;
>   'Twas mine, 'tis his, and has been slave to thousands:
>   But he that filches from me my good name,
>   Robs me of that which not enriches him,
>   And makes me poor, indeed.
>
> [III.iii.155–61]

In the same Scene, *Othello*, while his alarmed mind is struggling between confidence and conviction, delivers himself on the subject with a liberal and manly spirit.

> Thinkst thou I'd make a life of jealousy?
> To follow still the changes of the moon,
> With fresh suspicions? No – To be once in doubt,

---

1 The Posthumous Works of a late Celebrated Genius deceased.

Is once to be resolved. Exchange me for a goat,
When I shall turn the business of my soul
To such exsuffolate² and blown surmises,
Matching thy inference. 'Tis not to make me jealous,
To say my wife is fair, feeds well, loves company,
Is free of speech, sings, plays, and dances well;
Where virtue is, these are more virtuous.
Nor from mine own weak merits will I draw
The smallest fear or doubt of her revolt.
For she had eyes, and chose me. No, Iago,
I'll see before I doubt; when I doubt prove;
And on the proof, there is no more but this,
Away, at once, with love or jealousy.

Scene XII [III.iv]

It has often surprized me, to find the character of Desdemona so much mistaken and slighted, as it too generally is. It is simple, indeed, but that is one of its merits: for the simplicity of it is that of *innocence*, not of folly. In my opinion she seems to be as perfect a model of a wife, as either this author, or any other writer, could possibly have framed. She speaks little; but whatever she says is sensible, pure, and chaste. The remark she makes in this place, on the alteration of *Othello*'s manners towards her, affords a very proper admonition to all women in her situation and circumstances.

Something, sure, of state,
Hath puddled his clear spirit; and, in such cases,
Men's natures wrangle with inferior things,
Though great ones are their object. 'Tis even so –
For let our finger ake, and it endues
Our other healthful members with a sense
Of pain. *Nay, we must think men are not gods;*
Nor of them look for such observance always,
As fits the bridal.

[III.iv.140-50]

She had said to himself before,

Be't as your fancies teach you –
Whate'er you be, I am obedient.

[III.iii.88-9]

---

² 'Buzzing'.

And afterwards, in confessing herself before Iago and Æmilia,

> Here I kneel –
> If e'er my will did trespass 'gainst his love,
> Or in discourse, or thought, or actual deed,
> Or that mine eyes, mine ears, or any sense
> Delighted them on any other form;
> Or that I do not yet, and ever did,
> And ever will, though he do shake me off
> To beggarly divorcement, love him dearly;
> Comfort forswear me! Unkindness may do much,
> *And his unkindness may defeat my life,*
> *But never taint my love.*
>
> [IV.ii.151–61]

And further on, where Æmilia says to her, of Othello, 'I wish you had never seen him!', she replies,

> So would not I. *My love doth so approve him,*
> *That ev'n his stubbornness, his checks and frowns,*
> *Have grace and favour in them.*
>
> [IV.iii.18–21]

As the married state is both the dearest and most social connection of life, I think this a proper passage to conclude my observations with, on a work in which is comprehended the compleatest system of the oeconomical and moral duties of human nature, that perhaps was ever framed by the wisdom, philosophy, or experience of *uninspired* man.

Griffith's General Postscript quotes Elizabeth Montagu again and endorses her admiration for Shakespeare as a moral teacher. In a final bid for the superiority of English over Greek tragedies, Griffith claims that the former are more effective in inculcating morals than the latter: 'Theirs were performed in the morning; which circumstance suffered the salutary effect to be worn out of the mind, by the business or avocations of the day. Ours are at night; the impressions accompany us to our couch, supply matter for our latest reflections, and may sometimes furnish the subject of our very dreams.'

Joanna Baillie, 1762–1851

Joanna Baillie was born in Scotland and educated at a boarding school in Glasgow, but moved with her family to London in 1784. Her friends included Walter Scott and Robert Burns, and her collections of poetry, *The Family Legend* (1810) and *Metrical Legends of Exalted Characters* (1821), were influenced by their work. In London she became acquainted with the Bluestocking group who encouraged her to write. In addition to the *Plays on the Passions* (of which five editions had appeared by 1821) she published volumes of *Miscellaneous Plays* in 1804 and 1836 and individual plays in 1810 and 1826, a total of twenty-six plays in all. She became very popular as a writer of songs and ballads; Haydn provided music for some of her lyrics.

Baillie's plays were admired by her contemporaries (published anonymously, they were attributed to Scott by several critics), but very few were performed and none was a success, despite the presence of performers such as Sarah Siddons who starred as Jane in Baillie's best-known work, *De Monfort*, and took the leading role in *The Family Legend*, a Scottish Gothic drama which premiered in Edinburgh in 1810 with a Prologue by Scott. Byron is said to have remarked that 'women, saving Joanna Baillie, cannot write tragedy'.

A Series of Plays, in which it is Attempted to Delineate the Stronger Passions of the Mind: each Passion being the Subject of a Tragedy and a Comedy [Usually known as *Plays on the Passions*]. London: T. Cadell and W. Davies, 1798–1812

In the seventy-two-page 'Introductory Discourse' to the *Plays on the Passions* Baillie sets out her proposal to write a blank-verse tragedy and a comedy on each of the passions. She provides a general essay on the origins of drama and the nature of its popular appeal, together with an analysis of the ways in which both tragedy and comedy can be morally improving. She is a little defensive about the English tradition, and she appears to be thinking of Shakespeare when she writes, 'As in other works deficiency in characteristick truth may be compensated by excellencie of a different kind, in the drama, characteristick truth will compensate every other defect. Nay, it will do what appears a contradiction; one strong genuine stroke of nature will cover a multitude of sins, even against nature herself'. More explicitly, she comments a few pages later,

It appears to me a very strong testimony to the excellence of our great national Dramatist, that so many people have been employed in finding out obscure and refined beauties, in what appear to ordinary observation his very defects. Men, it may be said, do so merely to shew their own superior penetration and ingenuity. But granting this; what could make other men listen to them, and listen so greedily too, if it were not that they have received from the works of Shakspeare, pleasure far beyond what the most perfect poetical compositions of a different character can afford.

Conceding the impressive heritage of the Greek drama, she writes, 'Very strong genius will sometimes break through every disadvantage of circumstances: Shakspeare has arisen in this country, and we ought not to complain'. She argues, again with implicit rather than explicit reference to the Elizabethan and Jacobean drama, for the equality of male and female passions:

I believe there is no man that ever lived, who has behaved in a certain manner on a certain occasion, who has not had amongst women some corresponding spirit, who on the like occasion, and every way similarly circumstanced, would have behaved in the like manner. With some degree of softening and refinement, each class of the tragick heroes I have mentioned has its corresponding one amongst the heroines.

She concludes her Introduction on this note:

Shakspeare, more than any of our poets, gives peculiar and appropriate distinction to the characters of his tragedies. The remarks I have made, in regard to the little variety of character to be met with in tragedy, apply not to him. Neither has he, as other Dramatists generally do, bestowed pains on the chief persons of his drama only, leaving the second and inferior ones insignificant and spiritless. He never wears out our capacity to feel, by eternally pressing upon it. His tragedies are agreeably chequered with variety of scenes, enriched with good sense, nature, and vivacity, which relieve our minds from the fatigue of continued distress. If he sometimes carries this so far as to break in upon that serious tone of mind, which disposes us to listen with effect to the higher scenes of tragedy, he has done so chiefly in his historical plays, where the distresses set forth are commonly of that publick kind, which does not, at any rate, make much impression upon the feelings.

Elizabeth Inchbald (née Simpson), 1753–1821

Elizabeth Inchbald ran away from her farming family in Suffolk to become an actress, at first in Norwich and London but subsequently in Bristol where she made her debut as Cordelia to her husband Joseph Inchbald's Lear in 1772; the couple's theatrical friends included Sarah Siddons and John Philip Kemble, with whom Elizabeth apparently fell in love. Her husband died in 1779 and she continued to perform for a further decade but began to make a career as an author, writing plays, novels and articles for *The Edinburgh Review*. Her first play, *The Mogul Tale, or the Descent of the Balloon*, cashed in on the contemporary French fashion for ballooning and was a hit at the Haymarket in 1784. She subsequently wrote a number of reasonably successful comedies and farces including adaptations of French and German plays. Her dramas were admired by Sheridan, while Kemble encouraged her to write the fiction for which she is better known today. Her first novel, *A Simple Story* (begun in the 1770s but not published until 1791), drew praise from Maria Edgeworth, while her second, *Nature and Art* (1796), was indebted to Rousseau and Godwin for its educational and political philosophy.

The British Theatre: A Collection of Plays in Twenty-Five Volumes with Biographical and Critical Remarks by Mrs Inchbald. London: Longman et al., 1806–9

Longman employed Inchbald to write the prefaces for his *British Theatre* which includes twenty-four plays by Shakespeare in the first five volumes; the series goes on to cover Jacobean, Restoration and eighteenth-century drama. She subsequently made her own choice of *A Collection of Farces* (seven volumes, 1809) and *The Modern Theatre* (ten volumes, 1811), becoming in effect the first professional female editor and critic of drama. Some early editions carry an 'Address to the Reader' which is a thirty-page discussion of contemporary acting styles and theatre spaces. The prefaces to the individual plays included in the *British Theatre* collection are brief, but they occasionally draw on Inchbald's experiences as an actress and playwright and give evidence of her desire to take 'the woman's part'. (n.b. Most library holdings of the *British Theatre* consist of 'made-up sets' so that different plays appear in different volumes; references below are to the set at the Folger Shakespeare Library in Washington, D.C.)

Volume 1 contains *The Comedy of Errors* ('improbable'), *Romeo and Juliet* (demonstrates Shakespeare's 'just knowledge of the human heart'), *Hamlet*, *Richard III*, and *King John*:

> Constance is the favourite part both of the poet and the audience; and she has been highly fortunate under the protection of the actress. It was the part in which that idol of the public, Mrs. Cibber, was most of all adored; and the following lines, uttered by Mrs. Siddons in Constance,
>
> > Here I and sorrow sit;
> > This is my throne, bid kingdoms bow to it
> >
> > [III.i. 73–4]
>
> seem like a triumphant reference to her own potent skill in the delineation of woe, as well as to the agonizing sufferings of the mother of young Arthur.

Volume 2 begins with *1 Henry IV*:

> This is a play which all men admire, and which most women dislike. Many revolting expressions in the comic parts, much boisterous courage in some of the graver scenes, together with Falstaff's unwieldy person, offend every female auditor; and whilst a facetious Prince of Wales is employed in taking purses on the highway, a lady would rather see him stealing hearts at a ball, though the event might produce more fatal consequences. The great Percy ... pays some attention to his wife, but still more to his horse; and as the king was a rebel before he mounted the throne, and all women are naturally loyal, they shudder at a crowned head leagued with a traitor's heart.

Nevertheless, Inchbald criticises readers who are 'too refined to laugh at the wit of Sir John' and continues:

> It is impossible for puritanism not to be merry, when Falstaff is ever found talking to himself; or holding discourse over the honoured dead. It is nearly as impossible for stupidity to be insensible of the merit of those sentiments, delivered by the prince, over the same extended corse; or, to be unmoved by various other beauties, with which this work abounds.

The volume continues with *2 Henry IV*, *The Merchant of Venice* (Jessica 'proved in her disposition a strong resemblance to the wicked Shylock,

or though she had deserted him, she never would have robbed him'),
Henry V and *Much Ado About Nothing* (Beatrice and Benedick are
'highly entertaining and most respectable personages').

Volume 3 contains *As You Like It* (Inchbald criticises Rosalind's
dialogue for possessing 'no forcible repartee'), *The Merry Wives of Wind-*
sor (praised as a faithful report of 'the manners and usages of that age'),
Henry VIII (assumed to be an Elizabethan play), *Measure for Measure*
(the source is blamed for 'incredible occurrences') and *The Winter's Tale*.
Inchbald writes enthusiastically of Hermione and continues:

> High as this injured queen ranks in virtue and every endearing quality,
> she has a faithful attendant, who in that lowly capacity, reaches even the
> summit of her majesty's perfection. Paulina, in nature, and the best of all
> nature, tenderness united with spirit, has such power over the scenes in
> which she is engaged for the protection of the new-born child, that, like
> the queen, she confers honour and interest upon Leontes, merely by his
> keeping such excellent company.

Volume 4 contains *King Lear* (Inchbald prints Nahum Tate's 1681
adaptation of this play which was generally preferred in the eighteenth
century), *Cymbeline*, *Macbeth*, *Julius Caesar* and *Antony and Cleopatra*.
Inchbald compares Lear with James II, abandoned by his daughters Mary
and Anne. She agrees with Samuel Johnson in finding *Cymbeline* 'weak'
and lacking in 'magic', but comments

> Still, the impossibility, that half the events in this play could ever occur,
> cannot be the sole cause of its weak effect. Shakespeare's scenes are
> frequently such, as could not take place in real life; and yet the sensations
> which they excite are so forcible, that improbability is overpowered by
> the author's art, and his auditors are made to feel, though they cannot
> believe.

She calls *Macbeth* 'a grand tragic opera', and in her brief discussion of
its sources she refers to *Shakespear Illustrated*, though she does not
mention Charlotte Lennox by name. In *Julius Caesar* Shakespeare is
again praised as a 'penetrating and impartial commentator upon the heart
of man'. With *Antony and Cleopatra* Inchbald expresses a consciously
unfashionable preference for Shakespeare's play over Dryden's *All for*
Love:

> The reader will be also introduced to the queen of Egypt, in her undress,
> as well as in her royal robes; he will be, as it were, admitted to her toilet,
> where, in converse with her waiting-woman, she will suffer him to arrive
> at her most secret thoughts and designs ... But these minute touches of
> nature, by which Shakespeare proves the queen to be a woman, are,

FIGURE 2. Anne Seymour Damer, *Antony and Cleopatra*, V. ii: the death of Cleopatra; a bas-relief sculpture exhibited at Boydell's Shakespeare Gallery (1803). Damer (1749–1828) specialised in busts and in animal sculptures (particularly dogs). Her work was admired by Horace Walpole who bequeathed his house, Strawberry Hill, to her when he died.

perhaps, the very cause why Dryden's picture of the Egyptian court is preferred, on the stage, before this.

Dryden's characters, she remarks, are 'seen only in parade'.

Volume 5 contains *Coriolanus*, *Othello*, *The Tempest* and *Twelfth Night*. Volumnia in *Coriolanus* is 'a woman to the very heart ... admired and beloved' even for her inconsistencies; *The Tempest* is a drama which 'does *not* interest the passions' and here Inchbald agrees with her contemporaries in preferring Dryden's adaptation. As for *Othello*:

> So vast is the power of the author's skill in delineating the rise and progress of sensations in the human breast, that a young and elegant female is here represented, by his magic pen, as deeply in love with a Moor – a man different in complexion and features from her and her whole race – and yet without the slightest imputation of indelicacy resting upon her taste.

Henrietta Bowdler, 1754–1830

Henrietta Bowdler, usually known as Harriet, appears in Janet Todd's *A Dictionary of British and American Women Writers 1660–1800* as a writer of novels and of the highly successful *Sermons on the Doctrines and Duties of Christianity* (1801) which went through fifty editions by 1853. The Bishop of London contacted the publishers to offer a parish to the anonymous author. Harriet was also the sister of Thomas Bowdler under whose name *The Family Shakespeare* appeared in 1807, and Noel Perrin has demonstrated that this volume was really the work of Harriet (*Dr. Bowdler's Legacy*, 1969). Her anonymity, comparable to that of Mary Lamb in the *Tales from Shakespear* (also 1807), may perhaps be explained on the grounds that she 'wanted to avoid the odium of admitting that she, an unmarried gentlewoman of fifty, understood Shakespeare's obscenity enough systematically to remove it. Brothers were the recognized recourse when sisters wished to stay concealed' (Perrin: 76–7). The situation was complicated in the case of the Bowdlers since at least six members of the family over three generations were involved in what became almost the family business of expurgating Shakespeare. Surviving letters from friends and family members seem however to leave no doubt that the first *Family Shakespeare* was Harriet's, whereas the second, published in 1818, was her brother's. A friend of the Bluestockings, Harriet also published poetry, and a novel, *Pen Tamar, or The History of an Old Maid*, appeared posthumously in 1831.

The Family Shakespeare. Printed by Richard Cruttwell of St James's Street, Bath, for Hatchard of Piccadilly, London, 4 vols, 1807 [published anonymously]

While it is galling to have to present Henrietta Bowdler as the first woman to edit Shakespeare, it is appropriate to the spirit of her work that, unlike other writers in this collection, she must be represented negatively, by what she cut rather than by what she published. And her method was overwhelmingly to cut rather than to substitute acceptable alternatives for problematic words or lines as subsequent bowdlerists did. Her only substitutions are on the grounds of obsolescence, not obscenity.

The 1807 Preface explains that, 'while few authors are so instructive as Shakespeare, ... his Plays contain much that is vulgar, and much that is indelicate'. This is attributed to the age in which he lived, and Bowdler quotes Elizabeth Montagu: 'whatever is immoral, is equally blameable in all ages'. She explains that she has omitted 'many speeches in which Shakespeare has been tempted to purchase laughter at the price of decency', and points out that there are many full texts for those who want them, but this one is especially for those 'who wish to make the young reader acquainted with the various beauties of this writer, unmixed with any thing that can raise a blush on the cheek of modesty'. The canon is reduced to twenty plays and nothing has been added. 'I have endeavoured to remove everything that could give just offence to the religious and virtuous mind ... Many vulgar, and all indecent expressions are omitted; an uninteresting or absurd scene is sometimes curtailed; and I have occasionally substituted a word which is in common use, instead of one that is obsolete'. The edition is 'intended to be read in private societies, and to be placed in the hands of young persons of both sexes'.

Volume 1 contains *The Tempest, A Midsummer Night's Dream, Much Ado About Nothing, As You Like It* and *The Merchant of Venice*; volume 2 contains *Twelfth Night, The Winter's Tale, King John, Richard II* and *1 Henry IV*; volume 3 contains *2 Henry IV, Henry V, Richard III, Henry VIII* and *Julius Caesar*, and volume 4 contains *Macbeth, Cymbeline, King Lear, Hamlet* and *Othello*. It is noticeable that several of the plays that gave problems to the eighteenth-century moral critics, such as *Measure for Measure, Troilus and Cressida* and *Antony and Cleopatra*, are simply omitted in their entirety. Others are carefully pruned according to Bowdler's stated principles. In *Cymbeline*, for example, she omits Iachimo's references to prostitutes in his conversation with Imogen in I. vii, and all lines like 'That you have tasted her in bed' and 'She hath been colted by him' in the account of his visit to Britain in II. iv. She entirely omits Posthumus's soliloquy in II. v beginning 'Is there no way for men to be, but women / Must be half-workers?' In *Hamlet* she omits the hero's taunting asides to Ophelia in the play scene (III.ii) with their discussion of 'country matters' and 'the puppets dallying'. She gives only the first stanza of Ophelia's 'Valentine' song and omits her later song altogether. Throughout all twenty plays she is particularly careful to take out any references to God or Jesus which might be considered irreverent. Her cuts are far more sweeping than those made by Thomas in the second edition which contains thirty-six plays. He restores some of the cuts she had made of what she judged 'uninteresting or absurd scene[s]' on aesthetic grounds, but he tinkered a great deal more with verbal detail. It was his edition which became the best-seller, but he was building on foundations laid by his sister.

Mary Anne Lamb, 1764–1847

The second of seven children to a lawyer's clerk and servant, Mary Lamb received a brief education at an academy in Fetter Lane (London), and was responsible for the earliest education of her younger brother Charles (1775–1835). She began an apprenticeship in dressmaking, but in 1796, in a fit of insanity, she stabbed her mother to death. Charles managed to limit her asylum incarceration to three years, and continued to live with her for the rest of his life; 'I am wedded, Coleridge,' he wrote to his close friend, 'to the fortunes of my sister and my poor old father' (*Oxford Guide to British Women Writers*: 250–1). Charles and Mary collaborated on several successful books for children, including *Tales from Shakespear* (1807) and *Mrs Leicester's School, or, The History of Several Young Ladies, related by Themselves* (1809), while in 1815 Mary published a shrewd account of the condition of working women and the inadequacies of girls' education, an article 'On Needlework' for the *British Ladies' Magazine*, in which she argued that women 'may be more properly ranked among the contributors to, than the partakers of, the undisturbed relaxations of mankind' (258).

Tales from Shakespear: Designed for the Use of Young Persons, based on an idea by Mary Jane Godwin (second wife of William Godwin) and commissioned by Godwin's Juvenile Library, retold the stories of Shakespeare's plays for children. Although Mary's name did not appear on the title-page until the seventh edition of the *Tales* (1838), she was responsible for most of the work, writing much of the volume's preface and fourteen of the twenty tales: 'Mary has done them capitally', Charles wrote to Manning (*Letters of Charles and Mary Anne Lamb*: II.225). As Mary pointed out in a letter, Charles 'picked out the best stories first' (*Lear, Macbeth, Hamlet, Romeo and Juliet*, and *Othello*), and left her to tackle the 'more perplext and unmanageable' plays: *The Tempest, A Midsummer Night's Dream, The Winter's Tale, Much Ado About Nothing, As You Like It, The Two Gentlemen of Verona, The Merchant of Venice, Cymbeline, All's Well That Ends Well, The Taming of the Shrew, The Comedy of Errors, Measure for Measure, Twelfth Night,* and *Pericles, Prince of Tyre* (Gilchrist, *Mary Lamb*, 1889: 120). Charles reported that Mary complained 'of having to set forth so many female characters in boys' clothes. She begins to think Shakespeare must have wanted imagination!' (Gilchrist: 120). In the volume's preface, Mary explained (anonymously) that her intention was 'chiefly to write' for 'young ladies ... because boys are generally permitted the use of their fathers' libraries at a much earlier age than girls are' (vi–vii); many of her tales, such as *Measure for Measure* included here, focus upon the role of women in the plays and the constraints placed upon women in society (see Susan J. Wolfson, 1990).

The *Tales* first appeared in eight sixpenny numbers, but were soon collected in two small volumes, 'embellished' with illustrations which Charles Lamb deplored for their 'beastly vulgarity'. The success of the *Tales* was swift: a new edition was called for in 1809, and by 1900 Lambs' *Tales* had been reprinted some seventy-four times, including translations into French, German, Spanish and Swedish and 'an Indian imitation' in Bengali (*American Shakespeare Magazine*, 'Book Report', 1897: 94).

Tales from Shakespear: Designed for the Use of Young Persons. By Charles Lamb, 2 vols. London: Printed for Thomas Hodgkins at the Juvenile Library, 1807

Preface

I have wished to make these Tales easy reading for very young children. To the utmost of my ability I have constantly kept this in my mind; but the subjects of most of them made this a very difficult task. It was no easy matter to give the histories of men and women in terms familiar to the apprehension of a very young mind. For young ladies too it has been my intention chiefly to write, because boys are generally permitted the use of their fathers' libraries at a much earlier age than girls are; they frequently have the best scenes of Shakespear by heart, before their sisters are permitted to look into this manly book; and, therefore, instead of recommending these Tales to the perusal of young gentlemen who can read them so much better in the originals, I must rather beg their kind assistance in explaining to their sisters such parts as are hardest for them to understand; and when they have helped them to get over the difficulties, then perhaps they will read to them (carefully selecting what is proper for a young sister's ear) some passage which has pleased them in one of these stories, in the very words of the scene from which it is taken; and I trust they will find that the beautiful extracts, the select passages, they may chuse to give their sisters in this way, will be much better relished and understood from their having some notion of the general story from one of these imperfect abridgments.

[Charles's continuation of the Preface immediately follows.]

Measure for Measure

In the city of Vienna there once reigned a duke of such a mild and gentle temper, that he suffered his subjects to neglect the laws with impunity; and there was in particular one law, the existence of which was almost forgotten, the duke never having put it in force during his whole reign. This was a law dooming any man to the punishment of death, who should live with a woman that was not his wife; and this law through the lenity of the duke being utterly disregarded, the holy institution of marriage became neglected, and complaints were every day made to the duke by the parents of the young ladies in Vienna, that their daughters had been seduced from their protection, and were living as the companions of single men ...

[Lucio visits Isabel to tell her of Claudio's arrest:] Lucio then told her, Claudio was imprisoned for seducing a young maiden. 'Ah,' said she, 'I fear it is my cousin Juliet.' Juliet and Isabel were not related, but they called each other cousin in remembrance of their school-days friendship; and as Isabel knew that Juliet loved Claudio, she feared she had been led by her affection for him into this transgression. 'She it is,' replied Lucio ...

[Angelo is tormented by his desire for Isabel:] In the guilty conflict in his mind Angelo suffered more that night, than the prisoner he had so severely sentenced; for in the prison Claudio was visited by the good duke, who in his friar's habit taught the young man the way to Heaven, preaching to him the words of penitence and peace. But Angelo felt all the pangs of irresolute guilt: now wishing to seduce Isabel from the paths of innocence and honor, and now suffering remorse and horror for a crime as yet but intentional. But in the end his evil thoughts prevailed; and he who had so lately started at the offer of a bribe, resolved to tempt this maiden with so high a bribe as she might not be able to resist, even with the precious gift of her dear brother's life.

When Isabel came in the morning, Angelo desired she might be admitted alone to his presence; and being there, he said to her, if she would yield to him her virgin honour, and transgress even as Juliet had done with Claudio, he would give her her brother's life: 'for,' said he, 'I love you, Isabel.' ...

'To whom should I complain? Did I tell this, who would believe me?' said Isabel, as she went towards the dreary prison where her brother was confined. When she arrived there, her brother was in pious conversation with the duke, who, in his friar's habit had also visited Juliet, and brought both these guilty lovers to a proper sense of their fault; and unhappy Juliet with tears and a true remorse confessed, that she was more to blame than Claudio, in that she willingly consented to his dishonourable solicitations ...

The duke then more plainly unfolded his plan. It was, that Isabel should go to lord Angelo, and seemingly consent to come to him as he desired at midnight; that by this means she would obtain the promised pardon; and that Mariana should go in her stead to the appointment, and pass herself upon Angelo in the dark for Isabel. 'Nor, gentle daughter,' said the feigned friar, 'fear you to do this thing; Angelo is her husband; and to bring them thus together is no sin.' Isabel being pleased with this project, departed to do as he directed her; and he went to apprize Mariana of their intention. He had before this time visited this unhappy lady in his assumed character, giving her religious instruction and friendly consolation, at which times he had learned her sad story from her own lips; and now she, looking upon him as a holy man, readily consented to be directed by him in this undertaking ...

[At the City Gates 'to the amazement of all present, and to the utter confusion of Angelo, the supposed friar threw off his disguise':] The duke first addressed Isabel. He said to her, 'Come hither, Isabel. Your friar is now your prince, but with my habit I have not changed my heart. I am still devoted to your service.' 'O give me pardon,' said Isabel, 'that I, your vassal, have employed and troubled your unknown sovereignty.' He answered that he had most need of forgiveness from her, for not having prevented the death of her brother; – for not yet would he tell her that Claudio was living; meaning first to make a farther trial of her goodness. Angelo now knew the duke had been a secret witness of his bad deeds, and he said, 'O my dread lord ... let my trial be my own confession. Immediate sentence and death is all the grace I beg.' The duke replied, 'Angelo, thy faults are manifest. We do condemn thee to the very block where Claudio stooped to death; and with like haste away with him; and for his possessions, Mariana, we do enstate and widow you withal, to buy you a better husband.' 'O my dear lord,' said Mariana, 'I crave no other, nor no better man:' and then on her knees, even as Isabel had begged the life of Claudio, did this kind wife of an ungrateful husband beg the life of Angelo; and she said, 'Gentle my liege, O good my lord! Sweet Isabel, take my part! Lend me your knees ... Oh, Isabel, will you not lend a knee?' The duke then said, 'He dies for Claudio.' But much pleased was the good duke, when his own Isabel, from whom he expected all gracious and honorable acts, kneeled down before him, and said, 'Most bounteous sir, look, if it please you, on this man condemned, as if my brother lived.' ...

The duke commanded Claudio to marry Juliet, and offered himself again to the acceptance of Isabel, whose virtuous and noble conduct had won her prince's heart. Isabel, not having taken the veil was free to marry;

and the friendly offices, while hid under the disguise of a humble friar, which the noble duke had done for her, made her with grateful joy accept the honor he offered her; and when she became duchess of Vienna, the excellent example of the virtuous Isabel worked such a complete reformation among the young ladies of that city, that from that time none ever fell into the transgression of Juliet, the repentant wife of the reformed Claudio. And the mercy-loving duke long reigned with his beloved Isabel, the happiest of husbands and of princes.

Sarah Siddons (née Kemble), 1755–1831

The most celebrated actress of her day, Sarah Siddons came from a theatrical family; her father Roger Kemble and her brothers John Philip, Stephen and Charles were all actors, and her niece Fanny (daughter of Charles) followed her onto the stage. Her first public performance was as Ariel in the Dryden and Davenant adaptation of *The Tempest* at the King's Head in Worcester in 1767 when she was twelve. Despite initial opposition from her parents, she married William Siddons who participated in that production as Hippolito (a new character, heir to the Duke of Mantua, and 'one that never saw Woman') in 1773, and he became her business manager. A brief season for Garrick at Drury Lane in 1775–6 was judged a failure, but she became a success in the provinces with a number of roles including Shakespeare's Rosalind, Gertrude, Imogen, Isabella, Beatrice, Desdemona – and Hamlet. As her early biographer James Boaden put it, 'It may hardly be suspected by the followers of her maturer efforts, that one of her most applauded parts at Manchester was the character of Hamlet' (*Memoirs of Mrs. Siddons*, 1827: I. 281). She returned to London in 1783 and performed a wide range of parts until she retired in 1812, after which she gave private readings and benefit performances. William Hazlitt, who was too young to have seen her best stage performances, was particularly impressed with her readings of the tragedies: 'No scenic representation I ever witnessed produced the hundredth part of the effect of her reading Hamlet' (obituary in *New Monthly Magazine*, 1831: 31). She was hailed as the Muse of Tragedy and painted as such by Joshua Reynolds. Her most famous Shakespearean roles were Constance in *King John* (see Elizabeth Inchbald), Lady Macbeth, and Katherine of Aragon in *Henry VIII*; she told the elderly Samuel Johnson when she visited him in October 1783 that Katherine was her favourite part.

Sarah Siddons, 'Memoranda: Remarks on the Character of Lady Macbeth', in *The Life of Mrs Siddons* by Thomas Campbell. London: Effingham Wilson, 1834, 2 vols (vol. 2)

Sarah Siddons's Lady Macbeth remains her best documented performance. It is discussed in detail by James Boaden in his *Memoirs of Mrs. Siddons*, published before she died, and by her close friend Thomas Campbell in his *Life of Mrs. Siddons*, published three years after her death in 1834 and containing her own 'Memoranda' which she bequeathed to him. Both men clearly attended numerous performances and they are able to convey something of the extraordinary power she put into the part. Boaden writes:

> It has been said that, since the Eumenides of Eschylus [*sic*], tragic poetry had produced nothing so terrible and sublime as the Macbeth of Shakespeare. It may be said, with equal probability, that, since the happy invention of man invested dramatic fiction with seeming reality, nothing superior, perhaps equal, to the Lady Macbeth of Mrs. Siddons has been seen … The character of Lady Macbeth became a sort of exclusive possession to Mrs. Siddons. There was a mystery about it, which she alone seemed to have penetrated.

This might not have been predicted from her first performance in Bath in 1778 of which she recorded a vivid account:

> It was my custom to study my characters at night, when all the domestic cares and business of the day were over. On the night preceding that in which I was to appear in this part for the first time, I shut myself up, as usual, when all the family retired, and commenced my study of Lady Macbeth. As the character is very short, I thought I should soon accomplish it. Being then only twenty years of age, I believed, as many others do believe, that little more was necessary than to get the words into my head; for the necessity of discrimination, and the development of character, at that time in my life, had scarcely entered into my imagination. But, to proceed. I went on with tolerable composure, in the silence of the night, (a night I never can forget), till I came to the assassination scene, when the horrors of the scene rose to a degree that made it impossible for me to get farther. I snatched up my candle, and hurried out of the room, in a paroxysm of terror. My dress was of silk, and the rustling of it, as I ascended the stairs to go to bed, seemed to my panic-struck fancy like the movement of a spectre pursuing me. At last I reached my chamber, where I found my husband fast asleep. I clapt my candlestick down upon the table, without the power of putting the candle out; and I threw myself on my bed, without daring to stay even to take off my clothes. At peep

of day I rose to resume my task; but so little did I know of my part when I appeared in it, at night, that my shame and confusion cured me of procrastinating my business for the remainder of my life.

She was reluctant to play the part in London in 1785 and had a major argument with Richard Brinsley Sheridan, the manager at Drury Lane, on the first night over her 'innovation' (compared with the previously definitive performance by Susanna Pritchard) of playing the sleep-walking scene without holding a candle. Siddons sensibly argued that the 'Out, damned spot!' sequence required vigorous gestures with both hands. She refused to change her plan and the scene was a success: 'Mr. Sheridan himself came to me, after the play, and most ingenuously congratulated me on my obstinacy'. She also recalls on that occasion murmuring to herself as she undressed, 'Here's the smell of blood still', evoking from her dresser the response 'Dear me, ma'am, how very hysterical you are tonight; I protest and vow, ma'am, it was not blood, but rose-pink and water; for I saw the property-man mix it up with my own eyes'.

Siddons clearly finds Lady Macbeth a somewhat cold and difficult character to portray, but she does her best to present her in the most sympathetic light. Commenting on the first meeting of the Macbeths on stage [I. v], she says:

[Macbeth] announces the King's approach; and she, insensible it should seem to all the perils which he has encountered in battle, and to all the happiness of his safe return to her, – for not one kind word of greeting or congratulation does she offer, – is so entirely swallowed up by the horrible design, which has probably been suggested to her by his letters, as to have forgotten both the one and the other. It is very remarkable that *Macbeth* is frequent in expressions of tenderness to his wife, while she never betrays one symptom of affection towards him, till, in the fiery furnace of affliction, her iron heart is melted down to softness.

Proceeding through the part, she says of 'I have given suck' [I. vii. 54ff.]:

Even here, horrific as she is, she shews herself made by ambition, but not by nature, a perfectly savage creature. The very use of such a tender allusion in the midst of her dreadful language, persuades one unequivocally that she has really felt the maternal yearnings of a mother towards her babe, and that she considered this action the most enormous that ever required the strength of human nerves for its perpetration. Her language to Macbeth is the most potently eloquent that guilt could use. It is only in soliloquy that she invokes the powers of hell to unsex her.

Stressing Lady Macbeth's loneliness, she ascribes the 'appalling scene' of
the sleep-walking to an overflowing of suppressed emotion:

> Please to observe, that [Macbeth] (I must think pusillanimously, when I
> compare his conduct to her forbearance,) has been continually pouring
> out his miseries to his wife. His heart has therefore been eased, from time
> to time, by unloading its weight of woe; while she, on the contrary has
> perseveringly endured in silence the uttermost anguish of a wounded
> spirit.

Campbell claims that Sarah Siddons showed him her 'Remarks on the
Character of Lady Macbeth' some nineteen years before he published
them in 1834, indicating that they were in existence in 1815 (Campbell:
44). Both he and the author of an article in *Blackwood's Edinburgh
Magazine* (1834) nevertheless conduct an extended comparison between
her view of the character and that of Anna Jameson in *Characteristics of
Women* (1832), both of them anxious to deny any possibility of influence
or what we might call plagiarism. Campbell argues for a broad similarity
of approach: 'If there be any difference, it is that [Anna Jameson] goes
a shade farther than Mrs. Siddons, in her advocacy of Shakespeare's
heroine' (43). The *Blackwood's Magazine* writer (anonymous in 1834,
identified in the *Wellesley Index to Victorian Periodicals* as John Wilson)
finds more contrasts between the two accounts, but sets them together
against 'Lady Macbeth's male critics [who] have dismissed her with
ungallant haste and harshness' (365). He discusses what are seen as the
disparities between Siddons's performance of the role and her 'Memoranda' account: she argues on the page for a more vulnerable and
'feminine' character than her 'commanding', 'sternly beautiful' and
'stately' impersonation actually conveyed (359). Jameson is here described
as being 'in the first rank of our philosophical critics on Shakespeare'
(358) and 'the best female critic of the age' (365).

Elizabeth Wright Macauley, 1785–1837

An English actress, Macauley left the stage in 1817 to become a preacher at a London chapel; she subsequently returned to her acting career and it was in 'the varied and opposite characters of actress and preacher of the Gospel' that she was best known to the public (anonymous obituary appended to *The Autobiographical Memoirs of Miss Macauley*, 1834). Her publications included volumes of poetry (her 'Historical Poem' *Mary Stuart* was reprinted twice in 1823), and treatises on the theatre, such as *A Pamphlet on the Difficulties and Dangers of a Theatrical Life* (1812). In 1836–7 she toured England giving lectures on 'Domestic Philosophy' interspersed with readings from plays. Her last lecture, given in York, addressed 'Jealousy' and was illustrated by a recitation from *Othello* which, the *Gentleman's Magazine* reports, 'she delivered with an energy that drew forth the enthusiastic plaudits of her auditory' (July 1837: 96). The following day she died from a stroke.

Macauley's *Tales of the Drama: Founded on the Tragedies of Shakspeare, Massinger, Shirley, Rowe, Murphy, Lillo, and Moore, and on the comedies of Steele, Farquhar, Cumberland, Bickerstaff, Goldsmith, and Mrs. Cowley*, was published in London in 1822 and reprinted in New Hampshire in 1833. The preface to *Tales of the Drama* explains that Macauley converted 'the acted Drama to the more popular form of narrative, for the purpose of rendering the real beauties of the British stage more familiar, and better known to the younger class of readers, and even of extending that knowledge to family circles where the drama itself is forbidden' (1833: 5). The most important objective 'has been to render the whole strictly obedient to the most refined ideas of delicacy, subservient to the best purposes of morality, and conducive to the highest sense of religious awe, and love for a beneficent Providence' (1833: 6). *Tales of the Drama*, illustrated with woodcuts in the American 1833 edition includes discussions of *The Merchant of Venice*, *King John*, *Julius Caesar* and *Coriolanus*; the volume also includes two poems by Macauley in praise of Shakespeare's 'peerless worth' (1833: 71).

Miss Macauley, *Tales of the Drama: Founded on the Tragedies of Shakspeare, Massinger, Shirley, Rowe, Murphy, Lillo, and Moore, and on the Comedies of Steele, Farquhar, Cumberland, Bickerstaff, Goldsmith, and Mrs. Cowley*. Chiswick, London: Sherwood, Neely and Jones, 1822 and Exeter, New Hampshire: Robinson and Towle, 1833

The Merchant of Venice

Being of a liberal disposition, and something too anxious in doing honour to his father's memory by a show of rather too much magnificence, [Bassanio] had incurred many debts indiscreetly, which, from a sense of probity, he was now desirous to acquit himself of. They preyed upon his mind, and his prime of youth was clouded by the remembrance of those errors which he had committed in his less than prime. Bassanio was in truth an honest man – not according to the common acceptation of the term, but according to its real principle: for honesty, like many other terms used in this great world, is more talked of than understood, and rather practised than felt. It is a commendation all are ambitious to possess – but few desirous to deserve ...

In this extremity Bassanio and Antonio applied for three thousand ducats to Shylock, a wealthy Jew merchant, of usurious practices, but which were greatly checked by Antonio, whose benevolence and integrity reprobated the idea of taking advantage of his fellow creatures' necessities, and therefore he frequently lent out money gratis; thereby bringing down the rate of usance: and thus he, following the bent of his merciful inclination, had rescued many who had applied to him from the heavy penalty of their forfeitures to Shylock. The Jew therefore hated him; and finding he now required assistance at his hands, it was to him a subject of great exultation and of future hope ...

[At the trial Antonio demands that Shylock 'should record a deed of gift to his son in law of all he might die possessed of – and that he himself should immediately become a Christian!!!':] At this dreadful proposal a

FIGURE 3.
Original illustration of Shylock from *Tales of the Drama.*

cry of horror burst from the lips of the unfortunate Jew – all else might have been endured, but to become a Christian!! this was an affliction beyond calculation – a punishment the most severe which could have been imposed: yet he spoke no word in way of objection or appeal – his heart was swelled with anguish, too acute for utterance on this subject; and he could only make a faint request to retire, saying, if they would send the deed after him, he would sign it. He departed, and with an unsteady step slowly proceeded from court; but, when he reached the outer gates, his ears were assailed by the dismal yells, groans, hooting, hissing, and execrations of a numerous multitude. He stood still on the steps – looking with dismay on the rude rabble before him – but ere he could determine whether he should return and seek protection, or strive to make his way through the crowd – several of the mob rushed up the steps, and seizing the poor wretch, dragged him amongst them and buffeted him without mercy ... Overwhelmed with grief and shame, and hurt by some of the severe blows he had received – after a few hours of the most exquisite suffering both mental and corporal, he expired, having pronounced a pardon for his child, and signed the stipulated deed of gift. After his death the rabble razed his house to the ground – and piling up the rubbish in the form of a mountain, fenced it round, put a rude stone at the top, to signify that these ruins were once the dwelling of a merciless Jew whose life was the forfeit of his own malignity.

So perished this unfortunate man, one who amply possessed the bounteous gifts of heaven – and who, in seeking more, lost what he had. His name was execrated to posterity – and pity seldom deigned to bestow a tear on his fate. Yet surely, though his cruelty was great, and his revenge dreadful; his provocations were also great: and Antonio, however merciful he might be to his fellow Christians, evinced no mercy or forbearance towards the Jew, on whom he showered every indignity. He was Shylock's bitterest foe; hating his religion, he railed at him, and depreciated his value among his fellow merchants; he had disgraced him, spit on his beard on the Rialto, hindered him of half a million of money, called him dog, laughed at his losses, mocked at his gains, scorned his nation, thwarted his bargains, cooled his friends, heated his enemies: such were Shylock's accusations. And much of this because he was a Jew!! This was not Christianity, this was not the forbearance taught by that great Master of the faith, which we profess to follow ... If therefore the Jew was without mercy – little of mercy or favour had been shown to him, to teach him the bright example of

CHRISTIAN CHARITY!!!

... Nothing now occurred to interrupt the mutual happiness of all parties, save that the gentle Jessica, though she had been tempted by love to forsake her father, yet was deeply afflicted when she heard of his death. Time, however, blunted the poignancy of her grief, and her future life was comfortable, though probably not happy; for the painful remembrance of her disobedience could never entirely be obliterated from her heart ... Portia had no drawback upon her peace; her life with Bassanio was one continued scene of happiness ... Antonio's misfortunes were only transient. Three of his argosies, richly laiden, came unexpectedly into port, and all his previous losses were redeemed. Bassanio discharged every debt with large interest, suited to the circumstances of his creditors, and the extent of their kindness towards himself. The fame of his honour and integrity spread over the land, nor less the fame of Antonio's friendship. Their virtues were not merely nominal, they were solid and unchangeable; and when for ages after any one spoke of friendship – that of the merchant Antonio, for his kinsman the Lord Bassanio, was recorded as a precedent for all others.

Caroline Maxwell, active 1808–1828

Little is known of the novelist and historian Caroline Maxwell aside from her publications: 'an historical romance', *Alfred of Normandy* (1808), *Feudal Tales, Being a Collection of Romantic Narratives and Other Poems* (1810), *Beauties of Ancient English and Scottish History* (1825) and two 'abridgements' of the Bible (1827–8). *The Juvenile Edition of Shakspeare: Adapted to the Capacities of Youth* (London, 1828) adopts the format successfully established by Lambs' *Tales from Shakespear* (1807) of paraphrasing Shakespeare's plays for children; Maxwell also includes illustrative extracts from the text 'for study or recitation' (iii). 'Polite education cannot be complete', the Introduction argues, without 'an early knowledge of this excellent author' – but 'the perusal of the whole of Shakspeare's dramatic works might be deemed improper for juvenile readers' (iii). Hence *The Juvenile Edition of Shakspeare* adopts a policy of censorship: 'any incident, passage, or even word which might be thought exceptionable by the strictest delicacy, is entirely omitted, and on no occasion has the fair purity of the youthful mind been for one moment forgot' (iv). Submitted 'to the discernment of parents, of guardians, and preceptors', *The Juvenile Edition of Shakspeare* sought to convey 'much useful instruction, under the most pleasing garb, and shewing in the strongest light, the superiority of virtue, of honesty, discretion and goodness of heart, over the reverse of those amiable and honourable moral duties' (iv). The volume includes chapters on *Cymbaline* [sic], *Timon of Athens*, *The Story of Thomas Lord Cromwell*, *Anthony and Cleopatra* [sic], *Troilus and Cressida*, *Henry VIII*, *Titus Andronicus*, *King Lear*, *Richard II*, *Pericles* and *Sir John Oldcastle, the good Lord Cobham*.

Caroline Maxwell, *The Juvenile Edition of Shakspeare: Adapted to the Capacities of Youth*. London: Chapple, N. Hailes, Wells and C. H. Williams, 1828

Titus Andronicus

It has been previously remarked, that it is a matter of much doubt whether, or no, the Tragedy of Titus Andronicus was a legitimate dramatic work of Shakspeare's ... But as the play in question bears the name of the great Bard, we must take it for granted it is his, as none living can really prove to the contrary. And the outline of the story must be presented, to our young readers, as well as the horrid subject of the piece, and its compli- cated, and distressing circumstances will admit. The cruelty and ferocious manners, the want of noble and just principle and the savage sternness, exemplified in almost every character throughout this story, are such as we should suppose could never possibly have existed, even in the most uncivilized human societies, for amongst such we may imagine the sym- pathies of natural feeling would take place. Than how much less expect to find [*sic*] such barbarity amongst the polished Romans at the point of time, in which, this tragedy takes place. A period in which the Christian religion had made some progress in the Empire, the doctrines of which might have been expected to have tended more to soften the heart, and regulate the manners, (even though not completely established) amongst these intrepid, but still savage race of men, who were actuated by errone- ous ideas of false honour only. The deficiency in feelings of humanity, throughout, must ever render Titus Andronicus an unpleasant story: but given by so great a master of the human passions, both in their most amiable, or most degraded state, it must have its place in this selection; and the more so from its morally proving, that the most desirable gifts of nature, such as courage, beauty, sense or greatness, if not under the guidance of virtue and religion, humanity and justice, nothing avail to render the possessor himself happy – or to gain love or esteem either here, or hereafter ...

Titus Andronicus arrives from complete conquest of the Goths, a conquest of the utmost consequence to the Romans; and for which they were ready to decree him every possible honour. A long train of noble captives graced his victory, amongst the most conspicuous, of whom, was Tamora queen of the Goths: her majestic person, extraordinary beauty, and splendid apparel, struck all observers with admiration, whilst the haughtiness of her demeanour convinced them that her high spirit was unsubdued. The three sons of the queen were likewise of this train, and a Moor, also the great favourite and chief counsellor of Tamora, named Aaron. The grandeur of this procession was, however, greatly damped by a sorrowful one, which accompanied it, namely the bier on which was deposited the remains of one of Andronicus' sons, killed in the last final struggle, in which victory decided in favour of the Romans. And they were now bearing this youthful warrior to the tomb of his ancestors.

The mournful ceremony of enclosing him in this last receptacle, being performed with every possible attention and respect, which paternal af- fection could suggest; the remaining sons of Andronicus, with a savage brutality which would have disgraced the earliest period of the Roman empire, demanded of their father one of the noblest prisoners of the Goths, which he had there his captive, to sacrifice to the manes of their brother exulting at the same time, in the idea of the tortures they intended to inflict on him. This the inhuman father immediately consents to, as a just and proper measure, and names, as the victim the eldest son of Tamora, as the one most distinguished for nobility of birth, and stateliness of person. This order is given by Titus, without either pity, hesitation, or the slightest regard, to the tears and supplications of the wretched queen, his mother, who in a state of distraction, and kneeling at his feet, thus pathetically, and justly, addresses the powerful commander of his fate ['Stay, Roman brethren', I. i. 104–20] ...

The young prince therefore was destroyed, but (as may naturally be imagined) a deadly hatred against Andronicus, and all his family, entered the heart of Tamora, with a most determined resolution to seek revenge. The same idea was, likewise, entertained by her two remaining sons, Chiron and Demetrius. And, also of the crafty and designing Moor, who warmly attached to the queen and her children, secretly, and silently, vowed the destruction of the whole race of the Andronici, and to let no opportunity escape, for the execution of his deep revenge.

[Following Lavinia's wedding to Bassianus, Aaron, Tamora, Chiron and Demetrius enact their revenge during a hunt:] The hunt was to take place in a forest, celebrated for its gloom and intricacy, and by the wildness of the scenery, peculiarly adapted to the amusement of the chase, for such desperate hunters, who delighted to pursue the most ferocious, and terrific animals. And who could conceive no pleasures but such as were attended by personal danger, requiring to display bravery and skill.

Here it was, in this scene of desolation and terror, that the empress, her vile agent, and her two fiend-like sons, agreed to act their dreadful tragedy ...

> Revenge it, as you love your mother's life,
> Or be ye not henceforth called my children.
>
> [II.iii.113–14]

To which horrible accusation, her son Demetrius answers – 'This is a witness that I am your son.' – And instantly stabs Bassianus to the heart: Lavinia, who has been witness to this detestable action, in the bitterness of her grief and despair, (and totally regardless of the dangerous situation she was in, in the society of such dreadful, cruel, and wicked people,) threatens them with the vengeance, disgrace and punishment, which will follow on her disclosing the extent of their crime. When, with the feelings of demoniacs, they cut out her tongue to prevent her telling, and her hands to prevent her writing, any account of what they have perpetrated.

(This circumstance so horrible in itself, and so repugnant to nature, we may well suppose introduced only to heighten the tragic effect of the piece: as it is not to be imagined that a delicate young female, such as here described, could possibly have outlived such a dreadful mutilation, left as we are led to think without assistance or attention, in such a wild and solitary wilderness: but to proceed with the story, we must admit it.)

Anna Brownell Jameson (née Murphy), 1794–1860

The eldest daughter of Dennis Brownell Murphy, an Irish miniature painter, Anna Brownell Jameson was a respected and prolific writer on art, history, literature, travel, biography and women's employment. At the age of sixteen she became a governess to the sons of the Marquis of Winchester to support her family, and in 1825 she married the lawyer and friend of Hartley Coleridge, Robert Jameson; the marriage was unsuccessful from the start and in 1837, after Robert took up the position of Attorney-General of Upper Canada, they separated.

The rest of Anna Jameson's life was spent travelling and writing: in addition to *The Diary of an Ennuyée* (1826) and her highly successful volume of Shakespeare criticism, *Characteristics of Women* (1832), Jameson published several books on art history (including the extensive *Sacred and Legendary Art*, 1848–52), numerous periodical articles, histories of women (such as *Memoirs of Celebrated Female Sovereigns*, 1831) and social commentaries such as *The Relative Position of Mothers and Governesses* (1846). In the 1850s she sponsored reformers of women's education and position in society (including Adelaide Procter, Bessie Parkes and Barbara Bodichon) and suggested the idea for the early 'feminist' periodical, *The Englishwoman's Journal*. In 1855 she gave two public lectures, published as *Sisters of Charity and the Communion of Labour: Two Lectures on the Social Employments of Women* (1855; reissued 1856 and 1859), in which she argued for the breakdown of separate 'spheres' for men and women, with women being granted 'their *equal* but still *distinct* capacities and responsibilities in the great social commonwealth' (*Sisters of Charity*, 1859: xi and xvii). In 1893 Catherine Hamilton remembered Jameson as 'one of the first to claim for women that higher education and those wider opportunities which they now enjoy ... To her, and to those like her, the women of the nineteenth century owe a large debt of gratitude' (*Women Writers: Their Works and Ways*: 43). She died in 1860 after catching a cold while returning from a day's work at the British Library.

Jameson's *Characteristics of Women, Moral, Poetical, and Historical* – the first book to examine Shakespeare's female characters at length and consider 'women' as a legitimate category of Shakespeare criticism – first appeared in 1832 in two volumes, illustrated with fifty 'Vignette Etchings' designed by Jameson (see Figure 5); it was dedicated to Jameson's friend, Fanny Kemble (see Figure 4). Jameson's premise was to examine the moral, intellectual and emotional capacities of women – hence the general title of the book (only later in the century was the volume also known as *Shakspeare's Heroines*). 'It appears to me', she writes in the Introduction, 'that the condition of women in society, as at present constituted, is false in itself, and injurious to them, – that the education of women, as at present conducted, is founded in mistaken principles, and tends to increase fearfully the sum of misery and error in both sexes' (viii). Rather than write 'essays on morality, and treatises on education', Jameson (I.lii and xxi) used Shakespeare's heroines

> to illustrate the manner in which the affections would naturally display themselves in women – whether combined with high intellect, regulated by reflection, and elevated by imagination, or existing with perverted dispositions or purified by the moral sentiments. I found all these in Shakespeare ... his characters combine history and real life; they are complete individuals, whose hearts and souls are laid open before us – all may behold and all judge for themselves.

While observing that in Shakespeare's plays 'the male and female characters bear precisely the same relation to each other that they do in nature and society – [women] are not equal in prominence or in power – they are subordinate throughout' (I. xxiv), Jameson argued that Shakespeare's heroines were 'in truth, in variety, in power, equal to his men' (I. 35–6). In so doing Jameson redefined the status of Shakespeare's female characters within Shakespeare criticism; as Julie Hankey notes, 'after Jameson it became commonplace to describe Shakespeare as the "champion" of women' ('Victorian Portias', 1994: 427).

Characteristics of Women was received with enthusiasism: it was reprinted the following year (1833) in a 'corrected and enlarged' edition, published in New York in 1837, and by 1905 ran to over twenty editions. In 1834 John Wilson commended Jameson's book as a rare example of 'the eloquent and philosophic female criticism': comparing Jameson with Sarah Siddons, Wilson argued that

> the woman's heart, in both cases alike, revealed to them truths which seem to have escaped the perception of us male critics ... this is the service which in many particulars Mrs. Jameson has rendered to the female characters of Shakespeare; – in some cases placing the whole character in a new light, in almost all, elucidating and bringing out unsuspected beauties in individual situations or speeches ... it is hardly too much to say that

in these Characteristics the full beauties of Shakespeare's female characters have been for the first time understood. (181–6)

Henry Howard Furness, the Variorum editor, described the volume as 'delightful' (though he preferred Helena Faucit's *On Some of Shakespeare's Female Characters*, 1885), while on the publication of the second edition of the book in 1833 Fanny Kemble wrote to Anna Jameson from New York that 'you cannot think how extremely popular you are in this country. A lady assured me the other day, that when you went to heaven, which you certainly would, Shakespeare would meet you and kiss you for having understood, and made others understand, him so well' (Kemble, *Record of a Girlhood*, 1878: III. 316).

The introduction to *Characteristics of Women* is constructed as a dialogue between Alda (the author) and Medon (a male friend), while Jameson groups her character studies of Shakespeare's women into four

FIGURE 4.
Anna Jameson, Dedication of the second edition of *Characteristics of Women: Moral, Poetical, and Historical* to Fanny Kemble (1833). Jameson did the illustrations for the early editions of her book herself, learning to etch in order to be able to use her own drawings; later editions appeared with the drawings replaced by portraits and subsequently photographs of well-known actresses in Shakespearean roles. This drawing differs from the one in the 1832 edition and reflects Fanny's departure for an acting tour of America which she saw as an unhappy exile.

categories: characters of intellect (Portia, Isabella, Beatrice and Rosalind), characters of passion and imagination (Juliet, Viola, Helena, Perdita, Ophelia, Miranda), characters of the affections (Hermione, Desdemona, Imogen, Cordelia) and characters of history (Cleopatra, Octavia, Volumnia, Constance of Bretagne, Elinor of Guienne [*sic*], Blanche of Castile, Margaret of Anjou, Katherine of Aragon, and Lady Macbeth).

Anna Jameson, *Characteristics of Women, Moral, Poetical, and Historical.* With fifty Vignette Etchings, 2 vols. London: Saunders and Otley, 1832

Introduction. *Scene* – A Library [see Figure 5]

Medon. Then, in few words, what is the subject, and what the object of your book?

Alda. I have endeavoured to illustrate the various modifications of which the female character is susceptible, with their causes and results. My life has been spent in observing and thinking ... What I have seen, felt, thought, suffered, has led me to form certain opinions. It appears to me that the condition of women in society, as at present constituted, is false in itself, and injurious to them, – that the education of women, as at present conducted, is founded in mistaken principles, and tends to increase fearfully the sum of misery and error in both sexes; but I do not choose presumptuously to fling these opinions in the face of the world, in the form of essays on morality and treatises on education. I have rather chosen to illustrate certain positions by examples, and leave my readers to deduce the moral themselves, and draw their own inferences.

Medon. And why have you not chosen your examples from real life? ... you might have given us an epitome of your experience, instead of dreaming over Shakespeare ...

Alda. [Shakespeare's] characters combine history and real life; they are complete individuals, whose hearts and souls are laid open before us: all may behold, and all judge for themselves.

Medon. But all will not judge alike.

Alda. No; and herein lies a part of their wonderful truth. We hear Shakspeare's men and women discussed, praised and dispraised, liked, disliked, as real human beings; and in forming our opinions of them we are influenced by our own characters, habits of thought, prejudices, feelings, impulses, just as we are influenced with regard to our acquaintances and associates ...

Medon. But what have we here? – 'Characters of Imagination – Juliet – Viola.' Are these romantic young ladies the pillars which are to sustain your moral edifice? Are they to serve as examples or as warnings for the youth of this enlightened age?

Alda. As warnings of course – what else?

Medon. Against the dangers of romance? ... But seriously, do you think it necessary to guard young people, in this selfish and calculating age, against an excess of sentiment and imagination? ... The warning you speak of may be gently hinted to the few who are in danger of being misled by an excess of the generous impulses of fancy and feeling; but need hardly, I think, be proclaimed by sound of trumpet amid the mocks of the world. No, no; there are young women in these days, but there is no such thing as youth – the bloom of existence is sacrificed to a fashionable education, and where we should find the rose-buds of the spring, we see only the full-blown, flaunting, precocious roses of the hot-bed.

Alda. Blame, then, that *forcing* system of education, the most pernicious, the most mistaken, the most far-reaching in its miserable and mischievous

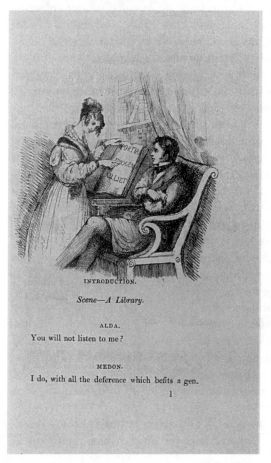

INTRODUCTION.

Scene—A Library.

ALDA.
You will not listen to me?

MEDON.
I do, with all the deference which befits a gen.

1

FIGURE 5.
Anna Jameson, Introduction to the second edition of *Characteristics of Women* (1833): 'Alda: "You will not listen to me?" Medon: "I do, with all the deference which befits a gentleman." ' Alda is clearly standing in for the author, while Medon is a male critic.

effects, that ever prevailed in this world. The custom which shut up women in convents till they were married, and then launched them innocent and ignorant on society, was bad enough; but not worse than a system of education which inundates us with hard, clever, sophisticated girls, trained by knowing mothers and all-accomplished governesses, with whom vanity and expediency take place of conscience and affection (in other words, of romance) ... Hence the strange anomalies of artificial society – girls of sixteen who are models of manner, miracles of prudence, marvels of learning, who sneer at sentiment, and laugh at the Juliets and the Imogens; and matrons of forty, who, when the passions should be tame and wait upon the judgment, amaze the world and put us to confusion with their doings.

Medon. Or turn politicians, to vary the excitement. – How I hate political women!

Alda. Why do you hate them?

Medon. Because they are mischievous.

Alda. But why are they mischievous?

Medon. Why! ... The number of political intriguing women of this time, whose boudoirs and drawing-rooms are the *foyers* of party spirit, is another trait of resemblance between the state of society now and that which existed at Paris before the Revolution.

Alda. And do you think, like some interesting young lady in Miss Edgeworth's tales [Maria Edgeworth, *Popular Tales*, 1804 and *Tales of Fashionable Life*, 1809–12], that 'women have nothing to do with politics'? Do you mean to say that women are not capable of comprehending the principles of legislation, or of feeling an interest in the government and welfare of their country? – of perceiving and sympathising in the progress of great events? – That they cannot feel patriotism? Believe me, when we do feel it, our patriotism, like our courage and our love, has a purer source than with you; for a man's patriotism has always some tinge of egotism, while a woman's patriotism is generally a sentiment of the noblest kind mixed up with her best affections ... As for the evil you complain of, impute it to that imperfect education which at once cultivates and enslaves the intellect, and loads the memory, while it fetters the judgment. Women, however well read in history, never generalize in politics; never argue on any broad or general principle; never reason from a consideration of past events, their causes and consequences. But they are always political, through their affections, their prejudices, their personal *liaisons*, their hopes, their fears.

Medon. If it were no worse I could stand it; for *that* is at least feminine.

Alda. But most mischievous. For hence it is that we make such blind partizans, such violent party women, and such wretched politicians ...

effects, that ever prevailed in this world. The custom which shut up women in convents till they were married, and then launched them innocent and ignorant on society, was bad enough; but not worse than a system of education which inundates us with hard, clever, sophisticated girls, trained by knowing mothers and all-accomplished governesses, with whom vanity and expediency take place of conscience and affection (in other words, of romance) ... Hence the strange anomalies of artificial society – girls of sixteen who are models of manner, miracles of prudence, marvels of learning, who sneer at sentiment, and laugh at the Juliets and the Imogens; and matrons of forty, who, when the passions should be tame and wait upon the judgment, amaze the world and put us to confusion with their doings.

Medon. Or turn politicians, to vary the excitement. – How I hate political women!

Alda. Why do you hate them?

Medon. Because they are mischievous.

Alda. But why are they mischievous?

Medon. Why! ... The number of political intriguing women of this time, whose boudoirs and drawing-rooms are the *foyers* of party spirit, is another trait of resemblance between the state of society now and that which existed at Paris before the Revolution.

Alda. And do you think, like some interesting young lady in Miss Edgeworth's tales [Maria Edgeworth, *Popular Tales*, 1804 and *Tales of Fashionable Life*, 1809–12], that 'women have nothing to do with politics'? Do you mean to say that women are not capable of comprehending the principles of legislation, or of feeling an interest in the government and welfare of their country? – of perceiving and sympathising in the progress of great events? – That they cannot feel patriotism? Believe me, when we do feel it, our patriotism, like our courage and our love, has a purer source than with you; for a man's patriotism has always some tinge of egotism, while a woman's patriotism is generally a sentiment of the noblest kind mixed up with her best affections ... As for the evil you complain of, impute it to that imperfect education which at once cultivates and enslaves the intellect, and loads the memory, while it fetters the judgment. Women, however well read in history, never generalize in politics; never argue on any broad or general principle; never reason from a consideration of past events, their causes and consequences. But they are always political, through their affections, their prejudices, their personal *liaisons*, their hopes, their fears.

Medon. If it were no worse I could stand it; for *that* is at least feminine.

Alda. But most mischievous. For hence it is that we make such blind partizans, such violent party women, and such wretched politicians ...

Medon. Then you think that a better education, based on truer moral principles, would render women more reasonable politicians, or at least give them some right to meddle with politics?

Alda. It would cease in that case to be *meddling*, as you term it, for it would be legitimized ... A time is coming perhaps when the education of women will be considered with a view to their future destination as the mothers and nurses of legislators and statesmen; and the cultivation of their powers of reflection and moral feelings supersede the exciting drudgery by which they are now crammed with knowledge and accomplishments.

Characters of intellect: Portia

We hear it asserted, not seldom by way of compliment to us women, that intellect is of no sex. If this means that the same faculties of mind are common to men and women, it is true; in any other signification it appears to me false, and the reverse of a compliment. The intellect of woman bears the same relation to that of man as her physical organization; – it is inferior in power, and different in kind. That certain women have surpassed certain men in bodily strength or intellectual energy, does not contradict the general principle founded in nature. The essential and invariable distinction appears to me this: in men the intellectual faculties exist more self-poised and self-directed – more independent of the rest of the character, than we ever find them in women, with whom talent, however predominant, is in a much greater degree modified by the sympathies and moral qualities ...

Portia, Isabella, Beatrice, and Rosalind, may be classed together as characters of intellect, because, when compared with others, they are at once distinguished by their mental superiority. In Portia it is intellect, kindled into romance by a poetical imagination; in Isabel, it is intellect elevated by religious principle; in Beatrice, intellect animated by spirit; in Rosalind, intellect softened by sensibility. The wit which is lavished on each is profound, or pointed, or sparkling, or playful – but always feminine; like spirits distilled from flowers, it always reminds us of its origin ... as women and individuals, as breathing realities, clothed in flesh and blood, I believe we must assign the first rank to Portia, as uniting in herself in a more eminent degree than the others, all the noblest and most loveable qualities that ever met together in woman ...

It is singular, that hitherto no critical justice has been done to the character of Portia: it is yet more wonderful, that one of the finest writers on the eternal subject of Shakspeare and his perfections, should accuse Portia of pedantry and affectation, and confess she is not a great favourite of his, – a confession quite worthy of him who avers his predilection for servant maids, and his preference of the Fannys and the Pamelas over the Clementinas and Clarissas.[1] ...

Portia is endued with her own share of those delightful qualities, which Shakespeare has lavished on many of his female characters; but besides the dignity, the sweetness, and tenderness which should distinguish her sex generally, she is individualized by qualities peculiar to herself: by her high mental powers, her enthusiasm of temperament, her decision of purpose, and her buoyancy of spirit ...

The sudden plan which she forms for the release of her husband's friend, her disguise, and her deportment as the young and learned doctor, would appear forced and improbable in any other woman; but in Portia are the simple and natural result of her character.[2] The quickness with which she perceives the legal advantage which may be taken of the circumstances; the spirit of adventure with which she engages in the masquerading, and the decision, firmness, and intelligence with which she executes her generous purpose, are all in perfect keeping, and nothing appears forced – nothing as introduced merely for theatrical effect.

But all the finest parts of Portia's character are brought to bear in the trial scene. There she shines forth all her divine self. Her intellectual powers, her elevated sense of religion, her high honourable principles, her best feelings as a woman, are all displayed ...

I come now to that capacity for warm and generous affection, that tenderness of heart which render Portia not less loveable as a woman, than admirable for her mental endowments. [At this point in the 'corrected and enlarged' second edition of *Characteristics of Women* (1833) Jameson inserts the following sentence: 'The affections are to the intellect what the forge is to the metal; it is they which temper and shape it to all good purposes, and soften, strengthen, and purify it.'] What an exquisite stroke of judgment in the poet, to make the mutual passion of Portia and Bassanio, though unacknowledged to each other, anterior to the opening of the play! ... Her subsequent surrender of herself in heart and soul, of her maiden freedom, and her vast possessions, can never be read without deep emotion; for not only all the tenderness and delicacy of a devoted woman, are here blended with all the dignity which becomes the princely heiress of Belmont, but the serious, measured self-possession of her address to her lover, when all suspense is over, and all concealment

---

1   Hazlitt's 'Essays', vol. ii, p. 167 [*Characters of Shakespear's Plays* (1817), p. 322. Fanny is the 'sweetheart' in Fielding's *Joseph Andrews* (1742); *Pamela* (1740–1) and *Clarissa* (1748) were novels by Samuel Richardson]
2   In that age, delicate points of law were not determined by the ordinary judges of the provinces, but by doctors of law, who were called from Bologna, Padua, and other places celebrated for their legal colleges.

superfluous, is most beautifully consistent with the character. It is, in truth, an awful moment, that in which a gifted woman first discovers, that, besides talents and powers, she has also passions and affections; when she first begins to suspect their vast importance in the sum of her existence; when she first confesses that her happiness is no longer in her own keeping, but is surrendered for ever and for ever into the dominion of another! The possession of uncommon powers of mind are so far from affording relief or resource in the first intoxicating surprise – I had almost said terror – of such a revolution, that they render it more intense. The sources of thought multiply beyond calculation the sources of feeling; and mingled, they rush together, a torrent deep as strong. Because Portia is endued with that enlarged comprehension, which looks before and after, she does not feel the less, but the more ...

[Added to the 'corrected and enlarged' second edition of *Characteristics of Women* (1833):] Many women have possessed many of those qualities which render Portia so delightful. She is in herself a piece of reality, in whose possible existence we have no doubt: and yet a human being, in whom the moral, intellectual, and sentient faculties should be so exquisitely blended and proportioned to each other; and these again, in harmony with all outward aspects and influences, probably never existed – certainly could not now exist. A woman constituted like Portia, and placed in this age, and in the actual state of society, would find society armed against her; and instead of being like Portia, a gracious, happy, beloved, and loving creature, would be a victim, immolated in fire to that multitudinous Moloch termed Opinion. With her, the world without would be at war with the world within: in the perpetual strife, either her nature would 'be subdued to the element it worked in,' [cf. Sonnet 111] and bending to a necessity it could neither escape nor approve, lose at last something of its original brightness; or otherwise – a perpetual spirit of resistance, cherished as a safeguard, might perhaps in the end destroy the equipoise; firmness would become pride and self-assurance; and the soft, sweet, feminine texture of the mind, settle into rigidity. Is there then no sanctuary for such a mind? – Where shall it find a refuge from the world? – Where seek for strength against itself? Where but in heaven?

Characters of passion and imagination: Helena

There never was, perhaps, a more beautiful picture of a woman's love, cherished in secret, not self-consuming in silent languishment – not pining in thought – not passive and 'desponding over its idol' – but patient and hopeful, strong in its own intensity, and sustained by its own fond faith ... The situation of Helena is the most painful and degrading in which a woman can be placed. She is poor and lowly; she loves a man who is far her superior in rank, who repays her love with indifference, and rejects her hand with scorn. She marries him against his will; he leaves her with contumely on the day of their marriage, and makes his return to her arms depend on conditions apparently impossible.[3] All the circumstances and details with which Helena is surrounded, are shocking to our feelings and wounding to our delicacy: and yet the beauty of the character is made to triumph over all ...

As her dignity is derived from mental power, without any alloy of pride, so her humility has a peculiar grace. If she feels and repines over her lowly birth, it is merely as an obstacle which separates her from the man she loves. She is more sensible to his greatness than her own littleness: she is continually looking from herself up to him, not from him down to herself. She has been bred up under the same roof with him; she has adored him from infancy. Her love is not 'th'infection taken in at the eyes,' nor kindled by youthful romance: it appears to have taken root in her being, to have grown with her years; and to have gradually absorbed all her thoughts and faculties, until her fancy 'carries no favour in it but Bertram's,' and 'there is no living, none, if Bertram be away' [I. i. 94–6].

It may be said that Bertram, arrogant, wayward, and heartless, does not justify this ardent and deep devotion. But Helena does not behold him with our eyes; but as he is 'sanctified in her idolatrous fancy.' Dr. Johnson says he cannot reconcile himself to a man who marries Helena like a coward, and leaves her like a profligate. This is much too severe: in the first place, there is no necessity that we *should* reconcile ourselves to him. In this consists a part of the wonderful beauty of the character of Helena – a part of its womanly truth, which Johnson, who accuses Bertram, and those who so plausibly defend him, did not understand. If it never happened in real life that a woman, richly endued with heaven's best gifts, loved with all her heart, and soul, and strength, a man unequal to or unworthy of her, and to whose faults herself alone was blind – I would give up the point; but if it be in nature, why should it not be in Shakspeare? We are not to look into Bertram's character for the spring and source of Helena's love for him, but into her own. She loves Bertram, – because she loves him! – a woman's reason, – but here, and sometimes elsewhere, all-sufficient ...

Bertram is certainly not a pattern hero of romance, but full of faults such as we meet with every day in men of his age and class. He is a bold, ardent, self-willed youth, just dismissed into the world from domestic indulgence, with an excess of aristocratic and military pride, but not without some sense of true honour and generosity ... He flies her on the

---

3 I have read somewhere that the play of which Helena is the heroine (*All's Well that Ends Well*) was at first entitled by Shakspeare 'Love's Labour Won.' Why the title was altered, or by whom, I cannot discover.

very day of their marriage, most like a wilful, haughty, angry boy, but not like a profligate. On other points he is not so easily defended, and Shakspeare, we see, has not defended, but corrected him. The latter part of the play is more perplexing than pleasing. We do not indeed repine with Dr. Johnson, that Bertram, after all his misdemeanours, is 'dismissed to happiness;' but notwithstanding the clever defence that has been made for him, he has our pardon rather than our sympathy; and for mine own part, I could find it easier to love Bertram as Helena does, than to excuse him: her love for him is his best excuse.

Characters of the affections: Hermione

The character of Hermione exhibits what is never found in the other sex, but rarely in our own – yet sometimes; – dignity without pride, love without passion, and tenderness without weakness ... The character of Hermione is considered open to criticism on one point. I have heard it remarked, that when she secludes herself from the world for sixteen years, during which time she is mourned as dead by her repentant husband, and is not won to relent from her resolve by his sorrow, his remorse, his constancy to her memory; such conduct, argues the critic, is unfeeling as it is inconceivable in a tender and virtuous woman. Would Imogen have done so, who is so generously ready to grant a pardon before it be asked? or Desdemona, who does not forgive because she cannot even resent? No, assuredly; but this is only another proof of the wonderful delicacy and consistency with which Shakspeare has discriminated the characters of all three. The incident of Hermione's supposed death and concealment for sixteen years, is not indeed very probable in itself, nor very likely to occur in every-day life. But besides all the probability necessary for the purposes of poetry, it has all the likelihood it can derive from the peculiar character of Hermione, who is precisely the woman who could and would have acted in this manner. In such a mind as hers, the sense of a cruel injury, inflicted by one she had loved and trusted, without awakening any violent anger or any desire of vengeance, would sink deep – almost incurably and lastingly deep ... Can we believe that the mere tardy acknowledgment of her innocence could ... heal a heart which must have bled inwardly, consumed by that untold grief, 'which burns worse than tears drown' [II.i.111–12]? ... is she one either to forgive hastily or forget quickly? and though she might, in her solitude, mourn over her repentant husband, would his repentance suffice to restore him at once to his place in her heart? to efface from her strong and reflecting mind the recollection of his miserable weakness? ... In a mind like Hermione's, where the strength of feeling is founded in the power of thought, and where there is little of impulse or imagination ... there are but two influences which predominate over the will, – time and religion. And what then remained, but that, wounded in heart and spirit, she should retire from the world? – not to brood over her wrongs, but to study forgiveness, and wait the fulfilment of the oracle which had promised the termination of her sorrows. Thus a premature reconciliation would not only have been painfully inconsistent with the character, it would also have deprived us of that most beautiful scene, in which Hermione is discovered to her husband as the statue or image of herself. And here we have another instance of that admirable art, with which the dramatic character is fitted to the circumstances in which it is placed: that perfect command over her own feelings, that complete self-possession necessary to this extraordinary situation, is consistent with all that we imagine of Hermione; in any other woman it would be so incredible as to shock all our ideas of probability.

The character of Paulina, in the 'Winter's Tale,' though it has obtained but little notice, and no critical remark, (that I have seen,) is yet one of the striking beauties of the play: and it has its moral too ... She is a character strongly drawn from real and common life – a clever, generous, strong-minded, warm-hearted woman, fearless in asserting the truth, firm in her sense of right, enthusiastic in all her affections; quick in thought, resolute in word, and energetic in action; but heedless, hot-tempered, impatient, loud, bold, voluble, and turbulent of tongue; regardless of the feelings of those for whom she would sacrifice her life, and injuring from excess of zeal those whom she most wishes to serve. How many such are there in the world! But Paulina, though a very termagant, is yet a poetical termagant in her way; and the manner in which all the evil and dangerous tendencies of such a temper are placed before us, even while the individual character preserves the strongest hold upon our respect and admiration, forms an impressive lesson, as well as a natural and delightful portrait.

In the scene, for instance, where she brings the infant before Leontes with the hope of softening him to a sense of his injustice – 'an office which,' as she observes, 'becomes a woman best' [II.ii.29–30] – her want of self-government, her bitter, inconsiderate reproaches, only add, as we might easily suppose, to his fury ... while we honour her courage and her affection, we cannot help regretting her violence ... It is admirable ... that Hermione and Paulina, while sufficiently approximated to afford all the pleasure of contrast, are never brought too nearly in contact on the scene or in the dialogue;[4] for this would have been a fault in taste, and have necessarily weakened the effect of both characters: – either the serene grandeur of Hermione would have subdued and overawed the fiery spirit of Paulina, or the impetuous temper of the latter must have disturbed in

---

4   Only in the last scene, when, with solemnity befitting the occasion, Paulina invokes the majestic figure to 'descend, and be stone no more,' and where she presents her daughter to her, 'Turn, good lady! our Perdita is found' [V.iii.120–1].

some respect our impression of the calm, majestic, and somewhat melancholy beauty of Hermione.

Historical characters: Cleopatra

I cannot agree with one of the most philosophical of Shakspeare's critics,
who has asserted 'that the actual truth of particular events, in proportion
as we are conscious of it, is a drawback on the pleasure as well as the
dignity of tragedy' [Hazlitt, *Characters of Shakespear's Plays*, 1817: 306].
If this observation applies at all, it is equally just with regard to characters:
and in either case can we admit it? The reverence and the simpleness of
heart with which Shakspeare has treated the received and admitted truths
of history – I mean according to the imperfect knowledge of his time –
is admirable; his inaccuracies are few; his general accuracy, allowing for
the distinction between the narrative and the dramatic form, is acknowledged to be wonderful. He did not steal the precious material from the
treasury of history, to debase its purity, – new-stamp it arbitrarily with
effigies and legends of his own devising, and then attempt to pass it current,
like Dryden, Racine, and the rest of those poetical coiners. He only rubbed
off the rust, purified and brightened it, so that history herself has been
known to receive it back as sterling ... It does not add to the pain, as far
as tragedy is a source of emotion, that the wrongs and sufferings represented, the guilt of Lady Macbeth, the despair of Constance, the arts of
Cleopatra, and the distresses of Katherine, had a real existence; but it adds
infinitely to the moral effect, as a subject of contemplation and a lesson
of conduct.[5] ...

Of all Shakspeare's female characters, Miranda and Cleopatra appear
to me the most wonderful. The first, unequalled as a poetic conception;
the latter, miraculous as a work of art. If we could make a regular
classification of his characters, these would form the two extremes of
simplicity [amended to 'the two extremes of simplicity and complexity'
in the second edition, 1833]; and all his other characters would be found
to fill up some shade or gradation between these two ... I have not the
slightest doubt that Shakspeare's Cleopatra is the real historical Cleopatra
– the 'Rare Egyptian' – individualized and placed before us. Her mental
accomplishments, her unequalled grace, her woman's wit and woman's
wiles, her irresistible allurements, her starts of irregular grandeur, her

---

5 'That the treachery of King John, the death of Arthur, and the grief of Constance,
   had a real truth in history, sharpens the sense of pain, while it hangs a leaden
   weight on the heart and the imagination. Something whispers us that we have no
   right to make a mock of calamities like these, or to turn the truth of things into
   the puppet and play-thing of our fancies' [Hazlitt, *Characters of Shakespear's
   Plays*: 306] – To consider *thus* is not to consider *too* deeply, but not deeply *enough*.

bursts of ungovernable temper, her vivacity of imagination, her petulant caprice, her fickleness and her falsehood, her tenderness and her truth, her childish susceptibility to flattery, her magnificent spirit, her royal pride, the gorgeous eastern colouring of the character; all these contradictory elements has Shakspeare seized, mingled them in their extremes, and fused them into one brilliant impersonation of classical elegance, Oriental voluptuousness, and gipsy sorcery.

What better proof can we have of the individual truth of the character than the admission that Shakspeare's Cleopatra produces exactly the same effect on us that is recorded of the real Cleopatra? – She dazzles our faculties, perplexes our judgment, bewilders and bewitches our fancy; from the beginning to the end of the drama, we are conscious of a kind of fascination against which our moral sense rebels, but from which there is no escape ...

To these traits we must add, that with all her violence, perverseness, egotism, and caprice, Cleopatra mingled a capability for warm affections and kindly feeling, or rather what we should call in these days, a constitutional *good-nature* – and was lavishly generous to her favourites and dependants. These characteristics we find scattered through the play: they are not only faithfully rendered by Shakspeare, but he has made the finest use of them in his delineation of manners. Hence the occasional freedom of her women and her attendants, in the midst of their fears and flatteries, becomes most natural and consistent; hence, too, their devoted attachment and fidelity, proved even in death. But, as illustrative of Cleopatra's disposition, perhaps the finest and most characteristic scene in the whole play, is that in which the messenger arrives from Rome with the tidings of Antony's marriage with Octavia ... The pride and arrogance of the Egyptian queen, the blandishment of the woman, the unexpected but natural transitions of temper and feeling, the contest of various passions, and at length, – when the wild hurricane has spent its fury, – the melting into tears, faintness, and languishment, are portrayed with the most astonishing power, and truth, and skill in feminine nature. More wonderful still is the splendour and force of colouring which is shed over this extraordinary scene. The mere idea of an angry woman beating her menial presents something ridiculous or disgusting to the mind; in a queen or a tragedy heroine it is still more indecorous;[6] yet this scene is as far as possible from the vulgar or the comic. Cleopatra seems privileged to 'touch the brink of all we hate' with impunity ...

In representing the mutual passion of Antony and Cleopatra as real

---

6 The well known violence and coarseness of Queen Elizabeth's manners, in which she was imitated by the women about her, may in Shakspeare's time have rendered the image of a royal virago less offensive and less extraordinary.

and fervent, Shakspeare has adhered to the truth of history as well as to general nature. On Antony's side it is a species of infatuation, a single and engrossing feeling: it is, in short, the love of a man declined in years for a woman very much younger than himself, and who has subjected him by every species of female enchantment. In Cleopatra the passion is of a mixt nature, made up of real attachment, combined with the love of pleasure, the love of power, and the love of self.

Mary Cowden Clarke (née Novello), 1809–1898

The daughter of Victor Novello, musician and composer, Mary Cowden Clarke grew up in a house frequented by artists, musicians and authors such as John Keats, Leigh Hunt, Charles Lamb and 'dear, kind Mary Lamb', who taught Mary Cowden Clarke Latin (*My Long Life*, 1896: 17). Charles Cowden Clarke (1787–1877), a journalist, drama reviewer, and lecturer on Shakespeare, was another family friend; Mary married him in 1828 and they enjoyed nearly fifty years of happy companionship and literary collaboration.

Mary Cowden Clarke must be one of the first women to make writing on Shakespeare her profession: her extensive publications on Shakespeare include concordances, annotated editions, critical studies and articles, alongside the popular *Girlhood of Shakespeare's Heroines* (1850–2). 'My affectionate veneration for Shakespeare began in childhood', Mary Cowden Clarke explained, 'when – a little girl – my father brought me home a new book, – "Lamb's tales from Shakespeare", and showed me the pictures, and told me something of the story' (preface to her edition of *Shakespeare's Works*, 1860: vi). Her mother also played an influential role: it was 'she who first inspired me with a love of all that is good and beautiful, and who therefore may well be said to have originated my love of Shakespeare' (preface to *Concordance*, 1845: v). Mary Cowden Clarke's first, massive, contribution to Shakespeare studies was her *Concordance* to Shakespeare's plays – the first of its kind – published in eighteen monthly parts during 1844 and 1845, then in a single volume in 1845. The idea for the *Concordance* came to Mary 'at the breakfast-table of some friends' (in fact, the Lambs), and took 'sixteen years of assiduous labour' to complete (preface to *Concordance*: v–vi); it was extensively and enthusiastically reviewed. Five years later appeared the highly successful *The Girlhood of Shakespeare's Heroines* (published serially from 1850 to 1852, then as a five-volume collection), fifteen long tales describing the childhood and early life of Shakespeare's heroines up until the point at which Shakespeare's play begins. The 'design' of the book, Mary Cowden Clarke explained, was 'to trace the probable antecedents in the history of some of Shakespeare's women; to imagine the possible circumstances and influences of scene, event, and associate [*sic*], surrounding the infant life of his heroines', and to place them 'in such situations as should naturally lead up to, and account for, the known conclusion of their subsequent confirmed character and afterlife' (I.iii–iv). In effect, the tales provide a novelistic 'subtext' to Shakespeare's female characters, and contain striking scenes of sex, violence and death; modern critics have condemned this naturalist approach to character as naive, but contemporary reviewers of the *Girlhood* were more appreciative, and respectful of the author of the *Concordance*, stressing the value of the tales for introducing young people to Shakespeare. An abridged edition prepared by Mary's sister, Sabilla Novello, appeared in three volumes in 1879, with many of the more sensational events omitted, but the full text was re-issued with a new preface in 1892.

In 1860 came Mary Cowden Clarke's edition of *Shakespeare's Works*. Understandably unaware of the work of Henrietta Bowdler, Mary wrote in the volume's preface 'I may be allowed to take pride in the thought that I am the first of his female subjects who has been selected to edit his works; and it is one of the myriad delights I owe to him, that I should be the woman upon whom so great a distinction is conferred' (vi). Despite Mary's firm position in the 1860 Preface that she eschews commentary on the grounds that it is intrusive and tedious – footnotes are 'mere vehicles for abuse, spite and arrogance' (vii) – she collaborated with Charles on an annotated edition which appeared in 1865. *The Shakespeare Key*, published jointly under the names of Charles and Mary, followed in 1879: the volume formed a companion to the *Concordance*, and consisted of entries ranging from lists of examples to substantial essays on topics such as 'Coins', 'Dramatic Time', 'Elliptical Style', 'Oaths', 'Punctuation', 'Soliloquies', and 'Power in Writing Silence', which praised the silences of Virgilia, Hermione and Perdita.

In addition to her major works on Shakespeare, Mary Cowden Clarke was an indefatigable contributor to journals and magazines and a prolific correspondent, writing articles on Shakespeare for *Shakespeariana* and *The Girl's Own Paper*, and including Shakespearean heroines in her quasi-historical *World-Noted Women* (1858). In 1850 she published a series on 'Shakespeare's Lovers' (male) in *Sharpe's London Magazine* (a periodical originally aimed at 'middle and lower walks of society' and advertised as 'safe and acceptable reading for the Family Circle'), and from 1849 to 1854 she contributed a series on 'Shakespeare – Studies of Women' to *The Ladies Companion*, in which she asserted 'in Shakespeare's page, as in a mental looking-glass, we women may contemplate ourselves. Of all the male writers that ever lived, he has seen most deeply into the female heart; he has most vividly depicted it in its strength, and in its weakness' (25). In her edition of *Shakespeare's Works* (1860), Mary argued that Shakespeare's insight into women stemmed from his respect for his wife, Anne Hathaway: 'the advantage in generosity which he has always assigned to women over men when drawing them in their mutual relations with regard to love, gives us excellent warrant for supposing that he had had reason to know this truth respecting her sex from the mother of his children' (x). In 1846 she proposed to erect a statue to Shakespeare by subscriptions invited from women only; she later confessed that she did not get much response to her newspaper advertisements (*Letters to an Enthusiast*: 46).

Mary Cowden Clarke had many admirers amongst American Shakespearean scholars, who showed their appreciation of her work by presenting her with a specially carved Testimonial Chair in 1852, made of rosewood and surmounted by a head of Shakespeare. The testimonial was organised by the self-professed 'Enthusiast' of Mary Cowden Clarke, Robert Balmanno of New York, who corresponded with Mary from 1850 to 1861 (reprinted in *Letters to an Enthusiast*, 1904); amongst the subscribers was the actress Charlotte Cushman (famous for her performances as Romeo and Hamlet). Mary Cowden Clarke's eminent correspondents included Horace Howard Furness of the Variorum series and his wife Helen Kate Furness, who published a concordance of the Poems in 1875 (Philadelphia) and whom Mary described as 'my sister in concordant deed!' ('Helen Kate Furness', *Shakespeariana*: 1883–4: 71). It was, however, the 'fraternity' of Shakespeare scholarship, and her acceptance within it, that Mary Cowden Clarke more often emphasised. *The Shakespeare Key* is dedicated to 'The True Shakespearian all over the world – in token of cordial fraternity', while in the Preface to the *Concordance* Mary expresses gratitude to John Payne Collier for letting her see the unpublished manuscript of the final volume of his edition of Shakespeare: 'Such a mark of confidence was a worthy type of the fraternity of feeling inspired by a close study of our Immortal Poet' (vii); she also acknowledges 'my "co-mates and brothers in 'labour'" – the Printers' (vii). Reflecting in 1896 on a visit to the Shakespeare Library in Birmingham in 1885 she comments 'I may here be permitted to mention that I have ever felt grateful for the liberal way in which distinguished Shakespearians have treated me with a cordial *fraternity* as one of their brotherhood' (*My Long Life*, 1896: 226–7).

Mary Cowden Clarke, 'On Shakspeare's Individuality in his Characters: Shakspeare's Lovers', *Sharpe's London Magazine* (1850), 3 parts: 168–72, 343–8, 138–75. Part 3

The character of Orlando, in AS YOU LIKE IT, is, perhaps, the most perfect examplar of manly gentleness and modesty that was ever drawn. He is so gentle-hearted, that the poet has endued him with a person of stalwart proportions, and a frame of great muscular strength, that no particle of effeminacy may mingle with the gentleness that distinguishes him ... In his replies to the two ladies, when they endeavour to dissuade him from venturing in so unequal-seeming a match, we still see the modest Orlando; concluding with that beautiful speech, profoundly touching in its youthful self-abnegation.

> 'I beseech you, punish me not with your hard thoughts ... I shall do my friends no wrong, for I have none to lament me: the world no injury, for in it I have nothing; only in the world I fill up a place, which may be better supplied when I have made it empty.' [I.ii.183–93]

Immediately after this speech, – almost womanly in its sweet spirit of resignation, – he wrestles with the strong man, throws him, and leaves him bereft of breath and motion on the earth ...

In the very midst of his kindly cheering of old Adam, on their journey, while he is soothing him with almost feminine tenderness, and proving his gentleness of heart by the most affectionate care, we find the poet reminding us of his manly strength of limb and muscle, by making Orlando raise the old man in his arms, and carry him to a place of rest, while he goes to seek food. Shakspeare has marked this pointedly; for he has made Orlando say ... 'come, *I will bear thee to some shelter;*' and afterwards, the duke says – 'Welcome; *set down your venerable burden.*'

In making one so passing gentle as Orlando a hero and a lover, the poet has well kept the image of the man before our eyes in his tall proportions, and his athletic strength. He is gentle-hearted, but high-spirited; he is modest, but firm and manly; his is the gentleness of bravery and magnanimity. Orlando is an embodiment of the power – the all-prevailing might of gentleness ...

The impression we have of the sincerity of Orlando's love is heightened by the qualities which constitute that of the other lovers in the play. There is more or less of extravagance in the love of all the rest. Oliver's is sudden; Silvius's desperate; Touchstone's whimsical. Oliver's affection offers no reason for its abrupt existence ... Till [Oliver] becomes [a lover], he is tyrannous and treacherous; practising against the very life of his younger brother. Afterwards, he is in all things changed. It is as if the magnanimity of his brother's rescue began the touching of his heart, and prepared it for the gentle influence of a first love – a love at first sight; this, in its softening and refining monition, advances his cure, and his coming into the sweet atmosphere of Arden and its simple happiness completes his reform ...

It is marvellous how consistently the poet has drawn this character of Claudio [in *Much Ado About Nothing*]. He has made him throughout a heartless fellow, with a ·constant eye to his own advantage; and yet so artistically as well as consistently is he drawn, that he passes for a gallant young soldier, a pleasant companion, a gentleman, and a LOVER! We are made to hear of his bravery in the wars, we are made to see that his friends like him, and we find him polished in manner and accomplished in speech. But on scrutinising his character, we discover his nature to be radically mean and selfish ... [He] is, in fact, a type of a large class of men who rank as lovers in the world. He loves the woman for his own sake, not for hers; for what she is worth to him, not for what she is herself ... That is quite the act of a worldly man, Claudio's asking Benedick, in the first instance, his opinion of Hero. A worldly man is apt to judge his mistress – or aught else he would appropriate – through the eyes of others. A worldly man likes to know the general estimate of a woman or a purchase he seeks to make his own. He rates them by the market-price of public opinion. If he discover that they stand high in the judgment of the world, they immediately rise in his own idea. To find that the lady he admires is thought a fine woman, is toasted as a beauty, is the prize sought by many suitors, – find that the horse he has thought of for his own riding has several other bidders, – to find that the lease of the house he has some notion of renting is likely to fall into other hands; – gives suddenly to each cent. per cent. additional value in his eyes, and excites his desire to become their possessor ...

Here are four individual lovers. Orlando, the impersonation of manly gentleness; Oliver, that of love at first sight, and reformation through love; Silvius, that of desperation in love; and Claudio, that of worldliness in love.

Mary Cowden Clarke, *The Girlhood of Shakespeare's Heroines: in a Series of Fifteen Tales*, 5 vols. London: W. H. Smith and Son, Simpkin, Marshall and Co., 1850–2

Portia: the heiress of Belmont

[Dedicated to John Rolt, Q.C. The Count Guido di Belmonte falls in love and marries Portia, the sister of his fellow student at the University of Padua, Bellario (in *The Merchant of Venice*, III.iv.50, Portia consults

Doctor Bellario, 'my cousin', in preparation for the trial). Twelve years later Portia dies giving birth to a daughter, named after her mother; distraught, Guido disappears for seventeen years leaving Bellario to bring up the baby Portia. See also Figure 6.]

[Bellario] would often laughingly tell [Portia], that though she had no regular schooling, no masters, no accomplishments, no womanly teaching, – no set education in short, yet that he should in time make her an excellent scholar, and a most capital lawyer.

Bellario was an enthusiast in his profession; and Portia loved to hear him dwell at length upon its attributes, its privileges, its powers, and its value. He would descant upon his favourite theme; and she, well-pleased to listen, would often introduce the subject, and urge and induce him to continue its disquisition ... 'The practice of Law,' he would say, 'induces magnanimity. It teaches us tolerance towards the infirmities of our fellow-beings; seeing how the best natures may be warped by unkindness, ingratitude, or injury. It engenders compassion for human frailty; forbearance on account of man's prejudices, mistakes, and ignorance; pity for his

FIGURE 6. Sabilla Novello, *The Merchant of Venice*: 'Porzia, in the Library at Belmont, receives her dying father's injunctions relevant to the caskets, which he resolved shall decide her future disposal in marriage'. Novello was the sister of Mary Cowden Clarke and abridged *The Girlhood of Shakespeare's Heroines* in 1879. She presented an album containing this and twenty-nine other pencil drawings illustrating *The Girlhood* to her niece Porzia Gigliucci on her birthday, 27 December 1884.

imperfections, and desire for his enlightenment. It inculcates benevolence, patience, consideration ... Accomplishment in oratory as well as sound-ness of judgment is essentially valuable, that you may not only carry conviction by the train of your reasoning, and the strength of your arguments, but that you may secure the attention, and win the favour of the more superficial among your auditors, so as at once to prepossess them in favour of your. cause.'

'Might not we women make good advocates, then, cugino mio?' Portia would playfully ask; 'you know we are apt to speak eloquently when our hearts are in a cause, and when we desire to win favour in its decision.'

'It is because your hearts generally take too active a part in any cause you desire to win, that your sex would make but poor lawyers, carina. Besides, women, though shrewd and quick judging, are apt to jump too rapidly at conclusions, and mar the power of their understanding by its too vivacious action ... To skilfully treasure up each point successively gained, and by a tardy unmasking of your own plan of action, to lead your opponent on to other and more sure committals of himself, is more consonant with the operation of a man's mind, than suited to the eager, impulsive nature of woman. Her wit is more keen, than her understanding is sedate.'

'Well, one day or other you may be brought to acknowledge that I could make a profound lawyer,' replied the smiling Portia; 'am I not your disciple? and must not the pupil of the learned Doctor Bellario needs become so if she choose?'

'My Portia will become quite as proficient as I could wish her, if she know enough of law to manage worthily and justly her own estate by-and-by,' answered he; 'and it is with the thought that she will hereafter be called upon as lady of Belmont, to rule her tenantry, to adjust their rights, to settle their differences, to decide their claims, and to secure their welfare, that I allow her to cross-question me upon the mysteries of law as she has done. And so now, that I may not make an absolute pedant of you, a jurisconsult in petticoats, a lawyer in a girl's white dress, instead of a sober silk gown, go call Nerissa to have a game at ball with you in the avenue, till I come and join you, that we may take a long walk together.' ...

It was the morning on which she completed her seventeenth year. She entered the library where Bellario sat, and as she stepped forward to present him with a rare old volume of poetry and a heap of blushing dew-covered flowers which she had just gathered as a birthday token, she looked so radiant with happiness and beauty, that he involuntarily gazed at her as he would have done at a beautiful vision – an impersonation of childhood on the verge of womanhood. Her fair hair, partly disordered by the eagerness with which she had collected her flowers regardless of thorns, spray, drooping leaves, or sweeping branches; her cheeks, glowing with morning air and exercise; her April eyes, bright with mingled smiles and tears, as she greeted him who had been father and brother both in one to her infancy and girlhood ... all made him fancy her a little fondling child again. But when, some minutes after, she stood at his side, discussing with enthusiasm the beauties of the poet whose richly-emblazoned volume she held in her hand; when her eyes beamed with intelligence, her figure dilated with the energy of her appreciation of lofty sentiment and daring imagination, her tone thrilled with admiration and awe, and her whole appearance was instinct with elevation and sublimity of thought, Bellario felt that he gazed upon a sentient, high-minded woman – one capable of bearing her part in the great drama of life, and of influencing the destinies of others by her intellect, her sentiment, her actions.

Desdemona: the Magnifico's child

[Dedicated to Alexander Christie 'in acknowledgment of the generous gift of his fine picture, "Othello's Despair"' (I.287). Brabantio courts the aristocratic but poor lady Erminia in secret against his father's wishes; when his autocratic father dies, Brabantio is finally free to marry the woman he loves.]

The gondola glided on. Beneath its black awning, – extended at full length upon its black leather cushions, – lay a young man, clothed in a suit of deep mourning. But in his face there was nothing that assorted with these swart environments ... For though the suit he wore was for a father, yet so harsh a parent, so unreasonable a tyrant had that father been, that his recent decease was felt to be emancipation from slavery, rather than a loss and a sorrow. Death had freed the young man from a more intolerable bondage than that of body – thraldom of spirit; and he was now hastening to claim the dearest privilege of human liberty – choice in love, in marriage, – which had hitherto been denied to him ...

[Brabantio inherits the title of Magnifico – and his father's haughty temper.] Amid a round of gaiety, of brilliant entertainments, of successive festivities, of growing emoluments and honours in the state, the magnifico's satisfaction seemed full to repletion; but perhaps it was this very plenitude which led to satiety, and then induced waywardness, and at length brought on recurring fits of his old temper, which had once produced such unhappy results. He had inherited a naturally haughty disposition from his father; his position fostered pride and wilfulness; unthwarted by fortune, idolized by his wife, he could scarcely fail to gain fresh conviction of his importance and irresponsible power; insensibly he became more and more capricious and domineering ...

So complete was the infatuation of Erminia's fondness for her husband, that she remained unaware of this growing evil in his humour ... She never dreamed that the ingenuous young man who had first won her heart in the obscure retreat where he had discovered her, content to sue for her love, to woo her humbly and perseveringly, and to make her his wife in unostentatious privacy and retirement, – who had consented to visit her by stealth, and abide in patience the release from a stern father's coercion, had in fact now become scarcely less imperious, or less of a domestic tyrant than that father.

But though unconscious of the change itself, its influence acted upon her. She did not trace the cause, but her gentleness merged into timidity; her submission into passiveness ... Instead of the honest remonstrance, the modest yet plain representation, – which surely beseem a wife, when reasoning a point with a husband, whose indulgence and justice equal his right of rule, and who will grant patient hearing to one whose interest in the ultimate good established should be no less than his own, – there was in the lady Erminia's conduct a subserviency, a temporizing, which will too often take the place of candour in a timid woman ...

Could the lady Erminia have taught [Desdemona] the honesty as well as modesty of innocence, – the unflinching candour which ought to belong to goodness and greatness, – have inspired the courage of transparent truth, she would have invested her daughter with a panoply that would have proved her best protection against the diabolical malignity by which she was one day to be assailed, and borne her scathless through the treachery which wrought her fate ... Accustomed to see her mother yield in silence even to things in which she did not acquiesce; to see her avoid doing what she tacitly seemed to agree to; to see her evade what she would not object to ... apparently consenting and approving, but in fact frustrating and censuring by a system of silent passiveness; the little girl insensibly acquired just such a system of conduct. It suited with her native disposition, – still, gracious, and serene; full of quiet sweetness, and unruffled calm. It secured her from the chance of opposition, of contest in will; it preserved her from the risk of exciting a father's displeasure ... [Erminia and Desdemona] hardly knew it – but so it was; they feared [Brabantio] more than they loved him; they dreaded his disapprobation, more than they hoped to win his approval. Over-strained respect engendered reserve. Had he been contended [sic] with a little less submission, he might have commanded more reverence; had he exacted less obedience, he might have obtained dearer regard; with somewhat less implicit observance, he might have had fonder affection. As it was, they honoured him as a husband, a father; but to neither of them was he a friend ... None of that loving trust, that spontaneous cordiality, – which should pour itself freely into the bosom of a woman's dearest male friend, – subsisted between them; but not one of the three was conscious of its non-existence. They each thought that love – perfect love, dwelt amidst them; but love, to be perfect love, must be free, unreserved, unfearing, equal.

Isabella: the votaress

[Dedicated to Douglas Jerrold. After the death of her mother, Isabella's
father joins a regiment outside Vienna and places Isabella with a careless
guardian, Frau Leerheim. Isabella befriends Nanni who, unbeknown to
the innocent Isabella, is a prostitute; Isabella's religious devotion later
inspires Nanni's repentance at her deathbed. Isabella attends school at a
local convent, and receives moral instruction from Sister Aloysia; one day
Isabella is shocked to hear from Bertha, one of Frau Leerheim's maids,
of the brutalisation in prison of a Bohemian boy and the consequent 'fall'
of his sister. Sister Aloysia takes the opportunity to explain to Isabella
the facts of prostitution.]

After a pause, Isabella repeated musingly: – 'The poor young thing
"went astray," Bertha said. "No brother to protect her!" From what, I
wonder?'

The good nun took this opportunity of giving Isabella the explanation
she had formerly promised, when she should be older and fitter to com-
prehend her meaning. She gently revealed to her, that by an inscrutable
ordination of the Almighty, sin and evil were permitted to exist; she spoke
to her of the degradation of vice, of the misery of crime; she told her of
the many ways in which frail humanity is beset … she showed how the
native greater weakness of women, both in frame and in heart, rendered
them peculiarly liable to fall away from virtue, and to yield to vice, and
that the very softness and flexibility of their natures, though originally
disposing them to good, yet also tended to make them easier victims to
sinister influence. She then unveiled to her, – as a tender mother might
do, – how the especial virtue, esteemed the crown of women, was fair
chastity; how it behoved them to preserve that crown untarnished; how
it was a duty to watch diligently their own hearts, lest solicitation from
thence should join with that they might meet elsewhere, to betray them;
how it was a glory and a grace to live unsullied; how it was irremediable
shame and dishonour to fall.

'But surely, where the glory is so great, on the one hand, and the penalty
so severe on the other,' said Isabella, 'the wonder is, that women should
ever yield, – should ever fall. Well may the sex be called weak, – foolish, –
frail, if they are so untrue to their own best interests.'

'Thus it appears to you, on the first glance. But consider. How many
are there, who have any one to represent to them their true best interest?
How many are there, who have the aiding strength of morality and
religion? How many poor girls are taught even simple right from wrong?
Too few, I fear. Remember, therefore … to be lenient when you judge
of error among the fallen of your sex … That rigid adherence to virtue
which in you, is mere duty, and scarcely more than a selfish regard to

your own advantage, is in them a high merit, – and too frequently the price of heroic self-denial, of sublimest sacrifice.'

'Sacrifice!' said Isabella. 'Surely, for highest gain.'

'Ay, sacrifice;' replied the nun. 'Sacrifice for highest gain, it is true – yet still, sacrifice. What should you know, my dear child, you, enclosed within a sanctuary of peace, know of the temptations, the almost irresistible temptations, of the daily world? How should you rightly estimate the promptings of passion – you, who have had your feelings regulated, your affections duly filled, your principles confirmed? … What idea can you form of the wisperings of vanity, the thoughts of a girl who sees herself in rags, while others are becomingly decked, – you, who have always had ladylike attire supplied for your wear. What are you to guess of the urgency of hunger, – you, who have your daily meals provided, and have never known the sting of more than a few hours' sharpened appetite, or a delayed unquenching of thirst? Think of these things, in their true force, – put yourself in the place of a poor young creature, day by day surrounded and beset by such influences, and then judge of her fall; then say, whether it be not almost a miracle, if she maintain her integrity.'

'A miracle, indeed!' whispered Isabella.

'Holy mother forbid, my dearest child,' said the nun, 'that I should for one instant seek to dethrone the sacred image of Chastity from the exaltation she occupies in your thoughts, or help to diminish your sense of the necessity firmly to abide by her laws, or in any way lessen your reverence for those who do hold fast by Virtue; all I would do is to teach you commiseration for those so unhappy as to abandon her service, to forfeit her privileges, to exchange her happiness, for the misery of Vice.' …

[After Nanni's death and the imprisonment of Ragozine, a notorious pirate, Isabella considers what her life might have been:] A life misspent, and an ignominious death … such might have been my brother's lot! Mine too, might have been no better than Nanni's, had I had only such instruction as the world awards to the lowly-born, instead of helping them to stem the tide of hostile circumstances which naturally surround them. Are there no means of averting this sore evil? Must a particular portion of humanity be acquiescently doomed to certain sin, as well as poverty? To starvation of soul as well as body? Can the intellect of the world devise no method of redemption? Will rulers ever continue to devote their energies towards fit correction of crime, rather than diligently to seek some system for its due prevention? Might not the discovery of how best to minister timely help, be a higher aim in policy, than the most equitable code of punishment that ever was designed? O that the poor could have early succour! Wholesome teaching – moral training – right guidance!

Then perchance, we might have fewer culprits, and worthier, happier citizens!'

As these thoughts passed through her mind, Isabella's attention was drawn, by the lay-sister, towards a carriage that came quietly but rapidly along the otherwise empty streets ... 'That is his grace, the Duke – our exemplary sovereign, Vincentio. He is going to early mass and confession, at the monastery hard by. Ah! he is indeed a worthy prince! So young a man, yet so strict in his religious observances; so modest and retired in his habits; so devoted to study; so unostentatious in the discharge of his duties. See how he avoids parade and display in this early hour, and in the plain equipage he chooses for going to his devotions. Holy virgin mother, assoil him, and have his soul in thy especial care!' ejaculated the nun.

'Amen!' murmured Isabella, with fervour. 'May he have all divine grace to fulfil his princely duties, in promoting the welfare and best happiness of his subjects. May he learn to enquire into their wants, to minister to their necessities, and to improve their condition ... To be the friend of such a prince, to aid him in his views, to inspire and sustain him in such designs would be high privilege, and tempt an ambition that should make a life of peace and retirement mere cowardice and self-indulgence. Were such a post of friendship possible, it were glorious enough in its prospects of patriotism and loyal help, to make the calm happiness of a convent-life, – which I fondly hope may be mine, – seem poor in the exchange! The vocation of a worthy prince, is not unlike that of the votaress; – it is a life dedicated to a sacred cause.'

Katharine and Bianca: the Shrew, and the demure

[Dedicated to 'the American Enthusiast' (see p. 83). Claudia, a vain and selfish woman from Genoa, marries Baptista Minola and has two daughters: Katharina and Bianca. Katharina's spirited temper goes unchecked by Claudia, and after Claudia's premature death Baptista allows Katharine to grow 'more hard and saucy than ever'. At a party given by Signior Gremio at his country house, Katharina loses her temper with a young boy, Giulio, and throws a large stone at him which strikes him on the temple, causing him to lose consciousness.]

Signior Baptista was so shocked at the injury that his daughter's rashness had caused; he was so much vexed at the scandal which this public exposure of the violence of her temper occasioned, that he resolved upon a step which he hoped might have the good effect of reforming her, while it offered the present advantage of removing her from the observation of society. He determined to place his two daughters as pensioners in a convent, for the finishing of their education ... Katharina and Bianca were accordingly placed as boarders among the Ladies of the Holy Petticoat;

such being the name of the fashionable sisterhood, in honour of a relic of great virtue and sanctity, which they possessed ...

[At the convent Katharine feels remorse over her mother's death and tries, briefly, to be more tolerant towards Father Bonifacio – but soon dismisses her 'generous impulses' as fanciful dreams.] Childish dreams of good and noble things! ... why are ye not more frequently, and more sedulously, watched for, fostered, and developed, by those who have the tutelage of youth? ... Is it because girls' schooling is mostly held to be comprised in the teaching of knick-knack making, accomplishments, and housewifery, with but little regard to the heart and mind which may one day be a wife's, – perhaps a mother's? Was it that these nuns – like many other school-teachers, were too intent on the culture of external qualifications, to pay any attention to the inward workings of their pupils' natures? Certainly, those of Katharina's were unnoted and unaided; and, left to themselves, they were insufficient to effect the redemption of her character.

Several successive vacations, – with their prize-distributions, their work-displays, their pincushions, their recitation-gabbles, their chorus-squeaks, their tinsel-crowns, their paper rose-wreaths, their frivolous anxieties, their important trifles, their absorbing insipidities, – had followed each other as the years came round. But the end of that time found the young ladies of the school little changed ... Their brains had remained stunted, while their bodies grew; their characters had been permitted to remained undeveloped; their ideas had been cramped and compressed into shell-baskets and rice-paper boxes; their thoughts had been pinned down to pincushions; their intellects had been put under glass cases with artificial flowers, – dwarfed and confined beneath glass lids with waxen effigies, and gilt filigree; they had never been suffered to entertain an opinion on a subject less flimsy than floss silk, catgut, or gauze; to speculate upon a higher subject than paste, wire, and gum; or to exercise their invention upon things of graver weight than feathers, – of greater moment than spangles, foil, and tinsel.

In all, save increased dexterity of finger, they were veriest babies still. Some of the most energetic among them ... could write flourished alphabets in three or four different texts, and add up sums the whole length of a slate; – but these were looked upon as the prodigies of the school – quite geniuses; girls almost unfemininely clever ...

[Signior Gremio holds a party in the grounds of his country house. See also Figure 7.] There was a large group dispersed round the grassy bank on which Katharina, Bianca, and her friend Elvira, had seated themselves. The gentlemen lounged at the ladies' feet, or lay a little in the rear, or leaned against the surrounding trees; while light talk, gay jests, and repartees, sometimes of compliment, sometimes of raillery, flew from one to another, and were bandied to and fro.

Suddenly signior Gremio said, 'I expect Giulio Vinci here to-day; he's not long returned from Naples, where he has been spending some time with an uncle of his, a captain in the marine service.'

Katharina's face flashed scarlet.

'And who may Giulio Vinci be?' said Elvira ...

'He's the boy I told you of, whom my sister was so unfortunate as to injure;' said Bianca in Elvira's ear; pressing her friend's arm, to draw her attention to Katharina's change of colour.

Katharina overheard the words, and said loudly and passionately: – 'If ever you speak of that again, I'll make your meek, blue eyes as red as a ferret's, with my nails.'

There was an awkward pause ...

Soon after, a game of ball was formed. A great number of the company engaged in it; and it proceeded with great spirit.

Giulio Vinci had just made a long run after the ball, and was tossing it up into the sky as high as he possibly could, and catching it, while he returned to the spot whence he was to pitch it into Bianca's hand, – her turn being to throw it next.

As she caught it from him, she said: – 'How active you are, signior Giulio! what a mercy it is, that you've no lameness – no weakness remaining from your accident! we ought to be very thankful.'

The words were hardly out of her mouth, before Katharina snatched the ball from her sister's hands, and flung it over the wall. 'I warned you not to allude to that again!' she exclaimed.

'Hey-dey, miss Miscetta! Are these your tricks still?' exclaimed Giulio, turning suddenly towards her. Then, seizing her by the wrists, he cried out: – 'Run, some of you, and fetch the ball. I'll hold this little fury fast, till you return.' She writhed, and struggled; but not one jot could she move her wrists in his firm grasp. He laughed at her fruitless efforts to free herself, and said: – 'You had to deal with a boy, then; I'm a man now, Miscetta, and stronger than you are.'

'I care not for your strength. Let me go, I say!' she exclaimed.

He unclasped his hold, saying: – 'There, you are free; but if you interfere any more with our game, you spoil-sport, I'll take care and prevent you effectually.'

She laughed a short mocking laugh, and her eyes flashed, as she said: – 'I make no promises!'

'But I do! and you'll see that I'll make them good;' said he. The ball was brought back; and the game was resumed; but the instant it became Bianca's turn to throw the ball, Katharina seized it from her, and threw it over the wall as before.

She had no sooner done so, than Giulio caught her up in his arms, and ran with her to a tree, at a little distance, near to which lay a cord that had been used for one of the swings. With this he proceeded to bind her to the tree, in spite of her frenzied stamping and struggling; while the company, half laughing, half concerned, at the scene, looked on, expecting to hear her flame out with her usual violence.

But not a single word did she utter.

At first, she panted, struggled, and strove her utmost, to prevent his effecting his purpose, her face, all the while, crimson with rage. But, after a time she grew deadly pale. For while Giulio was binding her to the tree, she suddenly became aware that it was the same from which her own violence had caused his fall, years before; in his exertions to secure her, the hair became pushed back from his forehead, and she caught sight of the deep-seamed scar that marked the place of the wound her hand had once given him.

A quite new and strange set of emotions overwhelm her, and hold her, as it were, paralysed in speech and motion. A perplexed feeling of shame

FIGURE 7. Isabel Scott, *The Taming of the Shrew*: Katherina and Guilio at Signor Gremio's ball: 'When you are tired of your bonds, you can cast them off by a word'. Little is known about Isabel Scott. Her sketchbook of illustrations of scenes from Mary Cowden Clarke's *The Girlhood of Shakespeare's Heroines* is amongst the Novello Cowden Clarke materials in the Brotherton Collection at Leeds University Library; she was possibly a friend of the family and an amateur artist.

and surprise take possession of her, at finding herself completely overcome, – *'mastered.'* As the strong, manly arms, hold her firmly, constrained there to abide, his will, she feels her spirit as well as her body give way, and own itself vanquished. One of the most singular features of this new state of feeling is, that the sense of defeat, for the first time in her life, is not altogether painful. As her woman's frame involuntarily yields to his masculine strength – as her feebler limbs bend beneath his will, and submit to his power, there is an inexplicable acquiescence, an absence of resentment and resistance, altogether unwonted, and surprising to herself.

Her silence, her turning pale, her ceasing from struggle and opposition, made Giulio, in his turn, relent. 'Say you'll not meddle with the ball again, and I'll undo the cords;' he said.

She looked into his face; but was literally unable to speak ... he was looking earnestly at her, watching her with curiosity and interest; and the thought came into his head, whether she might not be in some measure right – that the character of scold and shrew, so universally given to her, wrought the very evil it ascribed – that it worked upon such a disposition as hers in making her worse than she naturally was – that it made her sore and irritable, and chafed her into fury, rudeness, and violence. He saw that taunts and reproaches were so far from correctives, that they but served as stimulatives to her temper; when, to proper control, and a firmly-maintained authority, it might probably be taught to yield.

Ophelia: the rose of Elsinore

[Dedicated to John Forster 'in high admiration of his dramatic judgment' (II.181). Ophelia, the baby daughter of Polonius and the lady Aoudra, is nursed by a peasant-woman, Botilda, who sings old songs to her.]

The lady Aoudra's attendant, Kraka, one day saw fit to call the rustic nurse to account for the subject of one of these songs, which struck her town-bred notions as somewhat lacking in the matter of decorum. 'Hast thou ne'er a cradle-song, or proper nursery-rhyme, good Botilda, to chant to my lady's baby? The songs thou choosest for the child's lullaby, are none of the most seemly for the purpose, to my poor thinking ... There's no knowing how soon a babe may catch a meaning,' said the lady's-maid, tossing her head; 'meanings, – 'specially naughty meanings, – are sooner caught than you, in your country rudeness, might suppose, good mistress Botilda. There's no telling how early a child may spy out wickedness in words – they're so 'cute in listening, and pretending not to understand, and all the while making out a deal that they oughtn't. There's much more o' that going on, than you'd think, mistress Botilda.' ...

'As for my poor foolish old songs, can't think they'd do mischief to any one that isn't set upon seeing more in 'em than's meant – let alone a sucking-babe, that makes out naught of the words but the chime and the rhyme they make.'`

'No harm? no mischief?' exclaimed Kraka; 'why, there's that tawdry nonsense you sing about St. Valentine's day. I should like to know what you make out of that; good mistress Botilda?'

'I leave it to you, to make out what you have a fancy for from it, mistress Kraka;' said the nurse quietly. 'I can only say, as I said before ... it's no matter to me; and certainly no matter to the child, that can't make matter out of it.'

'What stupid animals these country folks are!' muttered the waiting-maid; 'little better than swine, in their brutish ignorance of what's what, and in their obstinate sticking to what they've once said.'

'Let them that like to ferret out filth, find what they have a mind to, in my old songs;' said the nurse to herself; 'only don't let 'em go and give their nasty notions to my innocent child; who, if ever she should chance to catch up the words by-and-by, from hearing me repeat 'em, would only do so like a prattling starling, for the sake of the sound, and without a thought of any bad meaning.' ...

[Polonius is called away to Paris and Aoudra reluctantly joins him. Aoudra places Ophelia in the care of Botilda, risking 'the want of refinement in the peasant home, for the sake of its simple food, its pure air, its kindly hearty foster-care'.] Amongst these rough cottage people, more and more did the child feel herself alone and apart. Her shyness and sparing speech grew upon her. She was not unhappy; but she became grave, strangely quiet and reserved for a little creature of her years, and so confirmed in her habit of silence, that she might almost have passed for dumb ... she did not know why she was disinclined to talk, but she seldom met with any inducement to open her lips, and insensibly she kept them closed. With her sweet, earnest eyes, her placid though un-smiling countenance, and her still demeanour, she had a look of reflection, of pensiveness, that better becomes womanhood grown, than childhood ...

[Ophelia befriends Jutha, Botilda's teenage daughter, who becomes pregnant. Jutha is too frightened and ashamed to tell anyone of her pregnancy; Ophelia observes her growing anxiety and illness, but remains innocent of the fact that Jutha is in fact heavily pregnant.] That evening, on their return to the cottage, it seemed to Ophelia, that those at home, first became aware of the change in her friend Jutha, which she had so long perceived and lamented. But it also strangely struck her that instead of this discovery awakening kindness and compassion towards the sufferer, it appeared to excite rather anger, reproach, and even invective. Their voices were raised in a confusion of questions, threats and expressions of wonder, with which they assailed the young girl, in an incoherent clamour, from which the child could make out nothing clearly. The mother bemoaned her own and her daughter's fate; the father murmured deep curses; the two elder brothers strode angrily to and fro, with menacing looks, ground teeth, and clenched hands ... Jutha had flung herself upon a chair in the midst; upon the back of which she leaned, burying her face in her arms. From time to time she uttered convulsive sighs; heavy sobs burst from her, each seeming to rend her frame asunder ...

Ophelia crept away softly to bed, unable to make out the meaning of this distressful scene; and marvelling much why they should show displeasure instead of sorrow at Jutha's illness ... She slept; but it was an uneasy sleep, full of dreams, and haunting ideas of wretchedness and perplexity. From this slumber she awoke strugglingly, and with a beating heart. It was pitch dark; she felt that many hours had elapsed, and that it was dead of night. She stretched out her arms, to feel for Jutha at her side; but no Jutha was there ...

In alarm for her friend, in an irresistible desire to learn how she was, and what detained her, Ophelia stole out of bed, and groped her way downstairs. On reaching the door of the sitting-room, she saw a bright streak from the crevice at the bottom, which showed her that there was light in the room ... She stood on the threshold, gazing in, trying to distinguish the objects the room contained. On the large table, which occupied the centre of the apartment, lay something extended, which was covered with a white cloth. At one end were ranged as many iron lamps as the cottage household afforded, burning in a semicircular row. Amazed at this strange sight, the child advanced; and with an uncontrollable impulse, walked straight up to the table, and raised the end of the white cloth, nearest to the lamps. Their light fell full upon the object beneath. Startled, and shuddering, the child looked upon that which was so familiar, yet so strange. Could that indeed be the face of Jutha? – that white, still, rigid thing? – with those breathless, motionless lips, and those eyelids, that looked fixed, rather than closed? And what was that, lying upon her breast, encircled by her arm? A little, little face – a baby's face! It looked so transparent, so waxen, – so pretty, though so strangely image-like, that the child involuntarily stretched forth her finger, and touched its cheek. The icy cold shot, with a sharp thrill, to her heart, and she screamed aloud, as she turned to Jutha's face, and flung herself upon it with wild kisses and tears.

Botilda, hearing the cry, came running in. She used her best efforts to calm the mourning and affrighted child, carrying her up to bed, lying down by her side, folding her in her arms, and speaking fondlingly and soothingly to her, until she dropped asleep. But it was long ere this was accomplished; and for many successive nights, the nurse had to sleep in the room with her charge, that she might be won to rest. The shock she had received, was severe; and long left its effects upon her sensitive organization. Naturally gentle, she became timid. She shrank about, scared, and trembling; fearful of she hardly knew what, but feeling unassured, doubtful, full of a vague uneasiness and alarm.

Hermione: the Russian princess

[Dedicated to Charles Knight 'in honor of his Shakespearean labours' (III.199). After leading the Emperor of Russia to safety in a snowstorm, Paulina is chosen as a childhood companion for the Emperor's daughter, Hermione. Several years pass, when Camillo and Antigonus arrive from Sicily to negotiate the marriage between their Prince, Leontes, and Hermione; they stay with Paulina and her father, the general Betzkoi.]

During their stay with general Betzkoi, the frank graces, the sensible conversation, and spirited beauty of his daughter Paulina, had made a powerful effect upon both the visitors. But Camillo, with the strict uprightness, and singleness of purpose that distinguished him, resolved to suppress his incipient passion, and to defer all consideration of its interests, until those of his royal master's wishes had been fulfilled. He determined neither by word or look to betray his feelings to Paulina or her father, until he should have returned from Sicily with the mutual agreement of the two courts respecting the projected royal marriage; and then he would endeavour to effect his own with the woman whom above all her sex, he desired to call his wife. The lord Antigonus was withheld by no such nice scruples from endeavouring at once to secure the prize he had in view; he thought he could not too early make sure of so beautiful a girl, who moreover, was the favourite of her who in all probability was destined to become his future queen; he therefore immediately, although privately, declared his love to the father of Paulina, and asked her hand of him ... Vladimir Betzkoi eagerly closed with the proposal ... and he told Paulina of the consent he had given, confident of her glad acquiescence with an arrangement that promised so happily.

'I knew a husband must be my fate, at some time or other;' was her answer to her father's intimation; 'I have long made up my mind to endure the impending evil, when its time shall arrive.' ...

[A few days later] the princess sat with her favourite lady, – the embroidery-frame furnishing a pleasant occupation for hands and eyes, while they were engaged in interesting talk.

'And now tell me, Paulina ... A capital, and a court, are sore places for the beguiling and losing of hearts. Hast thou thine safe yet?'

'Safe and sound; safe in mine own keeping, and sound from any scratch of the blindfold archer-boy's shafts;' said Paulina, laughing – though a little constrainedly. 'But though my heart's free, my hand's fettered. Fathers have a right to forge a golden link for our finger, that is apt to set an iron one upon the wrist; and we find ourselves bound hand and foot for life, before we've tried the use of our limbs, or found out whether we've a heart or not, to wish to guide them after our own fashion.'

'"Fettered! bound!" How mean'st thou?' exclaimed Hermione.

'My hand's fettered by a promise; I'm bound to become a wife, when-ever my husband comes to fetch me;' said Paulina. 'I'm engaged, – betrothed. My father has accepted the offer with which lord Antigonus honoured me; and has passed his word that I shall become his wife, when he shall come to claim me.' ...

'Then thou lov'st not this lord Antigonus?' said Hermione, after a pause.

'I love him not; neither do I hate him; he is too venerable a gentleman to be hated, – his years, if nothing else, secure him too much respect for hatred;' said Paulina. 'In sober earnest, he is a man to be both esteemed and liked; and I should have probably both liked and esteemed him more, had he not taken it into his head to like me – and to ask for me for a wife, before I had time to think whether I liked him better than any other man in the world, – which is what a wife should do, to be a good wife and a happy wife.' ...

[After several days Hermione discovers Paulina has been crying.] 'Tell me, dear friend; what is this?' Hermione began, in her benign voice. 'You have been in trouble, – in sorrow? ... Is it alarm, – anxiety, – or fatal certainty of evil?'

'Certainty should bring firmness; it is only suspense that ought to know agitation;' said Paulina, striving for her usual steadfastness of tone and man-ner, and as if in disdain of her present perturbed condition ... Paulina pressed her mistress's hand to her lips, to her bosom; then with an effort, spoke ...

'You remember, I once hinted to you, that, had not lord Antigonus been so premature in his proposal to my father, he might have been forestalled by, – there might have been one who, – had he spoken earlier, – that, in short, there was a man, whom I –'

'Whom you could have preferred?' said Hermione, finishing the sen-tence that died upon her friend's lips.

'Whom I could have preferred, – whom I did prefer; whom I liked better than I myself knew I did;' she returned; 'for whom my liking would have been love, had I known he loved me, – had I known he so much as thought of me. But he gave me no reason to suppose he cared for me one jot beyond ordinary courtesy and kindness of regard, – then. Now how-ever, – now, – this very morning – he, – that man ... It is for the last time I yield to the worse than folly of dwelling on this theme. It is because I would not let a shadow of reserve rest between myself and her who has been my royal mistress and tender friend in one, – it is because I will not have anything unexplained, or mysterious, in my conduct towards you, madam, that I tell you, at whatever cost, the whole of my secret. That

man whom I could have – that man whom I now mu.
from my thoughts, – he, who this morning avowed his lc
asked mine in return – too late, – is no other than Camillo.

Paulina's usually full, round, firm voice, sank to a whi.
pronounced the last word.

Mary Cowden Clarke, 'Shakespeare as the Girl's Friend',
Shakespeariana, vol. 4 (1887), 355–69 [reprinted from *The Girl's Own
Paper* (London), June, 1887]

Our great poet-teacher, who has given us 126 clearly-drawn and thoroughly individual female characters, who has depicted women with full
appreciation of their highest qualities, yet with accurate perception of
their defects and foibles, who has championed them with potential might
by his chivalrous maintenance of their innate purity and devotion, while
showing the points wherein their natural moral strength may be warped
and weakened by circumstance, who has vindicated their truest rights and
celebrated their best virtues – himself possessing keener insight than any
other man-writer into womanly nature – Shakespeare may well be esteemed a valuable friend of woman-kind.

To the young girl, emerging from childhood and taking her first step
into the more active and self-dependent career of woman-life, Shakespeare's vital precepts and models render him essentially a helping friend.
To her he comes instructively and aidingly; in his page she may find
warning, guidance, kindliest monition, and wisest counsel. Through his
feminine portraits she may see, as in a faithful glass, vivid pictures of what
she has to evitate, or what she has to imitate, in order to become a worthy
and admirable woman. Her sex is set before her, limned with utmost
fidelity, painted in genuinest colors, for her to study and copy from or
vary from, in accordance with what she feels and learns to be supremest
harmonious effect in self-amelioration of character. She can take her own
disposition in hand, as it were, and endeavor to mould and form it into
the best perfection of which it is capable, by carefully observing the women
drawn by Shakespeare.

From his youthful women she can gain lessons in artlessness, guile-
lessness, modesty, sweetness, ingenuousness, and the most winning
candor; from his wives and matrons she can derive instruction in moral
courage, meekness, magnanimity, firmness, devoted tenderness, high principle, noble conduct, loftiest speech and sentiment ...

For moral introspection and self-culture Shakespeare is a grand aid, as
well as for mental discipline; and, perhaps, peculiarly so, as regards women;
since he the most manly thinker and most virile writer that ever put pen

to paper, had likewise something essentially feminine in his nature, which enabled him to discern and sympathize with the innermost core of woman's heart. Witness his sonnets, – where tenderness, patience, devotion, and constancy worthy of gentlest womanhood are conspicuous in combination with a strength of passion and fervor of attachment belonging to manliest manhood ...

In Isabella, Shakespeare has shown us how warmly and earnestly a young maiden can plead, and dare to speak on most delicate and difficult subjects honestly and eloquently, when her appeal is to save a brother's life – a task most especially onerous in her case, who has been dwelling in the peace and security and purity of novitiate in a conventual life.

In Paulina he has given a specimen of womanly ardor in advocating a friend's cause – boldly confronting her royal master himself with plain-spoken remonstrance and rebuke, while vindicating her royal mistress's innocence, and striving to free her from the injustice of slanderous suspicion ...

With exquisite skill in the delineation of Virgilia's character has Shakespeare taught the mode in which a young wife with a proud husband and a dominant mother-in-law may best preserve peaceful feelings for herself, and gain both esteem and love from them; for Volumnia, though she is in the habit of rating her daughter-in-law – ay, and roundly, too – has evidently a sterling regard and respect for her; while Coriolanus, her lofty husband, has the most passionate and tender affection for her. The secret of Virgilia's own tranquillity, and of her preserved attachment for mother-in-law and husband, lies in her power of holding her tongue. She knows how and when to be silent – a knowledge rarer, yet more precious, than many women properly appreciate ...

In the brief but wonderfully characteristic scene [I.iii], where the mother and wife of Coriolanus, while he is absent, receive a visit from their friend, the Lady Valeria, we see how Virgilia resists her persuasion to leave her 'stitchery' [I.iii.69] and come out of doors, even though the visitor has ingeniously bribed her by praise of her little son, and by promised 'excellent news' [I.iii.90] of her husband, and though Volumnia enforces the persuasion; how Virgilia persistently abides by her resolution not to go 'over the threshold till my lord return from the wars' [I.iii.74–5]; and how, finally, Volumnia takes her part, gives way to her desire, by saying to Valeria, half-playfully, half-petulantly, 'Leave her alone, lady; as she is now, she will but disease our better mirth' [I.iii.104–5]. The sparing-speeched Virgilia is, indeed, a model of discreet conduct for a daughter-in-law; she avoids useless and unseemly word-contests, she refrains from talk when discussion or agitating event is going on, she placidly but usually gains her own way, and she secures the trusting attachment of those she most reveres and loves. Truly her character is worthy of serious consideration ...

Happy she who at eight or nine years' old has a copy of *Lamb's Tales from Shakespeare* [sic] given to her, opening a vista of even then understandable interest and enjoyment! Happy she who at twelve or thirteen has Shakespeare's works themselves read to her by her mother, with loving selection of fittest plays and passages! Happy they who in maturer years have the good taste and good sense to read aright the pages of Shakespeare, and gather thence wholesomest lessons and choicest delights!

Delia Bacon, 1811–1859

Author, teacher and populariser of the 'Baconian theory' which claimed Francis Bacon to be the true author of 'the Shakespearian works', Delia Bacon was born in Tallmadge, Ohio, to a Congregationalist missionary (she was not, nor did she ever claim to be, a descendant of Francis Bacon). She grew up in Connecticut, attending the celebrated school of Catharine Beecher, and from 1826–32 Bacon tried to establish a private school with her sister, teaching in Connecticut, New Jersey and New York City. In 1831 Bacon began to publish fiction, including *Tales of the Puritans* (published anonymously) describing extraordinary heroines in seventeenth-century New England, and in 1833 she gave dramatic readings for women and lectured on history; Caroline Dall recollects that 'men like Ralph Waldo Emerson, William Henry Chaning, and many of their compeers found delight in listening to her' (1886: 103–4). In 1845 'a terrible personal experience warped her mind' (Dall: 103): an unfortunate friendship with Alexander MacWhorter, a Yale theologian, which resulted in legal action against MacWhorter – the affair became the subject of Catharine Beecher's *Truth Stranger than Fiction* (1850).

In 1852 Bacon began to develop her theory 'that "Shakespeare" was the name of a *book*, and not the name of its author' (Appleton, 1880: 493), and after moving to London, Delia Bacon published an article questioning the authorship of Shakespeare's plays in *Putnam's Monthly* (1856). In 1857 her monumental *The Philosophy of the Plays of Shakspere Unfolded* was published with a preface by Nathaniel Hawthorne (American Consul in Liverpool at the time) who gave his guarded support to Bacon's project and helped secure a publisher for the volume. The book was poorly received: Delia Bacon was 'pelted with a storm of derision, abuse, and merciless malice' by her critics (Appleton, 1880: 493). Both mentally and physically ill, Bacon was taken back to America by her nephew, and in 1858 she was institutionalised at Hartford Retreat for the Insane; she died the following year.

The Philosophy of the Plays of Shakspere Unfolded (London, 1857), a volume of nearly six hundred pages, is divided into two books: the first outlines 'the Baconian rhetoric' of concealment, and the second offers extended studies of *King Lear*, *Julius Caesar* and *Coriolanus*. Delia

Bacon's thesis – or, as Hawthorne described it, 'the despotic idea that had got possession of her mind' (*Our Old Home*, 1863: 173) – was that a group of leading Elizabethan thinkers under the direction of Francis Bacon wrote the Shakespeare plays in order to promote, in a disguised and allegorical form, 'the New Philosophy'. 'The New Philosophy' sought the regeneration of the social order through political reformation, attacking in particular the royal prerogative. Because it was revolutionary in outlook – indeed, Delia Bacon commends Francis Bacon for apparently anticipating the English Civil War – the identities of the real author(s) of the Shakespeare plays had to be protected by the use of a pseudonym (Shakespeare). The Shakespeare plays thus become, for Delia Bacon, coded works by Francis Bacon and his circle that functioned as political critique at a time when open criticism of the government and of the social order was impossible.

Hawthorne was reluctant to see 'my name associated with the author's on the title-page' of *The Philosophy of the Plays of Shakspere Unfolded*, and he took pains to explain in his preface that his purpose was not to endorse Delia Bacon's theory but to place 'my countrywoman upon a ground of amicable understanding with the public' (xiv–xv). The book failed not only on account of Delia Bacon's central thesis – dismissed as heretical by most Shakespeare critics and scholars – but because of Bacon's laborious writing style: 'there was a great amount of rubbish', writes Hawthorne, 'which any competent editor would have shoveled out of the way' (1863: 188–92). None the less, Bacon received praise for her insights into the plays: 'we Americans', claimed Hawthorne, 'cannot afford to forget her high and conscientious exercise of noble faculties ... this bewildered enthusiast had recognized a depth in the man whom she decried, which scholars, critics, and learned societies, devoted to the elucidation of his unrivaled scenes, had never imagined to exist there' (1863: 179 and 192). *The National Magazine* (July 1859) concluded that Bacon's book was 'not the vehicle of a few flimsy remarks, but of some very eloquent criticism, and altogether, though written by a woman, the product of a mind thoroughly masculine in its grasp of thought and the energy of its style' ('New Books': 150).

After Delia Bacon's death in 1859, the 'Baconian theory' attracted increasing attention, particularly in America: 'the literature connected with the subject', wrote Caroline Dall in 1886, 'has now reached such proportions that wholly to ignore it is at once cowardly and absurd' (*What We Really Know About Shakespeare*: 103). Tracts such as Mrs C. F. Ashmead Windle's *Discovery of Lord Verulam's Undoubted Authorship of the 'Shakspere' Works* (San Francisco, 1881), addressed to the New Shakspere Society of London, continued to promote the

Baconian thesis, while clubs and societies debated 'the authorship question'. Among them was the Shakespeare Society of New York, established in 1884–5 with a membership consisting exclusively of men: 'a singular limitation', reported *Shakespeariana*, 'for a body permitting the discussion of the Baconian theory, a theory that originated with a woman, and whose most zealous and most learned advocate at the present time is also a woman [Mrs Henry Pott]' (J. V. L., 'Shakespeare Societies of America', 1885: 486). Today the Bacon Society is still active with members from both sides of the Atlantic.

Delia Bacon, *The Philosophy of the Plays of Shakspere Unfolded*. With a Preface by Nathaniel Hawthorne. London: Groombridge and Sons, 1857

The statesman's note-book – and the play [*King Lear*]

Brutus. How I have thought of this, and of *these times*,
I shall recount hereafter.
Hamlet. The Play's the thing.
Brutus. Tell us the manner of it, gentle Casca.
Casca. I can as well *be hanged* as tell *the manner* of it.
Posthumus. 'Shall's have a *Play* of this. –'

The fact that the design of this play [*King Lear*], whatever it may be, is one deep enough to go down to that place in the social system which Tom o'Bedlam was then peacefully occupying, – thinking of anything else in the world but a social revolution on his behalf – to bring him up for observation; and that it is high enough to go up to that apex of the social structure on which the crown was then fastened, to fetch down the impersonated state itself, for an examination not less curious and critical; the fact too, that it was subtle enough to penetrate the retirement of the domestic life, and bring out its innermost passages for scientific criticism; – the fact that the relation of the Parent to the Child, and that of the Child to the Parent, the relation of Husband and Wife, and Sister and Brother, and Master and Servant, of Peasant and Lord, nay, the transient relation of Guest and Host, have each their place and part here, and the question of their duty marked not less clearly, than that prominent relation of the King and his Subjects; – the fact that these relations come in from the first, along with the political, and demand a hearing, and divide throughout the stage with them; the fact of the mere range of this social criticism, as it appears on the surface of the play, in these so prominent points, – is enough to show already, that it is a *Radical* of no ordinary kind, who is at work behind this drop-scene ...

But notwithstanding that the subject of this piece appears to be so general ... it is not very difficult to perceive that it does, in fact, involve a local exhibition of a different kind; and that, under the cover of that great revolution in the human estate ... another revolution, – that revolution which was then so near at hand, was clearly outlined ... one towards which this Poet appears to *'incline'* in a manner which would not have seemed, perhaps, altogether consistent with his position and assumptions elsewhere, if these could have been produced against him ... This Play was evidently written at a time when the conviction that the state of things which it represents could not endure much longer, had taken deep hold of the Poet's mind; at a time when those evils had attained a height so unendurable, – when that evil which lay at the heart of the commonweal, so fearful, that it might well seem, even to the scientific mind, to require the fierce *'drug'* of the political revolution, – so fearful as to make, even to such a mind, the rude surgery of the civil wars at last welcome.

For, indeed, it cannot be denied that the state of things which this Play represents, is that with which the author's own experience was conversant; and that all the terrible tragic satire of it, points – not to that age in the history of Britain in which the Druids were still responsible for the national culture ... not to that time, but to the *Elizabethan* ... Down to its most revolting, most atrocious detail, it is still the Elizabethan civility that is painted here ... we all know what a king's favourite felt himself competent to undertake then; and, if the clearest intimations of such men as Bacon, and Coke, and Raleigh, on such a question, are of any worth, the household of James the First was not without a parallel even for that performance, if not when this play was written, when it was published.

It is all one picture of social ignorance, and misery, and *frantic* misrule. It is a faithful exhibition of the degree of personal security which a man of honourable sentiments, and humane and noble intentions, could promise himself in such a time. It shows what chance there was of any man being permitted to sustain an honourable and intelligent part in the world, in an age in which all the radical social arts were yet wanting, in which the rude institutions of an ignorant past spontaneously built up, without any science of the natural laws, were vainly seeking to curb and quench the Incarnate soul of new ages, – the spirit of a scientific human advancement; and, when all the common welfare was still openly intrusted to the unchecked caprice and passion of one selfish, pitiful, narrow, low-minded man.

To appreciate fully the incidental and immediate political application of the piece, however, it is necessary to observe that notwithstanding that studious exhibition of lawless and outrageous power, which it involves, it is, after all, we are given to understand, by a quiet intimation here and there, a *limited monarchy* which is put upon the stage here. It is a

constitutional government, very much in the Elizabethan stage of development, as it would seem, which these arbitary rulers affect to be
administering. It is a government which professes to be one of law, under
which the atrocities of this piece are sheltered ...

It is the king himself on whom the bolder political expositions are
thrust ... What the poor king might say between his chattering teeth was
not going to be very critically treated; and the Poet knew it. It was the
king, in such circumstances, who could undertake the philosophical expositions of the action ... under cover of the sensation which the presence
of a mad king on the stage creates ... And what surer proof of the king's
madness ... than those startling propositions which the poet here puts
into his mouth, so opposed to the opinions and sentiments, not of kings
only, but of the world at large; what madder thing could a poet think of
than those political axioms which he introduces under cover of these
suggestions, – which would lay the axe at the root of the common beliefs
and sentiments on which the social structure then rested. How could he
better show that this poor king's wits had, indeed, 'turned;' how could
he better prove that he was, indeed, past praying for, than by putting into
his mouth those bitter satires on the state, those satires on the 'one only
man' power itself, – those wild revolutionary proposals, 'hark! in thine
ear, – *change places*. Softly, in thine ear, – *which is the* JUSTICE, and which
is THE THIEF?' 'Take that of *me* who have the power to *seal the accuser's
lips*. None does offend. I say none. I'll able 'em. Look when I stare, see
how the subject quakes.' These laws have failed, you see. They shelter
the most frightful depths of wrong. That Bench has failed, you see; and
that Chair, with all its adjunct divinity ... Surely, the man who authorizes
these suggestions must be, indeed, 'far gone,' whether he be 'a king or a
yeoman.' And mad indeed he is. Writhing under the insufficiency and
incompetency of these pretentious, but, in fact, ignorant and usurping
institutions, his heart of hearts racked and crushed with their failure, the
victim of this social empiricism, cries out in his anguish, under that safe
disguise of the Robes that hide all: 'Take these away at least, – that will
be something gained. Let us have no more of this mockery. None does
offend – none – I say *none*' [see IV.vi.107–70] ...

It was to the 'far off times;' and not to the 'near,' it was to the advanced
ages of the Advancement of Learning, that this Play was dedicated by its
Author. For it was the spirit of the modern ages that inspired it. It was
the new Prometheus who planned it; the more aspiring Titan, who would
bring down in his New Organum a new and more radiant gift [Bacon's
Advancement of Learning and *Novum Organum* were published in 1605
and 1620 respectively]; it was the Benefactor and Foreseer, who would
advance the rude kind to new and more enviable approximations to the
celestial summits. He knew there would come a time, in the inevitable

advancements of that new era of scientific 'prudence' and forethought which it was given to him to initiate, when all this sober historic exhibition, with its fearful historic earnest, would read, indeed, like some old fable of the rude barbaric past – some Player's play, bent on a feast of horrors – some Poet's impossibility. And *that* – was the Play, – that was the Plot. He knew that there would come a time when all this tragic mirth – sporting with the edged tools of tyranny – playing around the edge of the great axe itself – would be indeed safe play; when his Fool could open his budget, and unroll his bitter jests – crushed together and infolded within themselves so long – and have a world to smile with him, and not the few who could unfold them only. And that – that was 'the humour of it' [*Henry V*, II.i.116].

Henrietta Palmer, (née Lee), 1834–1908

Henrietta Lee Palmer was born in Baltimore, Maryland, and educated at the Patapsco Institute (Maryland); in 1855 she married the prolific author and Confederate war correspondent for the *New York Tribune*, John Williamson Palmer. Henrietta Lee Palmer contributed to various New York, Philadelphia and Baltimore periodicals and papers (including the *New York Tribune*); she translated *The Lady Tartuffe* for the leading American actress known as Rachel, and published two books: *The Stratford Gallery; or the Shakspeare Sisterhood: Comprising Forty-Five Ideal Portraits* (New York, 1859) and *Home Life in the Bible* (Boston, 1882). In 1872 Mary T. Tardy included Palmer in her volume *Living Female Writers of the South*, a record of those women 'recognized as "writers" in the Southern States' (1).

The Stratford Gallery is an early American example of a book devoted entirely to character studies of Shakespeare's women. In the preface Palmer denies identifying herself with Shakespeare's 'wise and faithful scholars and expounders. Yet does she confidently claim the right to speak of these, his Sisterhood, as one woman may justly speak of another – judging them, not with sophisticated research nor oracular criticism, but simply, naturally, sympathetically, as she may regard her fellow-women whom she meets from day to day'. The book met with good reviews: the *Atlantic Monthly* praised Palmer's 'fresh' point of view, commenting that

> her observations, whether invariably just or not, are generally taken from a new standpoint. She is led to her conclusions rather by instinct than by reason. She makes no apology for her judgments: 'I have no reason but a woman's reason: / I think her so because I think her so' [*Two Gentlemen of Verona*, I.ii.23–4, quoted on the volume's title-page]. And it would not be strange if womanly instinct were to prove oftentimes a truer guide in following the waywardness of a woman's nature than the cold, logical processes of merely intellectual men. (see Tardy: 540)

The Stratford Gallery presents scene-by-scene plot summaries of each play followed by character studies of the play's heroine; the volume is lavishly illustrated, and contains chapters on Lady Macbeth, Juliet, Ophelia, Imogen, Miranda, Desdemona, Rosalind, Celia, Beatrice, Hero,

Julia, Silvia, Viola, Olivia, Maria, Portia, Jessica, Perdita, Hermione, Mistress Ford, Mistress Page, Anne Page, Isabella, Cleopatra, Cressida, Helen, Cassandra, The Shrew, Helena, Titania, Constance, Cordelia, The Abbess, Katharine of Arragon, Anne Bullen, the Princess of France, Margaret of Anjou, Joan of Arc, Lady Grey, Lady Anne, Lady Percy, Princess Katharine, Portia (wife of Brutus), Virgilia and Lavinia.

Henrietta Lee Palmer, *The Stratford Gallery; or the Shakspeare Sisterhood: Comprising Forty-Five Ideal Portraits.* New York: Appleton and Co., 1859

Beatrice

If this sharp-tongued young lady serve no better purpose to the humanity of this day and generation, at least she saves it from one graceless distinction, by proving in her own person that the 'fast' woman is by no means a modern 'institution:' not that we would detract from the perfected specimens of our own time, by comparison with this rudimentary example; but we contend that she possesses all the qualities necessary to a successful assumption of the character – her education, and the manners of the time, alone impede her.

Beatrice, like many another woman before and since, is the slave of a pert tongue; her intellect, though quick, is not strong enough to keep her vanity in subjection, and the consciousness of possessing in a ready wit the power of discomfiting others, proves a successful snare for her good taste and all the graceful effects of her gentle breeding. It is only in situations so inspiring as to compel her for the moment to forget her flippant affectations, that she appears as Nature made her – a spirited, generous, clever woman ...

The wit of Beatrice brilliant as it is, is but the dazzle of words – it has no imaginative element, none of the half-playful pathos which renders that of Rosalind so charming; the two compare as the cold, artificial glitter of a diamond with the cordial warmth of sunshine. To use Benedick's own words – and he, as chief sufferer, should be excellent authority – Beatrice 'speaks poignards, and every word stabs,' [II.i.247–8] while, in the poetic simile of Mrs. Jameson, 'the wit of Rosalind bubbles up and sparkles like the living fountain, refreshing all around' [I.80].

Beatrice has none of Rosalind's romantic susceptibility, nor passion; her love for Benedick we can never regard as more than an experimental freak; though, to do her justice, her soliloquy in the garden, where, concealed, she has overheard that Benedick loves her [III.i.107–16], is creditable alike to her heart and her good sense ...

But however the gratuitous impertinence and unseemly forwardness of Beatrice may jar with one's fine ideas of a lady, she nobly redeems herself by her chivalrous defence of her cousin Hero, on the occasion of her cruel disgrace; her hearty, clear-headed

Oh, on my soul, my cousin is belied! [IV.i.148]

in the face of her uncle's conviction of his daughter's shame, and Benedick's amazed suspicion, is worth whole volleys of her murderous wit.

Hero

In point of romantic interest and dramatic situation, Hero is undoubtedly the leading character in *Much Ado about Nothing*, although, adopting the popular appreciation, we have conferred the distinction of 'first lady' on her cousin Beatrice – not the first time, by the by, that loud and persistent vanity has succeeded in usurping the honorable place belonging to modest, graceful excellence.

A rare chasteness of thought and person is plainly the trait in Hero's character which expresses itself most distinctly in the affairs of her daily life; and in this particular she affords a lively contrast to her cousin's inherent vulgarity. Her emotions are as still as they are deep – her words few; yet, that she can express herself well on occasion is attested by her conversation with Ursula, designed to be overheard by Beatrice, in which her caustic description of that flippant young woman is quite equal to many of her renowned sallies; no wonder that Beatrice issues from her concealment with 'fire in her ears' [III.i.107] ...

It is noticeable that in the repartee – coarse even for the women of Shakspeare's time – bandied by the less fastidious tongues of her rattle-brain cousin and her gentlewoman, she never takes part, unless to repel some direct attack upon herself, with a

Fye upon thee! Art not ashamed?

[III.iv.28]

and that, too, with no affectation of prudery; her delicacy is as virgin as Desdemona's, that very snow-drop among women.

Portia

Portia is distinguished by a patrician elegance of person and presence, which is so innately her own that it depends but little for its effect on the aristocratic pretension of her surroundings. Although far from popular – her reputation for extraordinary mental endowments being sufficient to constitute a formidable obstacle to public favor – she is one of the most delightful of Shakspeare's women. Her intellectual quality is indeed marked; but that can never render a woman less lovable, when, as in Portia's case, it is subordinate to the affections. Schlegel, regarding her from a purely critical point of view, pronounces her 'clever;' and although Mrs. Jameson protests against the application of so dubious an epithet to this 'heavenly compound of talent, feeling, wisdom, beauty, and gentleness,' [*Characteristics of Women*, 1832: I.6] we must confess that to us it seems well chosen. 'Clever' does not, indeed, imply the possession of illustrious powers; but it does signify that nice 'dexterity in the adaptation of certain faculties to a certain end or aim' which is eminently graceful and feminine, and exactly describes the mental characteristics of Portia, as most conspicuously displayed in the trial scene, wherein her success is achieved, not by the exercise of inherent wisdom, or an educated judgment, but by the merely clever discovery of a legal quibble. That the word has fallen into disrepute, from unworthy associations, should not impair its legitimate value. True, it does 'suggest the idea of something we should distrust and shrink from, if not allied to a higher nature;' [Jameson, 1832: I.7] but we contend that, in Portia, cleverness is allied to a higher nature – to qualities which are, indeed, scarcely less perfect than her fair panegyrist has portrayed them – in a woman whose 'plenteous wit' [*Othello*, IV.i.201] and excelling accomplishments are more than equalled by her tenderness, her magnanimity, her graceful dignity, and her lofty honor.

Isabella

The character of Isabella presents a notable example of the inefficacy of a purely intellectual virtue to command our sympathy or admiration, or in any way to advance the cause of Religion.

In critical, as well as popular, appreciation, Isabella occupies a position of cool toleration – although in some opinions she has risen from that questionable status, to be denominated 'an angel of light,' and by another order of minds has been assailed with vituperative violence as a coarse vixenish prude ... [Charlotte Lennox, 1753: see p. 18] Cold, faultless, severe in moral rectitude, not liable to the weaknesses which 'make the whole world kin,' [*Troilus and Cressida*, III.iii.175] and utterly incapable of sympathy for them, this *religieuse* stands, in a manner, arrayed against her fellows: existing, not only physically, but morally, apart from them, permitting herself no tie of reciprocal feeling to keep her united with the human family – the type of a class of mistaken but sincere religionists of all sects, who, by their repulsive self-sufficiency, fatally subvert the very interests to which they have consecrated their lives.

Isabella is no hypocrite – that is, consciously; her flawless excellence commands our exalted respect, our honorable recognition, however it may repel any more enthusiastic admiration; to the impregnability of her chastity, the prominent feature of her strongly marked individuality, full honor must be awarded; yet self-sacrifice, without a reservation, has become so inseparably associated with all that is most lovable in woman, that it would have been far easier to forgive the actual offence, than conscientiously to applaud her moral grandeur, remembering the beautiless details of her victory ...

Isabella's complaints of the too lax discipline of her order are construed by her panegyrist, Mrs. Jameson, to signify that she desires a 'more strict restraint,' 'from the consciousness of strong intellectual and imaginative power, and of *overflowing sensibility*,' in herself, which require it [1833: 126]. With all respect, we would suggest that this 'very virtuous maid' is supplied with the latter qualities only from the abundant stores of the accomplished authoress herself. Isabella's strong intellectual power no one questions – it is conclusively established in her logical tilt of wits with the lord deputy; but of imagination, or sensibility, she is as destitute as an Audrey. Her appetite for severer penances and sharper mortifications is natural to the morbid devotee – and by no means peculiar to her, or of any special significance.

The Shrew

It is scarcely possible to consider the character of Katharina with gravity; her shrewishness is so wildly extravagant, so inconceivable in any maiden, 'young, beauteous, and brought up as best becomes a Gentlewoman,' [I.ii.86–7] that she may serve but as the heroine of the extravaganza wherein she figures – and as a burlesque 'moral and example' to those 'not impossible shes' who are curst, within the bounds of probability, with her unamiable proclivities.

The predicaments of this brawling Kate are extremely ludicrous; but we cannot be so charitable towards her peculiar sin against womanhood as to pity them, even when she is most hardly pressed – she deserves even more than she suffers, at the hands of her mad Petruchio; and the outward fruits of her trials and tribulations are highly satisfactory. Nevertheless, we own we have but little faith in the enduring quality of a 'taming' which is procured by almost the same means as are employed in the subduing of a wild animal, and by a husband who neither loves nor is loved by her; we much fear that – the keeper and his lash out of sight – this human wild-cat, 'convinced against her will,' would be 'of the same opinion still' ...

The final trotting out of his trained wife before his friends, for a wager, is worthy of the man who 'came to Padua to wive it wealthily' [I.ii.75] ... But she gets off her little speech, with which, by the by, no one out of the dangerous circle of Woman's Rights can possibly find fault; and she receives her reward – a kiss from the husband, whom we are sure, for all her fine talk, she hates cordially.

Frances Anne (Fanny) Kemble, 1809–1893

Actress, diarist and poet, Fanny Kemble was born into a prominent theatrical family: Sarah Siddons was her aunt, and her uncles (John Philip and Stephen) and father (Charles) played leading acting and managerial roles at Drury Lane and Covent Garden. Educated in France and England, Fanny Kemble was launched on a stage career by her father in 1827: she played Juliet opposite her father's Mercutio and her mother's Lady Capulet, and was an instant success. Fanny Kemble did not, however, have a high regard for the acting profession and disclaimed her theatrical achievements – 'the stage itself, though it became from the force of circumstances my career, was, partly from my nature, and partly from my education, so repugnant to me, that I failed to accomplish any result at all' (*Notes upon Some of Shakespeare's Plays*, 1882: 10). Kemble sought to write instead: her first play *Frances the First, an Historical Drama* (1832) was apparently successful, being reprinted seven times within the year, and in 1844 she published her first volume of *Poems* (Philadelphia).

In 1827 she met Anna Jameson and they became close friends; Jameson dedicated her *Characteristics of Women* to Kemble in 1832 (see also Figure 4, p. 68). In 1834, following a threat of bankruptcy at Covent Garden, Fanny reluctantly accompanied her father on a two-year tour of the United States (recorded in her *Journal of a Residence in America*, 1835). While touring America Kemble met and married Pierce Butler, a wealthy southern planter; she was later horrified to discover the conditions of slaves kept on his south-east Georgia plantations. With the outbreak of the Civil War and the British government's apparent support for the Confederate South, Fanny Kemble published her *Journal of a Residence on a Georgian Plantation in 1838–9* (1863), in which she made a powerful attack on slavery:

> scorn, derision, insult, menace – the handcuff, the lash – the tearing away
> of children from parents, of husbands from wives – the weary trudging
> in droves along the common highways, the labor of body, the despair of
> mind, the sickness of heart – these are the realities which belong to the
> system, and form the rule, rather than the exception, in the slave's expe-
> rience.

Thereafter her marriage became increasingly strained, and in 1848–9 she divorced, with Butler taking custody of their two daughters. In 1848 Fanny Kemble abandoned her acting career for public readings of Shakespeare throughout the United States and Britain, which she continued for over twenty years. She settled in Lennox (Massachusetts) and later in Philadelphia, finally returning to England in 1877 where she began to publish extensively: further journals, including *Records of a Girlhood* (three volumes, 1878) and *Records of Later Life* (1882); fiction, including *The Adventures of Mr John Timothy Homespun in Switzerland* (1889) and *Far Away and Long Ago* (1889); and in 1891 her poetry was anthologised in *The Poets and the Poetry of the Century*, edited by A. H. Miles (London). 'She was very frank and outspoken', remembers the *National Cyclopaedia of American Biography*, 'and had an almost manly love of independence' (1894: 3.414–15).

In 1867 Kemble published 'Notes on characters in the play of *Macbeth*' for *Macmillan's Magazine*, followed a year later by an article on 'Lady Macbeth'. *Macmillan's Magazine*, established in 1859, was a monthly British journal that carried political and religious articles with travel sketches, fiction (including serialised books) and poetry. It appealed to a predominantly Liberal middle- to upper-class readership, and by 1870 gained a circulation of eight thousand, with contributions submitted from writers such as Anthony Trollope, Henry James, Robert Louis Stevenson, Matthew Arnold, Walter Pater, Katharine Cooper and Frances Hodgson Burnett. In 1882 both of Fanny Kemble's articles for *Macmillan's* were reprinted in *Notes upon Some of Shakespeare's Plays*, together with an Introduction 'On the Stage', 'hints for acting' *Romeo and Juliet*, a discussion of *Henry VIII* and three chapters on *The Tempest*, in which Kemble makes a meticulous comparison of textual variants in editions of the play by Hanmer, Theobald, Rowe, Malone and Steevens, Johnson, and the current Oxford edition, against the 'so-called new readings' of John Payne Collier's 1632 forged folio of the *Works of Shakespeare*, 'discovered' in 1849 with 'contemporary' manuscript alterations (*Notes upon Some of Shakespeare's Plays*: 107).

Fanny Kemble, 'Lady Macbeth', *Macmillan's Magazine*, 17 (February 1868), 354–61

Lady Macbeth, even in her sleep, has no qualms of conscience; her remorse takes none of the tenderer forms akin to repentance, nor the weaker ones allied to fear, from the pursuit of which the tortured soul, seeking where to hide itself, not seldom escapes into the boundless wilderness of madness.

A very able article, published some years ago in the *National Review*, on the character of Lady Macbeth, insists much upon an opinion that she died of remorse, as some palliation of her crimes, and mitigation of our detestation of them. That she died of *wickedness* would be, I think, a juster verdict. Remorse is consciousness of guilt ... and that I think Lady Macbeth never had; though the *unrecognised* pressure of her great guilt killed her. I think her life was destroyed by sin as by a disease of which she was unconscious, and that she died of a broken heart, while the impenetrable resolution of her will remained unbowed. The spirit was willing, but the flesh was weak; the body can sin but so much, and survive; and other deadly passions besides those of violence and sensuality can wear away its fine tissues, and undermine its wonderful fabric. The woman's mortal frame succumbed to the tremendous weight of sin and suffering which her immortal soul had power to sustain; and, having destroyed its temporal house of earthly sojourn, that soul, unexhausted by its wickedness, went forth into its new abode of eternity.

The nature of Lady Macbeth ... is incapable of any salutary spasm of moral anguish, or hopeful paroxysm of mental horror ... Macbeth, to the very end, may weep, and wring his hands, and tear his hair and gnash his teeth, and bewail the lost estate of his soul, though with him too the dreadful process is one of gradual induration. For he retains the unutterable consciousness of a soul; he has a perception of having sinned, of being fallen, of having wandered, of being lost ... He may be visited to the end by those noble pangs which bear witness to the pre-eminent nobility of the nature he has desecrated, and suggest a re-ascension, even from the bottom of that dread abyss into which he has fallen ... But *she* may none of this: she may but feel, and see, and smell blood; and wonder at the unquenched stream that she still wades in – 'Who would have thought the old man to have had so much blood in him?' [V.i.40] – and fly, hunted through the nights by that 'knocking at the door' which beats the wearied life at last out of her stony heart and scared, impenetrable brain ...

Taking the view I do of Lady Macbeth's character, I cannot accept the idea (held, I believe, by her great representative, Mrs. Siddons) that in the banquet scene the ghost of Banquo, which appears to Macbeth, is seen at the same time by his wife, but that, in consequence of her greater command over herself, she not only exhibits no sign of perceiving the apparition, but can, with its hideous form and gesture within a few feet of her, rail at Macbeth in that language of scathing irony [III.iv.59–67] ... To this supposition I must again object that Lady Macbeth is no ghost-seer. She is not of the temperament that admits of such impressions; she is incapable of supernatural terror in proportion as she is incapable of spiritual influences; devils do not visibly tempt, nor angels visibly minister to her; and, moreover ... to have seen Banquo's ghost at the banqueting table ... and persisted in her fierce mocking of her husband's terror would have been impossible to human nature. The hypothesis makes Lady Macbeth a monster, and there is no such thing in all Shakespeare's plays. That she is godless, and ruthless in the pursuit of the objects of her ambition, does not make her such. Many men have been so; and she is that unusual and unamiable (but not altogether unnatural) creature, a masculine woman, in the only real significance of that much misapplied epithet.

Lady Macbeth was this: she possessed the qualities which generally characterise men, and not women – energy, decision, daring, unscrupulousness; a deficiency of imagination, a great preponderance of the positive and practical mental elements; a powerful and rapid appreciation of what each exigency of circumstance demanded, and the coolness and resolution necessary for its immediate execution. Lady Macbeth's character has more of the essentially manly nature in it than that of Macbeth. The absence of imagination, together with a certain obtuseness of the nervous system, is the condition that goes to produce that rare quality – physical courage – which she possessed in a pre-eminent degree. This combination of deficiencies is seldom found in men, infinitely seldomer in women; and its invariable result is insensibility to many things – among others, insensibility to danger. Lady Macbeth was not so bloody as her husband, for she was by no means equally liable to fear; she would not have hesitated a moment to commit any crime that she considered necessary for her purposes, but she would always have known what were and what were not necessary crimes. We find it difficult to imagine that, if she had undertaken the murder of Banquo and Fleance, the latter would have been allowed to escape, and impossible to conceive that she would have ordered the useless and impolitic slaughter of Macduff's family and followers, after he had fled to England, from a mere rabid movement of impotent hatred and apprehension. She was never made savage by remorse, or cruel by terror ...

In denying to Lady Macbeth all the peculiar sensibilities of her sex (for they are all included in its pre-eminent characteristic – the maternal instinct – and there is no doubt that the illustration of the quality of her resolution by the assertion that she would have dashed her baby's brains out, if she had sworn to do it, is no mere figure of speech, but very certain earnest) Shakespeare has not divested her of natural feeling to the degree of placing her without the pale of our common humanity. Her husband shrank from the idea of her bearing *women* like herself, but not 'males,' [I.vii.74] of whom he thought her a fit mother; and she retains enough of the nature of mankind, if not of womankind, to bring her within the circle of our toleration, and make us accept her as *possible*. Thus the solitary positive instance of her sensibility has nothing especially feminine about it. Her momentary relenting in the act of stabbing Duncan, because he resembled her father as he slept, is a touch of human tenderness by which most men might be overcome, while the smearing her hands in the warm gore of the slaughtered old man is an act of physical insensibility which not one woman out of a thousand would have had nerve or stomach for ...

I am not inclined to agree, either, with the view which lends any special tenderness to Lady Macbeth's demeanour towards her husband after the achievement of their bad eminence ... She has her end to gain by talking, and she talks till she does gain it; and in those moments of mortal agony, when his terrors threaten with annihilation the fabric of their fortunes ... she, like the rider whose horse, maddened with fear, is imperilling his own and that rider's existence, drives the rowels of her piercing irony into him, and with a hand of iron guides, and urges, and *lifts* him over the danger. But, except in those supreme instants, where her purpose is to lash and goad him past the obstruction of his own terrors, her habitual tone, from beginning to end, is of a sort of contemptuous compassion towards the husband whose moral superiority of nature she perceives and despises, as men not seldom put by the finer and truer view of duty of women, as too delicate for common use, a weapon of too fine a temper for worldly warfare ...

Nothing, indeed, can be more wonderfully perfect than Shakespeare's delineation of the evil nature of these two human souls – the evil strength of the one, and the evil weakness of the other. The woman's wide-eyed, bold, collected leap into the abyss makes us gulp with terror; while we watch the man's blinking, shrinking, clinging, gradual slide into it, with a protracted agony akin to his own ...

The preservation of Macbeth's dignity in a degree sufficient to retain our sympathy, in spite of the preponderance of his wife's nature over his, depends on the two facts of his undoubted heroism in his relations with men, and his great tenderness for the woman whose evil will is made powerful over his partly by his affection for her. It is remarkable that hardly one scene passes where they are brought together in which he does not address to her some endearing appellation; and, from his first written words to her whom he calls his 'Dearest partner of greatness,' [I.v.11] to his pathetic appeal to her physician for some alleviation of her moral plagues, a love of extreme strength and tenderness is constantly manifested in every address to or mention of her that he makes. He seeks her sympathy alike in the season of his prosperous fortune and in the hour of his mental anguish:

Oh, full of scorpions is my mind, dear wife!

[III.ii.36]

and in this same scene there is a touch of essentially manly reverence for the womanly nature of her who has so little of it, that deserves to be classed among Shakespeare's most exquisite inspirations: – his refusing to pollute his wife's mind with the bloody horror of Banquo's proposed murder.

> Be innocent of the knowledge, dearest chuck!
>
> [III.ii.45]

... from first to last he so completely leans on her for support and solace in their miserable partnership of guilt and woe, that when we hear the ominous words:

> My Lord, the Queen is dead!
>
> [V.v.16]

we see him stagger under the blow which strikes from him the prop of that undaunted spirit in whose valour he found the never-failing stimulus of his own.

Frances Anne Kemble, *Notes upon Some of Shakespeare's Plays.*
London: Richard Bentley & Son, 1882

On the stage

Things dramatic and things theatrical are often confounded together in the minds of English people, who, being for the most part neither the one nor the other, speak and write of them as if they were identical, instead of, as they are, so dissimilar that they are nearly opposite.

That which is dramatic in human nature is the passionate, emotional, humorous element, the simplest portion of our composition, after our mere instincts, to which it is closely allied, and this has no relation whatever, beyond its momentary excitement and gratification, to that which imitates it, and is its theatrical reproduction; the dramatic is the *real*, of which the theatrical is the *false* ...

The Italians, nationally and individually, are dramatic; the French on the contrary, theatrical ... our American progeny are, as a nation, devoid of the dramatic element, and have a considerable infusion of that which is theatrical, delighting, like the Athenians of old, in processions, shows, speeches, oratory, demonstrations, celebrations, and declarations, and such displays of public and private sentiment as would be repugnant to English taste and feeling ...

The combination of the power of representing passion and emotion with that of imagining or conceiving it – that is, of the theatrical talent with the dramatic temperament – is essential to make a good actor; their combination in the highest possible degree alone makes a great one ...

Every day lessens the frequency of this specific combination among ourselves, for the dramatic temperament, always exceptional in England, is becoming daily more so under the various adverse influences of a state of civilisation and society which fosters a genuine dislike to exhibitions of emotion, and a cynical disbelief in the reality of it, both necessarily repressing, first, its expression, and next, its existence. On the other hand, greater intellectual cultivation and a purer and more elevated taste, are unfavourable to the existence of the true theatrical spirit; and English actors of the present day are of the public, by being 'nothing if not critical,' [*Othello*, II.i.119] and are not of their craft, having literally ceased to know 'what belongs to a frippery' [*Tempest*, IV.i.226]. They have lost for the most part alike the dramatic emotional temperament and the scenic science of mere effect, and our stage is and must be supplied, if supplied at all, by persons less sophisticated and less civilised. The plays brought out and revived at our theatres of late years bear doleful witness to this. We have in them archaeology, ethnology, history, geography, botany (even to the curiosity of ascertaining the Danish wild-flowers that Ophelia might twist with her mad straws), and upholstery; everything, in short, but acting, which it seems we cannot have.

Some notes on *The Tempest* (Parts I, II and III)

The opening of this play is connected with my earliest recollections. In looking down the 'dark backward and abysm of time,' [*Tempest*, I.ii.50] to the period when I was but six years old, my memory conjures up a vision of a stately drawing-room on the ground-floor of a house, doubtless long since swept from the face of the earth by the encroaching tide of new houses and streets that has submerged every trace of suburban beauty, picturesqueness, or rural privacy in the neighbourhood of London, converting it all by a hideous process of assimilation into more London, till London seems almost more than England can carry ...

[In the drawing-room a lovely-looking lady] used to tell me the story of the one large picture which adorned the room. Over and over again, at my importunate beseeching, she told it, – sometimes standing before it, while I held her hand, and listened with upturned face, and eyes rounding with big tears of wonder and pity, to a tale which shook my small soul with a sadness and strangeness ... In the midst of a stormy sea, on which night seemed fast settling down, a helmless, mastless, sailless bark lay weltering giddily, and in it sat a man in the full flower of vigorous manhood. His attitude was one of miserable dejection, and, oh, how I did long to remove the hand with which his eyes were covered, to see what manner of look in them answered to the bitter sorrow which the speechless lips expressed! His other hand rested on the fair curls of a girl-baby of three years old, who clung to his knee, and, with wide, wondering blue

eyes and laughing lips, looked up into the half-hidden face of her father. –
'And that,' said the sweet voice at my side, 'was the good Duke of Milan,
Prospero, – and that was his little child, Miranda.'

There was something about the face and figure of the Prospero that
suggested to me those of my father; and this, perhaps, added to the
poignancy with which the representation of his distress affected my childish imagination. But the impression made by the picture, the story, and
the place where I heard the one and saw the other, is among the most
vivid that my memory retains. And never, even now, do I turn the magic
page that holds that marvellous history, without again seeing the lovely
lady, the picture full of sad dismay, and my own six-year-old self listening
to that earliest Shakespearian lore that my mind and heart ever received.
I suppose this is partly the secret of my love for this, above all other of
the poet's plays: – it was my first possession in the kingdom of unbounded
delight which he has since bestowed upon me ...

The *Tempest* is, as I have already said, my favourite of Shakespeare's
Dramas. The remoteness of the scene from all known localities allows a
range to the imagination such as no other of his plays affords ...

But chiefly I delight in this play, because of the image which it presents
to my mind of the glorious supremacy of the righteous human soul over
all things by which it is surrounded. Prospero is to me the representative
of wise and virtuous manhood, in its true relation to the combined
elements of existence – the physical powers of the external world, and the
varieties of character with which it comes into voluntary, accidental, or
enforced contact.

Of the wonderful chain of being, of which Caliban is the densest and
Ariel the most ethereal extreme, Prospero is the middle link. He – the
wise and good man – is the ruling power, to whom the whole series is
subject.

First, and lowest in the scale, comes the gross and uncouth but powerful
savage, who represents both the more ponderous and unwieldy natural
elements (as the earth and water), which the wise Magician by his knowledge compels to his service; and the brutal and animal propensities of the
nature of man, which he, the type of its noblest development, holds in
lordly subjugation.

Next follow the drunken, ribald, foolish retainers of the King of Naples,
whose ignorance, knavery, and stupidity represent the coarser attributes
of those great unenlightened masses, which in all communities threaten
authority by their conjunction with brute force and savage ferocity; and
only under the wholesome restraint of a wise discipline can be gradually
admonished into the salutary subserviency necessary for their civilization.

Ascending by degrees in the scale, the next group is that of the cunning,
cruel, selfish, treacherous worldlings – Princes and Potentates – the peers

in outward circumstances of high birth and breeding of the noble Prospero – whose villanous [*sic*] policy (not unaided by his own dereliction of his duties as a governor in the pursuit of his pleasure as a philosopher) triumphs over his fortune, and, through a devilish ability and craft, for a time gets the better of truth and virtue in his person.

From these, who represent the baser intellectual as the former do the baser sensual properties of humanity, we approach by a most harmonious moral transition, through the agency of the skilfully interposed figure of the kindly gentleman, Gonzalo, those charming types of youth and love, Ferdinand and Miranda – the fervent chivalrous devotion of the youth, and the yielding simplicity and sweetness of the girl, are lovely representations of those natural emotions of tender sentiment and passionate desire which, watched and guided and guarded by the affectionate solicitude and paternal prudence of Prospero, are pruned of their lavish luxuriance and supported in their violent weakness by the wise will that teaches forbearance and self-control as the only price at which these exquisite flowers of existence may unfold their blossoms in prosperous beauty, and bear their rightful harvest of happiness as well as pleasure.

Next in this wonderful gamut of being, governed by the sovereign soul of Prospero, come the shining figures of the Masque – beautiful bright apparitions, fitly indicating the air, the fire, and all the more smiling aspects and subtler forces of nature ...

Last – highest of all – crowning with a fitful flame of lambent brightness this poetical pyramid of existence, flickers and flashes the beautiful Demon, without whose exquisite companionship we never think of the royal Magician with his grave countenance of command – Ariel seems to me to represent the keenest perceiving intellect – apart from all moral consciousness and sense of responsibility. His power and knowledge are in some respects greater than those of his master – he can do what Prospero cannot – he lashes up the Tempest round the Island – he saves the King and his companions from the shipwreck – he defeats the conspiracy of Sebastian and Antonio, and discovers the clumsy plot of the beast Caliban – he wields immediate influence over the elements, and comprehends alike without indignation or sympathy – which are moral results – the sin and suffering of humanity. Therefore, because he is only a spirit of knowledge, he is subject to the spirit of love – and the wild, subtle, keen, beautiful, powerful creature is compelled to serve with mutinous waywardness and unwilling subjection the human soul that pitied and rescued it from its harsher slavery to sin – and which, though controlling it with a wise severity to the fulfilment of its duties, yearns after it with the tearful eyes of tender human love when its wild wings flash away into its newly-recovered realm of lawless liberty ...

Brought up in all but utter solitude, under no influence but that of her

FIGURE 8. Margaret Elizabeth Wilson, *The Tempest*, I.ii.409: Miranda's first sight of Ferdinand, with Ariel in a cloud above (watercolour, 1785). Little seems to be known of Wilson; she is not listed in any of the relevant British or American biographical dictionaries. The original watercolour is done in sombre but delicate shades of grey and brown.

wise and loving father on earth, and her wise and loving Father in Heaven, Miranda exhibits no more coyness in her acceptance of Ferdinand's overtures than properly belongs to the instinctive modesty of her sex, unenhanced by any of the petty pretty arts of coquetry and assumed shyness, which are the express result of artificial female training ... [She] offers her life to her lover with the perfect devotion and humility of the true womanly nature: –

> To be your fellow
> You may deny me, but I'll be your servant
> Whether you will or no.
>
> [III.i.84–6]

In the purity and simplicity of this 'tender of affection,' Ferdinand made acquaintance with a species of modesty to which assuredly none of those ladies of the Court of Naples, 'whom he had eyed with best regard,' [III.i.40] had ever introduced him; and indeed to them Miranda's proceeding might very probably have appeared highly unlady-like, as I have heard it pronounced more than once by – ladies ...

But Prospero was after all a mere man, and knew no better than to bring up Miranda to speak the truth, and the fair child had been so holily trained by him, that her surrender of herself to the man she loves is so little feminine after the approved feminine fashion, that it is simply angelic.

That Shakespeare, who indeed knew all things, knew very well the difference between such a creature as Miranda and a well-brought-up young lady, is plain enough, when he makes poor Juliet, after her passionate confession of love made to the stars, and overheard by Romeo, apologise to him with quite pathetic mortification for not having been more 'strange' [*Romeo and Juliet*, II.ii.101]. She regrets extremely her unqualified expressions of affection, – assures Romeo that nothing would have induced her to have spoken the truth, if she had only known he heard her, and even offers ... to 'frown and be perverse and say him nay,' [II.ii.96] – and in short has evidently shocked her own conventional prejudices quite as much as she fears she has his ... But then Juliet was the flower of Veronese young ladies, and her good mother, and gossiping nurse, were not likely to have neglected her education to the tune of letting her speak the truth without due preparation. Miranda is to be excused as a savage – probably Ferdinand thought her excusable.

Mary Preston, active 1869

Mary Preston's *Studies in Shakspeare* (Philadelphia, 1869) was listed in Steven Austin Allibone's *Dictionary of English Literature and British and American Authors* (1877), but little else is known of Mary Preston or her work. *Studies in Shakspeare* was registered in Maryland, and Preston signed the preface from Harford County, Maryland; her sympathies appear to be with the Confederacy – in the volume she attacks modern demands for the 'suffrages of the people', criticises *Othello* for its 'fault of color', throws scorn on the Massachusetts General Benjamin Butler, and describes New England Puritans as 'refugees of fanaticism' (37, 71, 131 and 138). The book, dedicated to her brother John Preston as 'a slight token of sisterly affection', included studies on *Macbeth*, *Julius Caesar*, *Romeo and Juliet*, *Richard III*, *As You Like It*, *A Midsummer Night's Dream* and *Timon of Athens*.

Mary Preston, *Studies in Shakspeare: A Book of Essays*. Philadelphia: Claxton, Remsen and Haffelfinger, 1869

Coriolanus

In modern times we hear so much about 'the suffrages of the people,' so much of the rights of *all* men to have a voice in public affairs, so much of 'the voice of the people being the voice of God,' as some profane writer has it, – we hear so much of this description of declamation, that it is refreshing to run to a truer philosophy, to follow the course of a purer and clearer stream of political sentiment, such as we discover in the play of Coriolanus.

'All men were *not* created free and equal,' however a Jefferson may have sought to inoculate a great people with such a doctrine. The world of nature, through all her laboratories, displays a silent protest against such teachings ... Who considers the sparrow *the equal* of the eagle that soars above the storm-cloud? Why, then, is it so unpopular to hold, that, among the Caucasian race, there are *essential* differences? – from the man of reason clear down to the man of passion; from the man capable of governing others, down to the man incapable of governing even his own appetites. Where, then, can be the wisdom of bestowing upon such *different* men *the same* rights and privileges? No, men were not *created equal*, and no human legislation can set at naught a divine decree. And as it is true, that men are not 'created equal,' so it is true, men are not 'created free.' We were born subjects to God's laws, slaves to 'Caesar's' decree, dependents on each other. Free! There are no animals made, by nature, by circumstances, by passion, such slaves as man! ...

Pride is man's besetting sin. From the low pride in mere superiority of wealth (which a *social necessity*, caused by the late war, has originated a new expression for – '*shoddy*,' [originally referring to yarn made from refuse woollen rags (1832), 'shoddy' was first applied to people or things that pretend to superiority in 1862]) – from this '*shoddy*' pride, which is the lowest grade, up through all its varieties ... we discover

> *This* trail of the serpent is *over us all* ...

Coriolanus's pride is so excessive that it actually devours all the man's adventitious and intrinsic virtues ... Indeed, his pride effaces from his judgment the memory, that his inferiors in station are men of like passions with himself ...

Coriolanus's judgment of the crowd's fitness for exercising an influence in the government, we think just; his contempt for their applause – as variable as the wind – we think *natural*. But Coriolanus's coarseness of manner and address to his inferiors was the exhibition of a pride that was mean and cruel in a great man.

King Lear

We hear a *great deal* of the *ingratitude* of children; *very little* of the *injustice* of parents. 'Honor thy father and mother,' is of frequent quotation. 'Parents, provoke not your child to wrath,' is seldom mentioned ... The world embraces and fondles in its false bosom many a father, upon whose unfilial treatment rests the faults of his miserable offspring. Cibber could be a vain fop, a literary dandy, welcomed in all the fashionable resorts of London. His daughter, meantime, was suffering, in that same London, the agonies of actual want and starvation [Charlotte Clarke, actress and writer, d. 1760]. I am persuaded that many of the errors, nay, of the crimes of humanity, spring from neglect of paternal duties – from unjustifiable harshness at a father's hand ...

It is then a proof of Shakspeare's correct reading of human nature, when he makes the play of King Lear teach a lesson to the unjust parent, as striking as to the ungrateful child ... This play, then, has a twofold meaning, upon which parents might reflect with equal benefit with the children their Creator has given them, to shield, not to expose them to the storms of adversity. From many a homeless man, from many a heart-

broken woman, from many a cheerless home, a mute appeal goeth up to
Heaven, against parental injustice, parental cruelty. And if at the bar of
the Just Judge there stands an accuser against his children, a white-haired
old man, a King Lear, near him is seen the saintly angel of the meek, the
lovely, the injured daughter, the Cordelia of domestic history ...

There have been tears over the white, discrowned Lear, driven from
those homes his injustice had showered upon ungrateful daughters. But
few seem to reflect upon the *greater wrong*, inflicted by a king, by a
father, whose judgment experience might have ripened, whose passions
time and reason should have cooled, turning from his door his youngest
daughter, *friendless*, as far as he could deprive her of friends; exiling an
old and faithful counsellor, also, because he remonstrated against such
injustice to Cordelia. And what was her offence? She is punished because
she 'most rightly said,' [I.i.183] as her courageous defender puts it. But
King Lear's outrages on his youngest daughter do not even stop here. His
ill-will seems to be nourished by his power to do Cordelia harm. His
wounded vanity is doubly hurt, by reflecting that he cannot alter the
judgment of his daughter, either by appeals to her self-interest, or threats
of his anger. And this is all true to real life. Let a parent once take offence
at his child's conduct, – without Charity drives out the vexing thoughts,
– the consequences are the same as those traced in King Lear. Everything
that malice or envy can invent to keep the flame of rage burning, is
hearkened to by the father. He desires to justify his unkind feelings to
his child, *to himself*, for he has a lurking suspicion that such feelings are
not right. Therefore, he regards all those who befriend his child as attacking him; all those who let him see they do not approve of harsh measures
to the offender, as being offenders themselves. All 'extenuating circumstances' are never to be mentioned in the unjust father's presence. They
are an offence unto him. And there are people *base* enough to pander to
such a parental state of mind.

Othello

How *natural* is the origin of *this love-match*. Othello and Desdemona
are entirely opposite in character. The histories of 'the course of true love'
teach us this apparent opposition of feeling is often the bond of union.
Two streams rushing from different directions find, at last, the same outlet
– the ocean. Two hearts, impelled by different motives, unite together in
love. Othello is brave; Desdemona is timid. Othello is a plain, artless
soldier; Desdemona is a beautiful, accomplished lady. Othello is obstinate;
Desdemona is yielding, where no great principle is at stake. Notice the
foundations of their intimacy, and let it be a warning to fathers. Othello
and Desdemona 'are thrown together.' 'Her father oft invited me,'

[I.iii.128] thus giving Othello an opportunity of knowing Desdemona, and of being known by her ...

We learn, then, from Shakspeare's great exemplar of jealousy, that it is a vice that may fasten upon a man of a great and of a generous heart, capable of winning the affections of a fascinating and virtuous woman. This instructs us, that jealousy often lodges in a fair temple, and accounts for many speeches and many actions in those from whom we hoped better things ...

In studying the play of Othello, I have always *imagined* its hero *a white* man. It is true the dramatist paints him black, but this shade does not suit the man. It is a stage decoration, which *my taste* discards, – a fault of color, from an artistic point of view. I have, therefore, as I before stated in my *readings* of this play, dispensed with it. Shakspeare was too correct a delineator of human nature to have colored Othello *black*, if he had personally acquainted himself with the idiosyncrasies of the African race.

We may regard, then, the daub of black upon Othello's portrait as an *ebullition* of fancy, a *freak* of imagination, – the visionary conception of an ideal figure, – one of the few erroneous strokes of the great master's brush, the *single* blemish on a faultless work.

Othello *was* a *white man*!

Richard III

The play opens at the close of the 'War of the Roses' ... peace once more spread its angel-wings over a land desecrated by fratricidal strife; now, brother no longer bears arms against brother, or father against son. The storm of civil strife dies out, and there is naught left to indicate its fury but the desolated homes, the broken hearts, the impoverished victims, the nameless graves which mark where its fury spent itself. Now the widow and the orphan may dry the tears of agony; for the soldier's battle's fought, and whether victory perched upon the standard under which he fought or on that of his foe, it can no more break his slumber ... Little can the dead be touched by praise or by censure, and if it be true that the departed spirit haunts the home once blessed by its bodily presence, the grave in which that body reposes until the resurrection, it is enough that the wife so fondly cherished, the child so tenderly loved, the friend so dearly prized, still offers, from the heart's sacred memories, the incense of grateful, honored, undying love.

Such are the feelings of most men as the curtain falls upon the awful tragedies of civil war. They have witnessed its harrowing scenes, and they hope never to behold them again.

There are *men* – shame to human nature that they must be classed as such – who, during a time of civil war, rise to high position, but must, with peace, return to their native obscurity. In war, false weights are used in estimating men's value. He who rushes into its blackest smoke, and makes himself conspicuous by leaping over the barriers of justice and compassion, – he who is thus forward where the great and good man pauses and dares not enter, is oftentimes styled a 'patriot,' 'a man of the times,' 'the exponent of the popular will.' When peace comes, such a character, no longer arrayed in its panoply of war, must retire into the background ... To relapse into his former obscurity – how dreadful the thought! To give time and opportunity for criticism of his military actions, with the dispassionate reasoning of a day of peace, – how agonizing the prospect! No. Anything but this. 'Stir up again the fires of sectional strife, rather than I should relapse again into my true position, the scorn of all men, the target at which contempt and revenge shall aim.'

As an example of *such men*, Shakspeare gives us King Richard the Third. In our own time we have had its truth brought home to us by Massachusetts' son, the famously infamous Gen. Ben. Butler. [General Benjamin Franklin Butler, a criminal lawyer and powerful state legislator from Massachusetts, was appointed military governor of Louisiana in 1862 after quelling riots in Baltimore. During his occupation of New Orleans he was accused of corruption and was dubbed 'Beast Butler' after issuing his notorious 'Woman's Order', which held that any New Orleans woman found insulting Union occupation troops was 'liable to be treated as a woman of the town plying her avocation'. After reports of financial scandal forced his removal from command in New Orleans, Butler went on to mismanage several military campaigns in 1864; in 1868 he became a Republican congressman.] ...

In this play Annie [*sic*] is introduced to us as a mourner, following the bier of her husband with sorrow to the tomb. Richard determines, for policy, to marry this widow ... He goes to meet this funeral procession; he stops it with threats; he listens, with well-assumed humility, to Annie's reproaches and insulting remarks on his deformities. Whenever a man permits himself to be downright villified and abused, and is *meek* under it, beware of him; for self-respect is always enforced by the honorable! Richard allows Annie to exhaust her scorn, and then he addresses himself to *her vanity*, as to woman's weakest point of attack ... We all know the *best of women* are prone to look with greater compassion on wrong committed through strong affection than upon wrong committed through anger or malice. There is something pleasing to most of women in the thought, that her charms are great enough to overwhelm man's judgment ... Pleased in spite of herself by his flatteries, vanity unconsciously rising supreme over reason and over just hatred, Annie accepts her husband's murderer, the deformed Richard. No wonder his estimate of woman is lowered by such unnatural success; for an inconstant woman is not respected, even by the man who avails himself of her fickleness ...

Richard proceeds to imprison and have executed the Queen-Dowager's brothers. He then causes Lord Hastings – a noble-man strong in the interest of his nephews, the heirs-presumptive to the throne – to be judicially assassinated on the plea of *witchcraft*. It is not a little strange to consider, that long after this play was written, this very excuse of witchcraft was made, by the New England Puritans, the foundation of persecutions and executions that the mind recoils from in horror. Perhaps if these refugees of fanaticism, 'when they moored their barks on the wild New England shore,' had brought with them an edition of Shakspeare, and made it one of their household treasures, they would not have stained their colonial history with the blood of the innocent; but it is one of the characteristics of fanaticism that it can bear with or seek light from no other source than that contained in its contracted limits. *It* allows of no argument except that in its own favor; *it* listens to no reasons save those it can torture in its own defence, *it* is a one-sided view altogether.

Annette Handcock, Countess of Charlemont, d. 1888

The daughter of the third Baron Castlemaine, Annette Handcock married the Earl of Charlemont (James Alfred Caulfield) in 1858; the Charlemont estates extended to some 8,000 acres in Armargh and Tyrone in Ireland. Very little is known of Annette Handcock; her only publication appears to be her paper on Lady Macbeth printed in the *Transactions of the New Shakspere Society*, originally read at the New Shakspere Society in January 1876.

The New Shakspere Society was founded in 1873 by the eminent Shakespeare scholar F. J. Furnivall, and met monthly at University College London. From its inception the New Shakspere Society appeared to welcome participation and papers from women (on English women's clubs see the entry for Julia Wedgwood, 1890; on American women's Shakespeare clubs see the entries for Elizabeth Wormeley Latimer, 1886, Kate Richmond-West, 1890, and Jessie F. O'Donnell, 1897). Papers read by women at the New Shakspere Society were reported or reprinted in full in the Society's *Transactions* and *Monthly Abstract of Proceedings*, often supplemented with a brief account of how the paper was received. They range from scholarly textual studies – such as 'The Relation of the First Quarto of *Hamlet* to the Second, and on Some of the Textual Difficulties of the Play' (November 1882) by Teena Rochfort Smith, editor of the Society's four-text edition of *Hamlet* – to more general studies: in April 1881, for instance, Constance O'Brien (author of the series 'Shakspeare Talks with Uncritical People' for *The Monthly Packet*, 1881–91) gave a paper 'On Shakspere's Old Men', while in October–December 1884 Miss Leigh-Noel gave a series of papers on 'Shakspere's Garden of Girls' (her book of the same name was published the following year). Other women to give papers at the Society's meetings included Grace Latham (represented in this anthology), Jane Lee (editor of the Society's parallel text of *Henry VI*) Miss E. H. Hickey (October 1882) Isabel Marshall (April 1883) and Emma Phipson, author of *Animal-Lore of Shakespeare's Time* (1883).

Lady Charlemont opens her article with a study of Lady Gruach's genealogy (later Lady Macbeth), observing that Lady Macbeth's grandfather (Kenneth IV) was deposed by Duncan's grandfather (Malcolm), and proceeds by offering a defence of Lady Macbeth as a woman whose good qualities were 'carried to excess' (195).

The Countess of Charlemont, 'Gruach (Lady Macbeth)', *Transactions of the New Shakspere Society*, 1st series, 3–5 (1875–8), 194–8 (read at the 21st Meeting of the Society, held 14 January 1876)

Mrs Jameson – like many others – gives Lady Macbeth credit for home affections. We learn from Gervinus, that German 'Romanticists have made Lady Macbeth a heroine of virtue' [*Shakespeare, Commentaries*: 598]. Others have looked upon her and upon her husband as an ancient Mr and Mrs Manning. [Frederick George Manning and his wife Marie de Roux were executed in 1849 for murdering a guest to their house in order to steal his money. Their execution, at which Mrs Manning wore a black satin dress on the scaffold, aroused considerable publicity.] The question is – Was Lady Macbeth only a woman, or, very woman *and* devil? ...

Many good qualities, when carried to excess, topple over and become faults. Generosity turns into extravagance, economy into stinginess, unselfishness becomes weakness; and an affectionate disposition ... well! ... has to be wretched. Does the Tragedy of Macbeth suggest that the familiar household affections may be turned into the handmaidens of Sin? Gruach had evidently loved her father: a look on a sleeping face that reminded her of him 'shook' her 'fell purpose' and stopped her 'keen knife' [I.v.52]. She had been a tender mother; but the essence of her being, was devoted to her husband. Gervinus describes this devotion in a masterly manner [*Shakespeare, Commentaries*, 1863: II.177]. All for Macbeth; – Gruach's lord – a throne won for him, and a world – ay, a heaven – well lost for her. She sees, feels, acts, but for him. Remember the age in which she lived. The letter telling of the witches and of their prophecy, seemed to her no more than the foreshadowing of Destiny ... The throne for Macbeth by the sacrifice of a life: so be it! She looks not beyond. Afterwards, when to secure his personal safety, her husband flies to other crimes, her soul-rending cry is – fearing to hear the answer – 'What's to be done?' The parts are changed. She now is passive; Macbeth active. All through the ordeal of the Coronation banquet, she bears up bravely; but, seeing the weakness of her husband, her spirit begins to fail.

See the end of the fourth scene of the third act. From this on, the great guilty heart sinks till we come to the 'Sleep-Walking scene.' Then, it is my belief that the strong brain had given way under the mental tortures endured by Gruach. It seems to me that the whole of the first scene of the fifth act is a *résumé* of all Lady Macbeth's part in the tragedy. And who can doubt but that in that scene she believed herself to be in Hell? ...

Mrs Siddons – so says Gervinus – believed Lady Macbeth to have been a fair beauty [1863: II.194]; and I have heard that a traditional picture of her existed years ago in an ancient Scottish Castle, belonging to a descendant, it was said, of Macbeth. It was the portrait of a small fair woman, with blue eyes, rather red (weak-looking?) about the lids ...

We believe that Gruach, after 'life's fitful fever' [III.ii.23], sleeps well. The last we hear of her is at the time of her death: '*A cry within of women*' [V.v.7]. She was not all evil. Her own sex and her servants mourned for her.

Mr Furnivall
... The notion that Lady Macbeth stirrd, nay forc't, Macbeth to his villainous murder, to gratify his ambition only, and not her own too, is so in the teeth of Shakspere's authority, Holinshed, 'but speciallie his wife lay sore upon him to attempt the thing, as she that was very ambitious, burning in unquenchable desire to beare the name of queen' – *Scottish Chronicle, i. 340, ed. 1805* [*Holinshed's Chronicles*: 211], and is, to me, so flatly contradictory to Shakspere's plain revelation of Lady Macbeth's tigrish nature, and her own words,

> I have given suck; and know
> How tender't is to love the babe that milks me:
> I would, while it was smiling in my face,
> Have pluck'd my nipple from his boneless gums,
> And dash'd the brains out, had I so sworn,
> As you have done to this ...
>
> [I.vii.54–9]

that I don't think the point worth arguing.[1] Any one desiring to spare Lady Macbeth, as Chaucer did Creseyde, 'for very routh,' may make excuses for her; but to ask us to think that love for her husband was her only motive, is going too far.

---

1 Lady Charlemont writes in answer, 'Of course Lady Macbeth had no objection to share the throne she helped her husband to get ...'

Anne (Mrs Jerome) Mercier, active 1872–1906

Little is known of Anne Mercier aside from her publications: religious works, including a history of *Christianity in England* (Edinburgh, 1886) and the successful *Our Mother Church: Being Simple Talk on High Topics* (London, 1872), which ran to five editions by 1886; histories for the Christian Knowledge Society; material directed at girls, such as *Pink Ribbons: Stories for Our Girls* (1876) and *Work, and How to Do It: A Practical Guide to Girls in the Choice of Employment* (1884; reissued in 1891) and religious material for the Girls Friendly Society. Anne Mercier's only published work of literary criticism appears to be her article on 'Oedipus and Lear' (signed under the name of Mrs Jerome Mercier) in *The Argosy* – a British fiction magazine appealing primarily to a genteel, middle-class readership of women; in 1870 it had a circulation of twenty thousand. In her article Mercier compares Greek and 'modern' tragedy: 'in the classic play the hero is Destiny; in the modern, it is the God-led Man'. This leads to the 'manifold complications' of modern tragedy: 'the simplicity of the older plot is laid aside; two or more plots are interwoven, like the tracery of a Gothic window, in confused harmony' (368). Mercier proceeds 'to verify these assertions' by comparing *Oedipus* with *Lear*.

Mrs Jerome Mercier, 'Oedipus and Lear', *Argosy* (November 1879), 368–72

> Then note in Oedipus the simplicity of plot – no plot at all according to our modern ideas, but rather one long scene; whereas in Lear we have two plots, both complex, and interwoven, as I said, like tracery. There is Glo'ster, whose pleasant vices have become instruments to plague him, suffering from the duplicity of his son: there the aged king, whose wilful, hot, proud, yet generous nature prepares the way for his daughter's [*sic*] cruelty, yet engages all our sympathy in his sufferings. Then the tender love of Cordelia, opposed to her sister's [*sic*] hardness, and their rivalries in love and hate, make a sort of third intrigue, co-acting with the former. Nor are either of these plots simple: each in itself is complicated by the mingled passions of every character, good and bad united, as in life, and tending to ultimate good or evil as the heart will or will not follow the

Divine impulse. Though there is no religion in the play properly so called, and it is implied that the king and his followers were still heathens, the Christianity of Shakespeare's day informs the whole. There is throughout a recognition of a higher spirit overruling all, and the lesson is strongly impressed on us that if man will but follow, however feebly, where his Maker leads, all things shall work together for good to him. So with Glo'ster. His bitter trials, the loss of his eyes, the treachery of Edmund, all lead his nature to a higher level: he sees his own folly, his Edgar's virtue, and we know that at the end of the drama a better Glo'ster is before us than he with whom it opens. It is the same with Lear. The words, 'Take physic, Pomp,' [III.iv.33] are, as it were, the motto of his part. Pride has been the real evil at the root of his sorrows, and we feel that his afflictions are all physic to expurgate this evil. The calm of Sophocles is not here: the play becomes a very hysterica passio of piled-up griefs, which would be unendurable and have too little of the pleasure which Aristotle prescribes even in tragedy, were it not for the sense we have throughout that the spirit of the king is being purified for a happier future. At first we feel more anger than love for him, as he curses and exiles his sweet child, *his* Antigone; but when we see him enter, his madness crushed out by the agony of sorrow, bearing her dead body, believing against hope in a breath to stain the mirror which he has held to her lips, our reverence and pity proclaim him a nobler king than before, and we eagerly hail the compensating frenzy which makes him die of joy in the belief that Cordelia still breathes.

In Oedipus there is no such aim. The monarch is not tamed and humanised by grief; his dying curse upon his son has no sign of remorse. We do not feel that he is rising to the level of greater spirits with whom his is to mingle in the shades. What we feel throughout is a calm conviction that a man, in himself noble and virtuous, can suffer no degradation even from the enmity of the gods. It is the struggle of grand humanity with fate, and the former is victorious.

Two such great works, so alike, yet so different; each showing an aged father and king, blessed in the love of one perfect child – the broken strength of the one leaning most touchingly on the tenderness of the other; the woes from false friends and from undeserved misfortunes; yet the spirit of the two so diverse; these can be compared; but the palm can scarcely be given to either. If the last scene appears the grander in Oedipus, the mystic disappearance of the blind king impressing us with an awe which the wholesale slaughter in Lear converts into a certain dissatisfaction, this is, perhaps, the only point in which such comparison can be made.

Reverting to our first figure, the simplicity of the Greek drama satisfies us with the sense of rest, of completion, of approval of that unconquerable dignity in manhood which reflects a lustre on our own humanity. On the other hand, the English play, like the English cathedral, charms and occupies our souls in unravelling so many lines combined in one exquisitely intricate web, the whole leading our thoughts through its beautiful complexities to a vision of holy calm above.

Dorothea Beale, 1831–1906

Principal of the pioneer girls' public school Cheltenham Ladies' College from 1858 to 1906, Dorothea Beale played an important role in the movement to improve women's education; she also served as a vice-president of the Central Society for Women's Suffrage. An early student of Queen's College for Women, Bedford (the first higher-education institution for women attached to an English University), Beale replaced the curriculum of accomplishments at Cheltenham Ladies' College with a course of rigorous education; she went on to encourage the professional training of women teachers by contributing essays to the Women's Education Union Journal, supporting professional associations of women teachers, and founding St Hilda's College, Oxford in 1893. In 1869 Beale edited the *Reports Issued by the Schools' Inquiry Commission on the Education of Girls* in which she argued that 'social tyranny – the force of unreasoning custom – [has] exercised a pernicious influence over women ... the old rubbish about masculine and feminine studies is beginning to be treated as it deserves. It cannot be seriously maintained that those studies which tend to make a man nobler or better, have the opposite effect upon a woman' (iii–v).

Although she never married, Beale had a high regard for family values and was a devout Christian. As Elizabeth Raikes remembers,

> Ophelia, to take an instance, was for all the generations of girls who read *Hamlet* at Cheltenham the woman who failed a man because she could not dare to be true. A matter like this was vital to Miss Beale ... Desdemona, again, was always marked as the wife who not unnaturally roused the suspicions of a jealous-minded husband, because he knew that in marrying him she had deceived her father. The misery that may follow a secret wilful marriage was always hinted at when this story was told (1908: 7)

Her monograph on *King Lear*, from which this extract is taken, was published at Cheltenham and was undoubtedly recommended reading for the students of the Ladies' College.

D. Beale, *King Lear: A Study*. Cheltenham, Thomas Hailing, 1881

Few plays of Shakspere seem perhaps less attractive at first sight ... We are allowed no respite: from first to last our feelings of indignation, terror, sympathy, are stirred, and the inward storms of passion are outwardly symbolised by the elemental conflict, and the noise of the battlefield. There is strife too within, for our judgment, our moral sense, condemns what our feelings excuse, and we are not able to be quite without compassion even for the darkest villain of all. Yet, though Greek in its conception and barbaric in scenery, the play is in its deepest spirit Christian. It is throughout a protest against the theory of blind fate: men reap the harvest they have sown –

> All friends do taste
> The wages of their virtue, and all foes
> The cup of their deservings.
>
> [V.iii.303–5]

And, if we except a very few irreconcilables, the agony is a purifying fire, and it is faith which gives the victory. The king recovers his lost faith in human virtue through the love of two faithful ones; he had never lost his faith in God ...

The first scene has shown us the fierce passion in the royal household, the second shows us how similar passions are stirred in the heart of Gloster; and then, like some intricate fugue, the two parallel themes are interlaced to the end, – and the tumult and clamour swells until it reaches its climax at the beginning of Act III. Through the whole of that act, the strife rages within and without. Then the exhausted sufferers sink into repose, the healing process has begun; and when, at last, faint and wounded, they are borne from the battlefield, we know by their changed voices, their altered tones, that adversity has done its work. The concluding act brings all once more upon the scene, the wicked are cast down, and the jarring discords cease, then a quiet cadence tells us that the sufferers are at rest, and some final notes recall the opening theme, and tell us that faith and love and duty will reign victorious over a renovated earth.

Yet grand as is the form and scenery of Lear, magnificent as it is in its conception as a whole, it seems to me unrivalled for its subtle analysis of feeling ...

But surely, we say, the old king loved his 'dog-hearted' [IV.iii.45] daughters! He gave them all, asking only in return their love. He was content to make his 'nursery' [I.i.124] with them; he had no other love, and, when theirs failed him, his poor heart broke.

Yet if love be the highest good, it must bless, and Lear's did not bless his daughters: it fed their selfishness, it taught them to lie, at last it cursed them. No, his was mere affection or fondness, not love. He thought himself loving, because he wanted to be loved. He is contrasted with Kent, who, for love's sake, threw away even the king's love. Shakspere would show how this greed of love degrades the character, and blinds the affections, making us value people not for what they are, but for their attachment (real or imaginary) to us ...

   But did Cordelia love her father? If so, why did she answer 'nothing,' and 'I love your majesty according to my bond: nor more nor less,' 'I obey you, love you, and most honour you' [I. i. 86–98]. Cordelia is not apt at definitions, and she deals in paradox. We must admit with Gervinus that she is unphilosophical in her mode of expression, since her husband could not carry away half the love which belonged to her father [*Shakespeare Commentaries*: 637]; yet she is evidently distinguishing between the filial love, which she gave to Lear, and that love which she bestowed on France, the elect of her soul ... There are two kinds of affection, the one social, the other personal, the one binds us together as members of a family, a nation, &c. It is dependent upon some kind of relationship – to be without this feeling is to be unnatural, and we hold in abhorrence those who break the bonds of loyalty or piety (in the Latin sense) – the undutiful child, the traitor to his country. It may be said that such love is more or less selfish; I would rather say it is love in its rudimentary state, it is the root out of which the larger love must grow, it developes [*sic*] into the highest, when we realise our oneness in the all-embracing love of God; then the soul goes forth of self, and is born to a new and larger life, it feels the enthusiasm of humanity. To begin with the nearest is to climb slowly but surely, to begin with the enthusiasm of humanity is to try to fly to a mountain-top. Now Lear demanded the personal affection which must be *won*, not *claimed*. Cordelia could not give to him such love as she gave to the noble king of France, but she did give to her father filial love, and so she answers,

>   Good, my lord,
>   You have begot me, bred me, loved me; I
>   Return those duties back, as are right fit.
>   [I.i.95–7]

And the special beauty of loyal love is this, that it is not destroyed by our faults, it is a steadfast, noble, God-like love, which loves on in spite of sin. Such love was kindled into a brighter glow in Kent, when he saw the wilful King casting himself down into misery, and it made Edgar bless the father who had outlawed him and sought his life. There are perhaps depths of wickedness which may destroy even this love, and make one renounce allegiance to a sovereign and even to a parent, but how terrible is the strife, how awful the burden, is shown in such dramas as Orestes and Hamlet ...

The subject of the play is not personal affection, but that loyal love or piety which draws us first to those who are nearest, as members of one family, or state, or church, but afterwards binds us to all whose needs we can fill, unites us to all humanity. Its bonds are not broken by sin, it is a Christlike redeeming love, which must mingle with sorrow, ere suffering can purify. Lear claimed at first, love rather than loyalty, he learned afterwards that it is authority, not merit, to which men bow, when he cried, 'a dog's obeyed in office;' [IV.vi.158–9] thus is society kept from anarchy by the rule even of the unworthy ...

If he retained a sort of faith in the gods, his faith in men was gone. All were 'sophisticated' Act III., sc. iv [III.iv.106]. There was wickedness concealed under every show of virtue [see IV.vi.164–7]. He has no power then to save himself; some holy and loving spirit must descend into the pit of misery, with the power of redeeming love, and bring forth the sinful, suffering soul. Then, even by the last reverse, he is not thrown into 'ill thoughts again' [V.ii.9]. He is able to bear all patiently; to believe that there is a mystery in God's dealings, which it will take a lifetime to understand. We see how changed he is when he dwells not on the sins of others, but his own; he is no longer a man 'more sinned against than sinning' [III.ii.60].

> ... I'll kneel down
> And ask of thee forgiveness: so we'll live ...
> And take upon us the mystery of things
> As if we were God's spies.
>
> [V.iii.10–17]

And at last he dies for love of her who had so loved him.

Constance O'Brien, active 1876–1912

Despite her long-running series of articles on Shakespeare for the English periodical *The Monthly Packet* (recommended by Elizabeth Wormeley Latimer in America in 1886), very little is known of Constance O'Brien; in 1881 she gave a paper 'On Shakspere's Old Men' to the New Shakspere Society, and in 1891 she published *Possible Plays for Private Players*, followed in 1912 by *The Guild of the Garden Lovers*.

The Monthly Packet, in which O'Brien's series 'Shakspere Talks With Uncritical People' appeared, was edited by the children's writer Charlotte Yonge primarily for an audience of young women aged fifteen to twenty-five, 'not as a guide ... but as a companion in times of recreation ... to make them more steadfast and dutiful daughters of our own beloved Catholic Church of England' (Mare and Percival: 140). The journal largely carried articles of instruction and romance, and series such as 'Ladies at Work. Papers on Paid Employment for Ladies by Experts in the Several Branches', to which Grace Latham contributed.

'Shakspere Talks With Uncritical People' was aimed at the non-specialist (or 'uncritical') reader. O'Brien argued that the best way for the 'uncritical' reader to study a Shakespeare play was to dispense with 'a quantity of theories, criticism and information' and enjoy its characters becoming 'real and alive' – by seeing the play acted, reading it alone or with 'a party of intelligent people', or 'when two or three enthusiasts gather round the fire, and talk over the dear people whose life seems as vivid as our own, and whose thoughts, words and deeds are as real to us as those of our everyday friends ... For unless you get to know the people themselves, all grinding at dates, succession in production, sources, in a word criticism generally, is simply staring at the picture frame and forgetting the picture' (*Julius Caesar*, 1886: 353). O'Brien hoped for a 'fresh and unhackneyed' approach to Shakespeare's plays (*Hamlet*, 1887: 70): her essays typically begin with a quick summary of Shakespeare's adaptation of his sources, followed by a scene-by-scene commentary on the play interspersed with lively character sketches and occasional surveys of criticism. The series included articles on *Romeo and Juliet* (1879), *The Merchant of Venice* (1881), *The Taming of the Shrew* (1882), *Henry V* (1883), *As You Like It* (1884), *Twelfth Night* (1885), *The Tempest* (1885),

Julius Caesar (1886), *Hamlet* (1887), *Measure for Measure* (1888), *Macbeth* (1890) and *Othello* (1891).

Constance O'Brien, 'Shakspere Talks With Uncritical People', *The Monthly Packet*, 1879–91 (February 1879: 186–97; February 1882: 175–86; September 1885: 275–89; July and September 1887: 70–86 and 258–70; November 1891: 536–52)

Romeo and Juliet (1879)

[Lady Capulet] is frozen with pride, cold, hard, and stiff; herself a Capulet, her family feelings are her strongest feelings; she comes sweeping over the scene, a determined, unlovable woman, who might prevent her old husband from thrusting himself into the fray, but has little tender softness in her otherwise. Her child should not have been sweet Juliet, but fierce Tybalt; his haughty and vindictive nature has some family likeness to that of his aunt; both are equally relentless and unscrupulous ...

The intercourse of mother and daughter is not one of Shakspere's favourite subjects; he only touches it twice, as if he was not quite sure of the ways of women together, and certainly Lady Capulet is not shown in attractive relation to her daughter, even here [I.iii] where she is all graciousness, and intending to get the girl's confidence; but she cannot really unbend to her child, and the passage where she praises Paris is about the most strained in the whole play. 'Read o'er the volume of young Paris' face,' [I.iii.81] etc. There is no real confidence between Juliet and her mother; the girl listens, and makes her demure little answers, the properest of the proper, showing no trace of that power of passion which lies concealed within her. Perhaps she herself is unconscious of it; the touch is still wanting that would open the lily bud. But another figure moves in this scene too important to be over looked, especially as she is the one example of her class which Shakspere shows to us, Juliet's easy-natured, affected, foolish old nurse. Her character displays itself at once, the fussy, curious, chattering old body, who identifies herself completely with the family in which she has lived so long; not by any means a model nurse, but a fair type of many since the time when Shakspere drew her, entirely without any principle except a curious sort of affection for her employers, and quite convinced that they could not get on without her. She is a thoroughly coarse-minded woman, yet she loves her foster-child in her foolish fashion; to her is transferred all the affection which the nurse would have given to her own dead child who, as she says with a pathetic touch, 'was too good' [I.iii.20] for her. After, doubtless, doing her best to spoil Juliet, she takes unbounded pride in her beauty, and thinks nothing too good for her darling ...

Perhaps the best-known scene in the whole play is the next interview between the lovers [the 'balcony scene', II.ii], when Mercutio's saucy conjuring has died away into silence; and then follows the lovely garden scene. Now we really see Juliet as she is, no longer repressed by external influences, no longer the shy girl, but suddenly developed by the new feeling that has come upon her; the lily-bud opens and shows her gold heart. All the vindictiveness instilled into her mind by the long family feud disappears before this new passion; her only love destroys her only hate. Juliet's nature combines the most exquisite tenderness with a curious directness and strength of purpose. Not only is she strong to endure in misfortune, but she faces the facts of her position, and is absolutely clear and honest about them ...

Romeo too is altered by the touch of real feeling; his old talk, which had gone terribly near rant, changes into the words of deep affection; he means all he says, as he gazes up at the bright vision in the balcony; he dares anything now, walls are no obstacle, all the Capulets in a body should not keep him from Juliet. Yet in spite of his love and earnestness, Juliet is the leading spirit of the two; perhaps it should not be so, but she has the stronger nature and guides, where Romeo is content to worship her. Sometimes she is too quick for him; her wishes change with her flitting fancies; she wants him to swear he loves her, and then stops his vows; she is happy, alarmed, joyous, foreboding, all at once; the uncertain foundation of her happiness troubles her even in her flush of joy, while Romeo is absorbed in the bright present. From this it comes that she reverses the order of things, and asks Romeo if he means to marry her – which somehow does jar a little; she has her wits so very much about her, considering her youth and perfect inexperience. Still, it may be that Romeo was not quick enough in thinking about this point, and she asks him very simply and naturally, with an innocent confidence of getting the truth in reply. He is a graceful pleasant sort of lover, full of ardour and devotion; but is he quite man enough for Juliet?

The Taming of the Shrew (1882)

Concealed under [Bianca's] demureness is the less pleasing feature of a certain aptitude for intrigue. She is in no hurry to be married when we first see her; no one yet has caught her fancy, and indeed she somehow gives a feeling that she is one of those slight, delicate, fairy creatures who are hard to please, and whom most men instinctively want to protect and caress. Very different is our notion of the stormy heroine, the tall nut-brown maid, handsome, scowling Katharina; there is nothing conventional about her at all events! Everything is upside down with her; and to her feeling nothing can happen rightly, as she has got out of her own control, and that of everybody else. She is a spoilt child on a large scale, not able to manage herself, and too strong for those about her. Baptista has no authority, and Bianca no influence over her, so there is no check on her wild passion ... Perhaps Shakspere did not mean us to take her very seriously, but with all the childish absurdity of her rages, one is half sorry for her as one is for a child or animal in a passion; it is so much worse for her than for the objects of the storm. She has put herself entirely out of her natural position as a woman, and as nobody can do anything with her in an ordinary way, something extraordinary is required to right her, which is the key to Petruchio's success ...

After making her father's house miserable for so long, it is only fair she should suffer something too, but one feels sorry for her in her comical misfortunes ... All this elaborate scheme for wearing out Kate's physical power of resistance seems barbarous; but hitherto she has been able to tyrannise over her surroundings in the pride of her strong will, so she has now to realise her true weakness. In the bullying, overbearing line which she took at home, Petruchio can easily beat her, and never give her a chance to quarrel with him, and slowly she is forced to the conviction that it is best to yield with a good grace and not struggle hopelessly. The process of conviction is necessarily slow, and Grumio has no business to mock at her hunger in the famous offer of 'the mustard without the beef' [IV.iii.30]. We confess to being glad Kate boxes his ears for the impudence, if it is unladylike ...

Everybody knows the [final] scene ... Of course the vehement girl goes right to the utmost extreme of submission, and pushes her doctrine of the inequality of the sexes as far as it will possibly go; this is just what we might expect from her. And then her fair picture of the man, toiling, fighting, enduring for the woman's safety and comfort, readily leads to the idea of the woman's willing tribute of 'love, fair looks, and true obedience to his honest will' [V.ii.153]. Kate has no idea of making all the sacrifice come from either side, or of erecting her husband into an eastern sultan; but she must have fallen far in love with Petruchio before she imagined him to correspond with the ideal husband of her speech. Her self-surrender is so complete that one gets a sort of feeling that it should have been to somebody higher than Petruchio.

Twelfth Night (1885)

It seems to be impossible to present a man in a lovesick condition without making him a little bit ridiculous. Not even Romeo, nor our present hero, Orsino, can escape, and the impression is deepened when, without preparation, we have to begin our acquaintance with him when he is in this condition. His beautiful sentiments, poured out before we well know who

he is, startle us, and create a slight prejudice against him, which we have
some difficulty in overcoming afterwards ... Perhaps this gentle and
romantic Duke was thus introduced to us at the very outset, to prevent
any anxiety as to the hands into which our heroine is to fall, when we
become acquainted with her in the next scene. Here she stands, a fair,
girlish creature, pathetically lonely among the rough group of sailors,
eliciting the chivalry of their honest captain by her friendless position ...
but she is far from helpless. We should say that, being early left an orphan,
she is used to thinking for herself, for after taking the facts of the situation
into consideration, she composedly decides on the one possible course to
take, not without a longing for the unattainable refuge of Olivia's house.
In resolving on her strange plan for safety, she evidently reckons with
confidence on her own powers to carry it out, and all along her character
blends strength and softness. Such determined perseverance as she displays
in carrying out a most painful task, forcing her own wishes aside with a
will as of iron, combined with such sensitive tenderness of feeling, such
a warm and constant heart, invest her with a peculiar charm even in
Shakspere's 'rosebud garden of girls' [M. Leigh-Noel's *Shakspeare's Garden of Girls* was published in the same year as this article, 1885]. We
wonder at the courage and audacity with which the pretended page plays
her part, and in an instant we see her quivering with feeling or natural
timidity, the girl's heart throbbing fast beneath the boy's doublet. Viola
seems fitted by nature for Orsino, both by the likeness between their
poetic and cultured characters and the difference between her unhesitating
devotion and his dreamy sentiment. We could not fancy Viola loving
twice; she is too thoroughgoing to change her mind, when her affections
have once been fixed, and she realizes this fact in her situation without
disguise. Indeed, most of Shakspere's girls, however romantic they may
be, know their own minds, and have an honesty and straight-forwardness
in their wishes which is thoroughly delightful when compared with the
imbecile shilly-shallying of many modern heroines. His maidens are sometimes deceived into taking a woman for a man, but their knowledge of
their own sentiments is unhesitating ...

Maria has a kind of regard for her lady and understands her moods,
but her principal desire in life seems to be to amuse herself, pay off those
who offend her, and rise in the world. Olivia's seclusion makes her waiting
woman of more importance in the household, and gives her more liberty
than is usual in such cases, and evidently the clever and unscrupulous
young woman understands making the most of the position ... For instance, when she is playing demure propriety in Olivia's presence, who
would imagine that she had any connection with the saucy piece of
impudence who bandied jests with Sir Toby and filled up his tankard only
a few hours previously? Altogether, we could not call Maria a very

desirable inmate for a respectable household, and the thought will some-times intrude that the Lady Olivia would have been better employed in looking to what passed in her house than in indulging in such unlimited grief even for her brother. It is clear that everybody in that establishment does what pleases them best; the clown wanders hither and thither, and Maria's standing flirtation with Sir Toby is open to the notice of all but her mistress ...

The point about [Sebastian] which is most insisted on is that nameless charm possessed by some happy natures, which works like witchcraft unconsciously exerted. Without any effort or design Sebastian completely masters the valiant sea captain Antonio, so that he cannot bear to part with him. Antonio feels towards this youth whom he rescued from the sea, such tender affection as is usually supposed to be only felt between man and woman, but there is abundant proof that Shakspere at least, believed in such friendship, and knew the heights and depths of which it is capable. Here it is natural enough that Antonio should love Sebastian because he has saved him, and then the bright, loveable creature becomes infinitely dear to the sea rover who has knocked about the world so long, fighting hard, working hard, with more enemies than friends. He is a good representative of the Elizabethan adventurer, whom his foes called a pirate, but who regarded himself as a defender of his country and faithful servant of his Queen.

Hamlet (1887)

[Hamlet's] position is truly an intolerable one. He finds himself not only excluded from the throne, but actually dependent on the usurper, whom, till now, he seems to have regarded as beneath contempt, his deepest feelings hurt, his taste continually offended, and no escape left for him. Then, worse than all, comes his mother's marriage. The agony of shame and grief which this causes him far outweighs his previous sorrow and disappointment, it seems to blacken not only his future, but even his past, his pure memories are poisoned, the mother he seemed to know has utterly disappeared, she never has been at all ...

[With Gertrude] we are met by one of those natures which perplex, not from depth but shallowness, people who seem hypocritical, but are more truly changeable, and therefore utterly puzzling to steadier minds. This fickle temperament is not incompatible with a good deal of charm, and we could easily imagine Gertrude to be, like the Queen in the 'Historie,' [*The Hystorie of Hamblet*, 1608 trans. from Belleforest: STC 12734.5] 'as courteous a Princess as any living, who had never offended any of her subjects'; that is, a pretty, good-tempered woman, with graceful manners, softly easy-going, desiring above everything to have all comfortable around her. No doubt she made King Hamlet an affectionately admiring wife, enjoying his passionate devotion without troubling herself to understand it; and no doubt she felt very flat and miserable without it when he was dead; but found the cajoleries of Claudius a very good substitute, and accepted them without more ado. In the same easy fashion she is, doubtless, attached to her son, sorry if anything ails his health, and wishing to see him happily married; but she has no hesitation in keeping him out of his rights, nor in doing him the deepest injuries. Talking to such a woman of honour or conscience is to waste breath; she simply fails to understand it. She follows her own inclinations, and sincerely wonders how anybody can be found to object. Naturally her perception of anything not absolutely on the surface is very slow; for instance, the state of tortured feeling in which Hamlet lives after his father's death and her re-marriage, is a perfect mystery to her. Not that she is exactly callous, for with a great effort it is possible to make a temporary impression on her, and disturb her complacency; but it does not last long, the impression is effaced, and she is just as before. In fact, Gertrude is just the character to drive a sensitive and passionate nature to despair in any struggle with her, simply by her shallowness; every force brought against her would spend itself in vain before it could really change her.

Othello (1891)

This old Senator [Brabantio] is as fiery as most of the elderly men in these Italian stories, blazing up into uncontrolled wrath on very slight provocation. Not that he has no grounds for excitement when he discovers Desdemona's flight, for the unexpected blow hits him hard. Evidently it has never occurred to him that his sweet daughter could have a will of her own, or that anything could come of her constantly seeing and hearing Othello in the privacy of her own home. The difference of colour seemed to Brabantio an all-sufficient bar, and in his blind pride he overlooked all the other qualities which drew Desdemona to the Moor. Still it is hard on the old man, and we cannot help feeling that he is not well used by the lovers, and that it is especially a trifle treacherous on Othello's part to repay his friend's hospitality by taking away his daughter without leave or license, or any effort to get Brabantio's consent. He would certainly not have given it, but for them to begin by running away is hardly honourable. There is something to be said for Brabantio's objections to his son-in-law; it is not surprising that he dislikes giving his daughter to one of a race and colour so different from her own, not altogether suitable in age and other respects. But his wild rage goes far beyond reason, because if Othello was fit to represent the Republic, to govern her dependencies, and lead her armies, it is folly to talk as if Desdemona had picked him out of the gutter, and therefore he must have ensnared her affection by magic ...

While [Othello] has the wild passions of a southern man latent in him, he has also a touch of Oriental dignity, and does not easily let himself lose his composure ... With all his love for Desdemona, it is a strange thing that he has no real trust in her, the old Oriental contemptuous feeling towards women underlies all his knowledge of her goodness and purity, and lays him open to attack. Then, as his hot blood gets fevered, he loses all sight of justice in his dealings with the helpless girl ... All the ferocity latent in Othello's nature bursts into flame as he craves for vengeance, the half-tamed savage in him breaks loose from the restraints of civilisation. Not that the Italian noble of the period would have seen anything remarkable in Othello's taking the law into his own hands on such an occasion, it might even seem the only thing to do, but not with this wild storm of fury.

Amelia Edith Barr (née Huddleston), 1831–1919

A prolific novelist and committed episcopalian, Amelia Barr was born in Lancashire (England), but emigrated to America with her husband Robert Barr in 1853, at the suggestion of Henry Ward Beecher and his suffragist sister Harriet Beecher Stowe (whom the Barrs met at Glasgow). In 1867 Amelia's husband and three sons died during a yellow fever epidemic in Texas; unable to make ends meet, Amelia moved to New York to seek Beecher's support – he encouraged her to write, and published her first pieces in his paper, the *Christian Union*. Barr began her career as a novelist in 1872, but it was not until the publication of *Jan Vedder's Wife* in 1885 that she achieved popularity or prosperity. By the time of her death she had written over seventy-five novels: many, like *Prisoners of Conscience* (1897), dealt with English and American history and reflected her interest in the struggle for liberty in both countries, but her work is usually dismissed as romantic and sentimental. In her autobiography, *All the Days of My Life* (New York, 1913), Amelia Barr made clear her commitment to women's suffrage: 'All my life long I have been sensible of the injustice constantly done to women. Since I have had to fight the world single-handed, there has not been one day I have not smarted under the wrongs I have had to bear, because I was not only a woman, but a woman doing a man's work' (468).

The Young People of Shakespeare's Dramas: For Youthful Readers (New York, 1882) sought to 'allure' young people 'into the paths of virtue and nobleness. No more perfect and gracious types of youthful life exist than the few scattered (mainly) through Shakespeare's Historical Dramas; and surely they may most fitly introduce young readers into that splendid world of the imagination which the great poet created for us' (3). The volume consists of scene-by-scene character studies of children and their parents in *King John, 3 Henry VI, Richard III, Coriolanus, Cymbeline* and *Lear* (in which Barr argues the Fool is a young boy), followed by 'historical sketches' of each play.

Amelia E. Barr, *The Young People of Shakespeare's Dramas: For Youthful Readers*. New York: Appleton and Co., 1882

Marcius, son of Caius Marcius Coriolanus

Coriolanus brings before us the better days of the first military greatness of the Roman people. The monarchy has given way to a republic, but the aristocratic and democratic elements are still at war; and the play is full of the struggle of the two powers – patricians and plebeians, senate and people, consuls and tribunes. In this struggle Coriolanus, in the might of his passions, surpasses even the heroes of the heroic age. But Shakespeare has taken pains to make this exceptional pride and passion possible by giving him a mother glowing with patriotism, and who has centered all her love, pride, and strength in making her only son the chief hero and ruler of his country. She trains him for dangers and ambitions; and is well pleased 'to let him seek danger where he was like to find fame.'

When Caius Marcius is introduced to us he is in the height and glory of his life. If he can control his passions he is loved and prized by all; senators stand bare-headed before him, soldiers follow him to battle gladly – he is their god! But, when he is angry, all his good qualities disappear; he disdains his enemies without cause, and they insult him without reason ...

The third scene introduces us to the home of the great soldier. The Roman houses at this time were very simple – a number of rooms all opening into a court. This court, or *atrium*, was the sanctuary of the dwelling, the place of the hearth and the domestic deities; in short, the home-room of the family. For these reasons it was, even at this early date, roofed over. Benches, chairs, and couches stood in it; simple seats, low, and without backs, not unfrequently made of bronze, with rude ornamental designs.

In such a room we first see the mother and wife of Caius Marcius. They are sitting sewing, and talking about the war with the Volces, and the absence and danger of the beloved son and husband. The haughty, daring temper of the mother, Volumnia, is finely contrasted with the modest sweetness and tender solicitude of the wife, Virgilia ... Shakespeare has thrown over this little scene the very spirit of antiquity. Valeria, like a courtly lady, knows that nothing can better please the mother and grandmother than to talk about and praise the young Marcius; and an admirable picture she draws of the boy, who would 'rather see the swords and hear a drum than look upon his schoolmaster.' And could any two words convey better the idea of a self-willed child than Valeria's description of his appearance – 'he has such a *confirmed countenance*?' [I.iii.59–60]. The boyish passion in which he 'mammocked' the gilded butterfly is but the mimic of the father, 'fluttering the Volscians about, like an eagle in a dove-cote' [V.vi.114–15] – while the grandmother can think of no higher compliment than to proudly pronounce the child to have been in 'one of his father's moods' [I.iii.66] …

An American poet – Walt Whitman – says that Coriolanus is incarnated, uncompromising feudalism in literature [*Democratic Vistas*, 1892: 367, 388, 393, 407 and 421]. But Coriolanus is not altogether a political play; for, though it is the history of a struggle between patricians and plebeians, it is also the history of a struggle between Coriolanus and his own self. And it is not the Roman people who bring about his destruction; it is his own haughty pride and passionate self-will. The lesson that Shakespeare teaches us in Coriolanus is the lesson Plutarch found there – 'the Muse has imparted nothing finer to mankind than the taming of Nature by moderation and wisdom.'

The boy Fool in *King Lear*

The play of 'King Lear' belongs to the heathen period of British history, but to a time far anteceding that of 'Cymbeline.' Quite intentionally in this play, Shakespeare has depicted Lear's bursts of rage, Cornwall's cruelties, the rude vehemence of Kent, the unnatural hard-heartedness of Lear's two eldest daughters, for they are the legitimate fruits of an age when impulses had an ungovernable strength, and crime a gigantic enormity.

In 'Lear' we have no splendid furniture, and elegant costumes, and Roman courtesy of manners; we must imagine its scenes in narrow chambers of rude masonry, on wild, barren moors, and amid stout Gothic coarseness and barbarity – a heathenish time, when chance reigned above, and power and force below, and when the wicked met death without a pang of remorse. Selfishness and self-will dominate, and the play would be too painful and tragic for perusal, if it were not for the 'fairest Cordelia,' and for the Fool, a boy who is a gracious emanation of all that is gentle and constant and cheerful and true …

> *Knight.* Since my young lady's going into France, sir, the fool
>   hath much pined away.
> *Lear.* No more of that; I have noted it well. [I.iv.73–5]

These two remarks are the key to the whole tender connection between Lear and his boy Fool. They show us how the boy's loving gentle nature clung to the 'sweetest Cordelia'; and we are aware that the King's sympathy with it is the one unselfish and redeeming spot in the old passionate monarch's breast. And after this, through all his melancholy wanderings, his care of the Fool is constant and loving. In his explosions of rage and invective, he never forgets his faithful companion's tenderness. The unkindness of his daughters, the unpitying elements, can not quench this spark of love in his wretched heart. In the depths of his misery, he turns from his own sufferings to think of him:

> Poor fool and knave, I have one part in my heart
> That's sorry yet for thee.

[III.ii.72–3]

The word 'knave' signifies only a 'boy.' It is a Saxon word which has gradually come to have a much worse meaning. The constancy of attachment between the two opposite natures of Lear and his Fool is one of the most beautiful and masterly creations that ever entered the mind of any poet. The 'poor knave's' struggles between his *'heart's sadness'* and his *'duty's jesting'* form a vivid self-contrast, while his evidently forced humor is a powerful heightening of the mournful and tragic in the play. Thus, we are no sooner made to feel the affectionate tenderness of the lad's character, by hearing, just before his first entrance, that since Cordelia's 'going into France the fool hath much pined away,' than we see him come in with a playful manner, assumed to hide his concern from his old master; and, from that time to the close, he maintains a constant endeavor by sportive words to veil his profound interest and sorrow in all that takes place.

Kate Richmond-West, active 1882–1890

Very little is known of Kate Richmond-West: she is not listed in contemporary or twentieth-century biographical dictionaries, and her only publications appear to be *An Interpretation of 'A Winter's Tale'* and *An Interpretation of King Lear* (Chicago, 1882, reprinted in 1890). These were originally presented by Richmond-West as a study course to a 'group of illiterate people, a class of fifty colored men and women' (1890: 3); they represent an early example of how Shakespeare was introduced to black men and women after emancipation. There were few opportunities for black men and women to study Shakespeare in nineteenth-century America: although in the North black children had attended segregated schools since the early nineteenth century, it was only after emancipation (1863) that black men and women throughout the United States were given the right to read. With a few notable exceptions, educational provision for black students was generally poor.

For literate black women, however, the woman's club or literary society provided an informal and supportive forum for reading and studying Shakespeare. In the late nineteenth century local self-help and study groups for black women proliferated, and in 1896 the National Association of Colored Women was formed from a membership of five thousand women, with the objectives of securing unified action among black club-women and uplifting home, moral, and civic life. Among the two hundred clubs that joined the NACW was the Coterie, established in 1889 in Topeka (Kansas) for the study of Shakespeare and other authors its black women members considered to be 'the best known writers of this country and England' (*The Plaindealer*, 30 November 1899, cited by Brady: 21). Unlike Kate Richmond-West's audience, the members of the Coterie were likely to be literate and relatively wealthy black women; white women in Topeka were apparently served by another women's Shakespeare study club, the Friends in Council Shakespeare Class of Topeka (see Adelaide Wood, 1887: 326).

Kate Richmond-West, *Interpretation of 'A Winter's Tale'*. Chicago: Knight & Leonard Co., 1882, reprinted in 1890 under the name Kate Richmond-Green.

Introduction

The ever-growing influence of Shakespeare's genius, the sympathy it secures from all classes of people, the power it infuses into the heart and brain of those who enter into the Shakespearean world, fill us with longing to lead humanity to its heritage; to make as familiar as household words the breathings of this mighty spirit; trusting some imagination may be kindled, some life enriched, through these interpretations of the great genius, William Shakespeare.

This work is the outgrowth of such successes within smaller circles that we feel sure an effort to reach the masses will be keenly appreciated. The strongest impulse to this course came from a group of illiterate people, a class of fifty colored men and women. Their earnest attention and marvelous appreciation of each story as it was unfolded to them, and the direct knowledge of the uplifting and joy those hours brought them, proved how universal is the craving for food that shall satisfy the busy working throng; lifting them above the cares of the day into a new world, where they are strengthened and refreshed.

Simply, then, this publication may be considered an introduction into the Shakespearean world: – a world where humanity never disappoints you; where all the forms are truth and nature, where as long as literature shall last it will feed the hungry soul. Count it a priceless advantage to become a member of this exalted community; to quit your politics, your shop, your kitchen and your ballroom, and enter at will the royal palace and the shepherd's hut.

Humanity ordinarily lacks the opportunity to meet with a sublime soul: yet through the power of Shakespeare any one of us can illumine a quiet hour with the companionship of souls more choice than we would meet with in experience if we lived for centuries.

And this is the privilege of humanity – not narrowed to a class, but the common heritage of all.

A Winter's Tale

Of Hermione, the central figure of the play, the grand, womanly woman ... she has our heart sympathy at once. Fair, beautiful, heroic queen! Would your spirit could be spread abroad, that every mother, wife and daughter might catch but a breath and rejoice, to claim you as their own. It is the feminine element in Shakespeare which, beyond all others, insures the immortality of his genius. For as woman is closer to nature than man, so a literature that would endure must combine the masculine and feminine.

This is the one play of the great master's where the force of the sympathy, truth, and patience of a woman's invincible spirit holds her above all the contending elements of the moving drama about her ...

One of the most remarkable feminine characterizations of Shakespeare is Paulina, who in her devotion to the queen, in her courage and self-reliance, in her vindication of the truth, and her fearless 'holding up the glass' to Leontes, stands unrivalled among the whole feminine creation of the Shakespearean world. Her motives will bear the closest investigation, the sunshine of a loving spirit gleams through her every word. But know her well, make her your friend, she will be as faithful to you as to her king and queen. You may trust her infinitely ... Here is a tender, womanly heart that pleads for another, an intrepid soul whose fearlessness is born of the truth of her convictions, and she will not be restrained ... Is she not justice personified, holding aloft the scales and the sword? Is she not upholding a race of women in her justification of Hermione? We confess to have breathed deeper, truer breath of freedom for the comprehension of this huge spirit ...

If students or readers glean but a part of the lessons these lives teach, they are broadened mentally and morally. If Leontes, in his passion, seems to demand more of mercy and charity than jealousy commonly demands, we must remember Leontes' soul was laid bare before us, and we were allowed to see every motion of heart and brain ... Who of us are ready to believe 'there is more joy in heaven over one sinner that repenteth than over ninety and nine just men who need no repentance?' [St Luke 15:7]. We say it over and mumble it, but we do not live up to it. A deep moral lesson has been taught us in this dramatic form of King Leontes, real life can rarely give to us; and then we owe to this grievous fault such a train of towering virtues as else might never have grown so dear.

Emma Lazarus, 1849–1887

A Jewish American poet, translator and essayist, Emma Lazarus is perhaps best remembered for her poem 'The New Colossus' (1883), five lines of which were inscribed on the pedestal of the Statue of Liberty in 1903. Born to a wealthy New York family, Lazarus received a private education and became proficient in several languages, gaining a wide knowledge of medieval Hebrew poetry (which she translated) and American literature. In 1866 she privately published her *Poems and Translations*, which won praise from Ralph Waldo Emerson (who became a close friend and critic), and throughout the 1870s she contributed poems to *Lippincott's* and *Scribner's Monthly*; Lazarus also wrote a novel (*Alide*, 1874) and a tragedy (*The Spagnoletto*, 1876). In 1879 following the persecution of Jews in Russia she began to write on Jewish identity, contributing articles to *The Critic*, *The Century Magazine* and *The American Hebrew*, in which she called for a 'closer and wider study of Hebrew literature and history', and in 1882 she wrote on persecution in her critically acclaimed *Songs of a Semite: The Dance to Death, and Other Poems* (New York, 1882). Her life was cut short by her death from cancer in 1887, when she was thirty-eight.

Lazarus's review of Salvini's *King Lear* appeared in the *The Century Illustrated Monthly Magazine* (previously *Scribner's Monthly*), a lavishly illustrated and highly successful American periodical with an enormous circulation (two hundred thousand by 1890), which had 'an almost incalculable influence on American society' (Fred W. Robbins, 1986: 368). *The Century* printed fiction, poetry, articles, reviews and memoirs by many well-known American and European writers (including Mark Twain, Henry David Thoreau, Frances Hodgson Burnett, Walt Whitman, Matthew Arnold, Thomas Carlyle and Julia Ward Howe); it had a religious and upright moral tone set by the founding editor (and popular nineteenth-century American poet) Josiah Gilbert Holland, and claimed to print nothing that might offend the sensibilities of women in the family circle. Arguably *The Century* underestimated the degree of social change for American women at the turn of the century, and the journal declined in popularity in the early twentieth century until it was disbanded in 1930.

Emma Lazarus, 'Salvini's "King Lear"', *Century Magazine*, 26:10 (May 1883): 89–91

Salvini [a leading Italian tragedian] understands the *motif* of *Lear* to be, not the local peculiarities of a king of ancient Britain, but the passion of fatherhood. 'Is not a father in Italy the same as a father in Britain?' are his own words upon the subject, and they clearly illustrate his conception. For him the whole tragedy rests upon the fact that the royal martyrdom is *undeserved*; the moment a thought is entertained that it was occasioned by the king's own lack of foresight or justice, its sublime quality disappears ...

What wiser and more appropriate act than, while retaining the title and honors of royalty, to renounce its duties and cares, rendered irksome by the inevitable weariness of a ripe old age? His own nature is exuberantly and demonstratively affectionate, and in presence of his whole court he asks his daughters who among them loves him best, simply for the delight of hearing their filial, graceful replies. From *Regan* and *Goneril* he receives dutiful response; then, overflowing with paternal pride and love, he turns to his darling youngest child, the gentlest and meekest of the three, and receives a rebuff discourteous and irreverent enough to affront even a modern and non-royal father: 'I love you according to my bond, neither more nor less. I am not yet married, but the first stranger who appears and claims me as his wife will obtain from me a greater meed of affection than you can possibly expect' [see I.i.92–3]. Whoever transports himself mentally into the period, place, and circumstances of this scene will not consider the wrath of *Lear* exaggerated. Only because of our own difficulty in laying aside the knowledge of Cordelia's true character, which the later portions of the play reveal, do we here sympathize with her, and condemn the perfectly justifiable indignation of the aggrieved parent and monarch.

Lear, as conceived by Salvini, is a man of noble generosity, of exquisite tenderness and sensitiveness, of powerful intellect and imagination. His robust physical force is beginning to wane, though still as a man of eighty he delights in the pleasures of the chase. But there is no trace of senility in the vigorous richly endowed mind. This conception is amply borne out by the text; for, if the insanity of *Lear* were occasioned by dotage and decrepitude, instead of by the stunning blows of unparalleled misfortunes, there could be no return of reason before his death. Yet, in the last two scenes, Shakspere represents him to be as lucid and sane as though his brain had never been clouded. By accumulating the black and subtle crimes of *Regan* and *Goneril*, the poet emphasizes for us the fact that *Lear* was not imbecile in misjudging them, but that he was dealing here with unnatural monsters such as no human foresight, much less the loving heart of a parent could have divined ...

After every new Shaksperean interpretation offered by Salvini, a chorus of critics promptly exclaim against its non-Shaksperean inspiration, its essentially *Italian* quality. If it could be urged as a fault against Salvini's *Othello* that it was 'not Anglican,' all the more emphatic is the dissatisfaction expressed with a so-called 'Italian *Lear*.' It is but a repetition of truisms to say that Shakspere's personages are human, universal, that they move in a world of passion, of dramatic and psychological complications over and above all distinctions of race, country, creed, and even sex ... Any actor, therefore, who brings out for us the profound human significance of his great characters, is the true interpreter of Shakspere, and such a one is Salvini. It has always seemed to us a curious fact that any who speak the tongue of Shakspere should wish to rob him of his chief claim to immortality. There are those who insist upon his being insular and local, rather than comprehensive and universal; who resent as an impertinence the very suggestion that his genius may speak as clearly and as intimately to an Italian or a Frenchman as to an Anglo-Saxon. If it were not so – 'the less Shakspere he,' as Browning puts it. They might as well attempt to confine him to the limits of Stratford, and assert that outside of Warwickshire he could not be properly understood, as to restrict him to the English-speaking or Teutonic races.

Charlotte Endymion Porter, 1859–1942

Author, editor and literary critic, Charlotte Porter was born in Towanda, Pennsylvania, and lived in Cambridge, Massachusetts; she was an early graduate of Wellesley College, and went on to study Shakespeare and French drama at the Sorbonne (Paris). In 1889 she launched *Poet-Lore* – a quarterly 'devoted to Shakespeare, Browning, and the Comparative Study of Literature' – with her friend Helen A. Clarke; both women contributed a course of 'Shakespeare Studies' to the journal in which they questioned the 'masculine dictation' of the plays (see the entry on Elizabeth Wormeley Latimer, 1886, for more details). By the turn of the century Porter was engaged in editing the complete works of Robert Browning (Camberwell edition, 1898), Elizabeth Barrett Browning (Coxhoe edition, 1900), and Shakespeare (Pembroke edition, 1903, and First Folio edition, 1903–12) for both American and English publishers; she also contributed three volumes to an American 'Shakespeare Studies' series, *Macbeth* (1901), *The Tragedies* (1911), and *The Comedies* (1912). Porter was responsible for putting on the first American stage performances of Browning's *Return of the Druses* (Boston, 1902), and played an active role in literary societies: she was Vice President of the Boston Browning Society, Director of the Boston Authors' Club, President of the American Drama Society (Boston) and a member of the Poetry Society of America (New York City). She was also interested in the Intercollegiate Socialist Society, and was noted to support women's suffrage.

In 1883 Charlotte Porter became editor of *Shakespeariana* with the support of Horace Howard Furness, the eminent Philadelphia Shakespeare scholar. The journal was launched in 1883 and published in Philadelphia, and in 1886 claimed to be 'the only Shakespearian Magazine in the world' (anon., 'The Drama': 36). *Shakespeariana* catered for a specialist audience of Shakespeare scholars, critics and enthusiasts, and carried essays, book reviews, theatre reviews and listings, and notes on American Shakespeare societies. In 1887 Porter's plans for broadening the scope of the journal were rejected, and she resigned as editor.

Charlotte Porter, 'An Unprized Maid', *Shakespeariana*, 1 (1883–4): 12–14

Some of us play-goers who have been most sensitive to Salvini's masterly interpretation of *Lear* have paid a certain penalty for the pleasure ... the dignity and fondness of the royal father as Salvini acts it, draws our attention to much aside from the petulance and unreason which also characterizes Shakespeare's *Lear*, beside and in spite of this same admirable dignity and fondness. In consequence, *Cordelia's* part loses much of the consistency of its revolt against lip-service and all of its attractive loveliness.

Can it be, perhaps, that Salvini himself has not so thorough a liking for *Cordelia's* reserved and self-respecting character as he has for *Desdemona's* more yielding and less-upright nature? ... It is evident that the author of a recent magazine article [Emma Lazarus on 'Salvini's Lear' in *The Century Magazine*, 1883] has felt this and felt it strongly, even so far as to her confusion of the sober memory of Shakespeare. This author, in describing Salvini's characterization of *Lear* says: ... '[Lear] receives a rebuff, discourteous and irreverent enough to affront even a modern and non-royal father: "I love you according to my bond, neither more nor less, I am not yet married, but the first stranger who appears and claims me as his wife will obtain from me a greater meed of affection than you can possibly expect."'

Did Shakespeare's *Cordelia* indeed reply thus? Surely this strange paraphrase of her answer reminds us rudely of the few first words of 'the unprized, precious maid' [I.i.259].

Let us get this speech of *Cordelia's* at first hand again ... Shakespeare makes clear to us in just what temper of righteous indignation against her sisters' extravagant deceit and provoked disdain of submitting her own purer love to so sordid a test, *Cordelia* answers to the question, -

> ... 'What can you say to draw
> A third more opulent than your sisters?'
> 'Nothing, my Lord.'
>
> [I.i.85–7]

With obstinate uncompromising honor she persists in this reply. Then *Lear* makes another appeal to selfish interests to prove that disinterested love which he craved blindly, no doubt, but, certainly in his first undisciplined state, valued very inadequately.

'Nothing will come of nothing' – he reminds her, – 'speak again' [I.i.90] ... One could not blame *Cordelia*, now, if some inherited ready anger and arrogance should prompt her reply. We find, however, that hers is one of those rare purely-truthful natures whose yea is yea, and nay nay, who love measure and follow honesty at the expense of policy ...

> Haply when I shall wed
> That lord whose hand must take my plight shall carry
> Half my love with him, half my care and duty
> Sure I shall not marry like my sisters,
> To love my father all.
>
> [I.i.100–4]

We can see how this refreshing moderation and uncompromising honesty makes the exacting *Lear* furious, but we cannot see how it can justify the paraphrase of this speech quoted above ...

A character like *Cordelia's* is rare in Shakespeare, and rare enough in life. The more's the pity that when its main lines are finely and firmly indicated as in this wonderful play of King Lear, we should not get at once an inspiring glimpse of its spiritual beauty and understand the firm and vital fiber of its relation to the moral motive and momentum of the play ...

If it is assumed that in this first act we get no indication of what manner of woman this is, then we are authorized in condemning *Cordelia* and sympathizing thoroughly 'with the perfectly justifiable indignation of the aggrieved parent and monarch'; then Salvini is right in giving us so commanding a representation of royalty and fatherhood that we lose all sight of *Lear's* defects and the unreasonable and petty nature of his exactions, and witness with a just aversion the revolt of *Cordelia's* self-respecting integrity and self-honoring love ... [But] is it true? Is *Cordelia's* real character only revealed in the later portions of the play? Take the book, – Shakespeare, like *Cordelia*, means his words, – and see whether the dozen or two lines he gives *Cordelia* mean nothing in particular, or whether they do not mean to embody the expression of a quiet, womanly, true-hearted, self-respecting soul: one which promises to be not easily hoodwinked, to repay the truest loving, and to be depended upon if need be in the evil day that this first scene of the play forebodes.

Margaret Isabella Tucker, active 1883–1884

Very little is known of Margaret Isabella Tucker: she is not listed in contemporary or twentieth-century biographical dictionaries, and her only publications appear to be her two articles on Lady Anne and Constance for *Shakespeariana* (see the entry on Charlotte Porter (1883–4) for more on *Shakespeariana*).

Margaret Isabella Tucker, 'Shakespearian Characters. I. – Constance', *Shakespeariana*, 1 (1883–4): 229–30

Among all the heroines of Shakespeare, there is no figure that stands out before us more vividly, touched with more dramatic power, than that of Constance ...

She appears as a generous, high-spirited impulsive woman; a pure and loving wife; ardent and impetuous in feeling, often rash and inconsiderate in action: just the one to find her confidence betrayed, taken advantage of, by unscrupulous enemies, and to be maddened by the consciousness of her own utter helplessness ... Nor is she a mere scolding, frenzied woman. When brought face to face with her great injurer, Elinor, who bore her personal envy and hatred, she indeed meets scorn with scorn, defiance with defiance; but her anger is loftier far, as it is more unselfish in its motives and bears down the rancorous spite of her mother-in-law ...

Nowhere else has Shakespeare so depicted the maternal character with all its forceful springs of action: its deep tenderness, its loving pride, its self-abnegation, its tenacity of purpose, its measureless indignation, and its passionate despair ... We see her as the wounded lioness, caught in the toils, despairing of escape, yet battling to the death in defence of her off-spring. Her one object in life is her boy; bereft of him, she cares nothing for lands or crown or life ...

And yet, we find a want in her character, which seems to have been vehement rather than strong – highly sensitive, easily moved by external forces, whether friendly or hostile, but with a certain want of wariness and reserve, lacking self-reliance and resource, fortitude to 'underbear' [*King John*, III.i.64] her woes, and resignation to the will of Heaven ... Her religious faith too, though real ... was yet not a practical power in her life, and failed to teach her patience.

Margaret Isabella Tucker, 'Shakespearian Characters. II. – Lady Anne',
Shakespeariana, 1 (1883–4): 305–6

The character of Anne, as Shakespeare has drawn it, casts a slur upon
feminine nature which I am glad to believe the true historic Anne does
not deserve ...

A loving wife, a tender and duteous daughter, a kind and affectionate
aunt (we notice with pleasure her maternal love for the little Princes who
stood between her and greatness), she seems to have possessed a kindly,
sympathetic nature, easily moved to passionate sorrow, yet in which the
higher womanly virtues of constancy and self-respect were altogether
wanting. Apparently without motive ... she 'is grossly led captive by his
honey words' [IV.i.79]. We can hardly believe any woman could have
been so cozened. With what consummate art the tempter plays upon her
personal vanity! A few dissembling looks, a few flattering expressions of
admiration for her beauty and of love for herself, and she casts behind
her the memory of her angel husband and his saintly father, and with
God, her conscience, and *such* bars against her, accepts their murderer as
her plighted husband! We reflect the scorn with which, even in the moment
of conquest, her successful wooer seems to have regarded her. 'Was ever
woman in this humor wooed? was ever woman in this humor won? I'll
have her, but I will not keep her long' [I. ii. 227–9]. She richly deserved
the verdict pronounced upon Elizabeth after a similar scene of audacity
and weakness – 'relenting fool, and shallow, changing woman' [IV. iv.
431]. We only do not hate her as we realize her fearful punishment ...

But the Lady Anne of contemporary history does not appear to have
been such a libel on her sex. In accordance with the spirit of the times,
which paid court to the reigning house by depreciating its defeated rivals,
Shakespeare has cast more than just odium upon the hero of this drama.
The truth appears to have been that Richard was an unscrupulous villain,
but not more diabolical than other nobles of his age ...

In proportion as we rescue Richard from the stigma of those deeds of
darkness, as we restore him to human shape and comeliness, so Anne's
conduct finds excuse. Richard was her early lover and had been ardently
attached to her from youth ... Her violent death was one of those crimes
which were wrongfully imputed to him. She languished and died of grief
at the loss of her only son; and if Shakespeare was ever visited by ghosts,
he must sometimes have seen in his dreams the pale countenance of Anne,
reproaching him for having made her infamous to posterity and sacrificed
her womanly dignity to dramatic effect, which demanded a contrast to the
imperious, high-spirited Margaret, and the resolute, remorseless Richard.

Grace Latham, active 1883–1893

Little is known of Grace Latham; she perhaps worked in the theatre, contributing an essay on 'The Stage' to *Ladies at Work. Papers on Paid Employment for Ladies by Experts in the Several Branches* (London, 1893), a collection of essays reprinted from *The Monthly Packet* edited by Charlotte Yonge (on *The Monthly Packet* see the entry for Constance O'Brien, author of the journal's popular series 'Shakspere Talks With Uncritical People', 1879–91). Latham was a prolific contributor to the New Shakspere Society, and from 1883 to 1892 she read numerous papers which were reported or reprinted in full in the Society's *Transactions* and *Monthly Abstract of Proceedings*. In her Shakespeare criticism Latham refers to Anna Jameson, and takes issue with the thesis put forward by Mary Cowden Clarke (1850–2) and Helena Faucit (1885) that Ophelia 'was put out to nurse, and passed her childhood in a farmhouse' (1884: 404). She also attacks the effects of patriarchal repression upon women, arguing that 'from their subordinate position' women have been subject to a discipline of restraint that acts

> like iron chains, cramping and weakening, instead of strengthening; just as a scholar may be reduced to a mere machine, with all originality crushed out of him, by an education which is too deep or extensive for his mind to digest. It is among certain of Shakspeare's women that we must look for this aspect of discipline, not among his men; for the reason that it is much more rare to find a boy who has been crushed in this way (1891: 334).

Grace Latham, 'O Poor Ophelia!' (*Hamlet*, Act IV, Scene II. Acting Edition), *Transactions of the New Shakspere Society* (1880–5), Pt II, 401–30 (read at the 94th Meeting of the Society, Friday, 8 February 1884)

It has been suggested that Ophelia was put out to nurse, and passed her childhood in a farmhouse; but not only is there no line in *Hamlet* to warrant our adoption of such a theory, but the girl herself lacks the healthy practical tone of mind, the self-reliance in little things, which a rough open-air rearing would have given her. It is more probable that she grew up under Polonius's own eye, and that with the same want of perception of character which distinguishes him in his dealings with Hamlet, while he pushed forward his independent son, he kept his gentle, timid daughter under stern control at home. We must certainly remember that in Shakspere's day children were kept in far greater subjection to their parents than now; Lady Jane Grey suffered 'nips and bobs and pinches' at the hands of hers; and we find Portia, a woman of very different mould to poor Ophelia, strictly carrying out her father's will in the matter of the caskets. Still in Ophelia's silence in her father's presence, in her short unwilling answers to his questions, we may learn that his rule was one of no ordinary repression or severity ... As he set spies upon his son, he probably did so upon his daughter also, and he may have been alluding to them when he mentions those who 'Put on him' [II.i.19] the story of Hamlet's love in way of caution. Ophelia would thus grow up with the knowledge that she was not trusted, and the sense that she was being watched ... While such a rearing would have roused an energetic courageous girl to a more or less decided opposition, it would cause a nervous, timid one, like Ophelia, to become most reserved, to live as much as possible alone, and, while outwardly most obedient and submissive, carefully to conceal all the hopes and fears, thoughts and feelings, that made up her girl's life ...

Various commentators have found great fault with Ophelia for her conduct during the interview with Hamlet of which she tells her father, holding that as she certainly gives us the impression that there was something that he desired to say to her, she also must have known it, and should have encouraged and helped him to tell her his troubles. This does not follow, especially in so unperceptive a girl as Ophelia. But even if it were so, the sad thing is that she is not to blame, as Professor Dowden has said [Edward Dowden, *Shakspere: A Critical Study of His Mind and Art*, 1875: 138–9 and 151]. It would have been most unnatural that a girl, whose bringing-up had repressed all spontaneity of speech and action, whose moral courage, never very great, had been crushed out of her, should have done anything but fail at such a crisis, and it is probably to remind us of her upbringing that the scene opens with Polonius's interview with Reynaldo [II.i].

Then, again, Ophelia lacks the passion which might have lifted her for the moment beyond her fears; and we feel the want of it in all her scenes; throughout the play she is pure, sweet, and highbred, but somewhat cold. This scene, for instance [II.i], leaves us with the impression that her feeling for Hamlet was tender and pitiful; a very real affection, but not deep enough to give her the power of self-sacrifice, and without the strength and fire of passion. Thus, fully believing Hamlet to be out of his mind, she stands dumb with terror, and then runs away. The fault must be laid not on herself, but on her character and bringing-up. For in a weak woman who has been thoroughly cowed, a kind of paralysis of the will takes place, and her acts come not from her own volition, but from that of the stronger nature, under whose domination she lives; should its influence be for a moment withdrawn, she knows not what to do, and stands without resource, the sport of circumstances ...

Much has been written about these closing scenes [IV.v] as to whether Ophelia were in truth pure or no. That she sang such a song as 'To-morrow is St. Valentine's Day,' is easily accounted for; not only by the cautions of her family, of which, to her, poor soul, it is the echo, but also by the well-known sad fact that in madness, the very things are sung and said that would be farthest from the lips of the poor patients when in their sane senses. That she should ever have heard such a song, by the customs of Elizabeth's days, which permitted broad reference to subjects now studiously ignored among us. This and Hamlet's conversation in the play-scene is the only real evidence against her, and this is fully explained, if we remember, that he was then in the full belief that she was abetting his uncle in his schemes against him. The cautions of Laertes and Polonius are only such as, under the circumstances, would be given to any girl by rather coarse-minded men in a free-spoken age. All her own words and actions show us a pure, sweet woman with modesty of heart and mind, as well as of manner. We must also consider that it would be very unlike Shakspere's method of working to draw such a creature as Ophelia, fair, good, and gentle, and then at the last, just when she most needs the sympathy of the audience, to throw her from her high pedestal into the mud. True, he has depicted good and bad men and women, with a great and wonderful toleration; but sin itself he hates with the hate of a thoroughly healthy mind; and he does not lead us to love and sympathize with unhappy vice. Also, we must remember that in his time harmless lunatics were allowed to live with their friends, and wander freely through the towns and villages; so that an English audience of that date would understand a representation of madness far better than a modern one, and would not need explanations of points now dark to us.

After all, the poor child had a sufficiently large number of faults to link her with ordinary human beings. True, she possessed an unusually large number of those passive virtues, which are so noble, because for their full development they require perfect self-rule, and which form a necessary part of every beautiful female character. Thus she had obedience to lawful authority, as represented in her father; gentleness, patience, and purity; and if active courage is lacking in her, she has at least the essentially feminine virtue of quiet endurance. Still we cannot but feel in her a total lack of all those active virtues which are equally necessary to woman in the proper guidance of her life; but which in a truly strong character are never perceived till the moment comes for their use. With great endurance, she has no courage; with self-control, no presence of mind; she can give a tender, clinging affection, but not a great trusting love; and though she shows perfect filial obedience, she has no judgment to discern where her duty to her father ends, and that to her lover begins; and we must feel that hers was a one-sided, unbalanced character. Committing no deliberate sin, the evil she does and is the cause of all comes from the same want of balance.

But do not let us blame her, or if so, very gently; Perdita's rearing had taught her to stand alone, at least, to a certain extent; Miranda had the power to do so by nature as well as by education; Ophelia had it by neither; her life has been that of a slave, and she has the virtues and the vices of one.

Grace Latham, 'On Volumnia', New Shakspere Society, *Monthly Abstract of Proceedings* (February 1887), 69–90 (read at the 122nd Meeting of the Society, Friday, 11 February 1887)

He did it to please his mother – *Coriolanus*, Act I, sc. 1 [I. i. 38–9]

This the first mention of Volumnia immediately follows that of Coriolanus, as though to link the two characters indissolubly together, and when we examine the great tragedy we find them so closely connected that any study of the one must needs include the other. Volumnia's daily thoughts, her joys and sorrows, the whole work of her life are so centred in her only son, that she can hardly be said to have any existence independent of him, while if he has a separate life of his own, most of his faults, and many of his gifts, are either inherited from her, or have been developed under her training, so that his character may truly be said to be rooted in hers ...

Although the outlines of [Volumnia's] character are to be found in Plutarch, the touches and details which give it life remind us of great English ladies, such as Shakspere must have met by the time he wrote this play. It is hard to find examples of them in history. Unless forced into publicity by circumstances, the life of a woman is unknown beyond her own immediate circle, great as may be her influence in it, and Volumnia, who devoted her life to her one son, would not have been mentioned by history had his career been more prosperous. The civil wars brought to the front patriotic and high-souled women, like Lucy Hutchinson; but in Elizabeth's reign we can only find such as in one respect or another may be said to have resembled Volumnia ... In the Duchess Dowager of Somerset we meet with the pride of rank and station; in Bess of Hardwicke, the clever managing woman with great influence over her male kindred, while Elizabeth herself crowns the list as one of the truest patriots England has ever known. To this day Volumnias are not by any means uncommon in England, especially in periods of national struggle and danger, combining with great pride of place an intense devotion to their country, to which they will sacrifice not only their pride, but the family ties which are yet dearer to their women's hearts ...

In Virgilia Shakspere has provided Volumnia with a good dramatic contrast. She is one of those quiet, gentle, persistent women with whom we often meet, who seem all submission, but who in the long run mostly get their own way ... Virgilia has had some experience of her husband's moods, sees the harm they do him, and would crush them in her child. Volumnia, to whom its masterful ways are an earnest of future greatness, cannot endure to see them checked, and makes its mother's efforts useless. This is the way in which Shakspere works out Plutarch's hint as to the father's lack of education, apparently intending us to infer that, absorbed in training up her promising boy as a warrior, and fearing lest she should break his spirit by correcting his self-willed temper, Volumnia neglected, or forgot to teach him the virtues of self-discipline and self-control, necessary to all, but doubly so to a public man; and although this might not have greatly harmed a gentler, better-balanced nature, it was fatal to one so like her own, leaving him at the mercy of every chance circumstance which grated against his preconceived opinions, and of every enemy who had the wit to rouse his stormy temper. True, she gave him high ideals of honour and duty, but even these he holds with such distorted exaggeration, that they became in him the personal pride and self-will which compass his ruin, and almost that of Rome ...

By nature very like her son, Volumnia's position as woman, wife, and mother has forced self-control upon her; and this, combined with her fiery impulsiveness, is one of the secrets of her strength of character, and of the influence she exercises over him ... In treating of the character of a civilized woman in contradistinction to that of a man, this element of self-control must always be taken into account. It is forced upon us from our very earliest baby-hood, when we are told that tears are naughty. It pervades our whole life, to an extent which no one who has not gone through the training can quite realize. We are taught to restrain every look and act, voice, walk, gesture, the manner as well as the matter of our speech, our very thoughts are all made to come up to a certain standard. Thus the most trivial details of daily life become, to use a monastic term, part of a rule, which every woman, who in the least degree respects herself, will keep in some fashion or other. Observe, we are not now speaking of religion or morality, but of the mental discipline which every woman receives; we might call it conventional training, and it is so in part, but it goes far deeper than any mere conventionality. Its outward forms vary greatly, every period and country, every layer in the social strata having many peculiar to themselves; and it is carried to very different lengths in individuals, according to the character and circumstances of the teachers, and the capacity of the pupils for receiving it; but more or less of it we find, with hardly an exception, in every civilized woman we meet.

Sometimes, where carried to excess with a weak nature, it is most harmful, crushing all originality and independence of thought and action; such a woman will commit a great wrong rather than violate her rule, and as it serves her instead of a moral sense she will be quite unconscious she has done so. But where the severity of the training has been at all proportioned to the strength of the character, it is an infinite blessing, for it gives that habit of constantly considering the effect of every word and action, that self-restraint which is strength, and which often brings with it wisdom and happiness.

Ophelia is a specimen of a case in which this training has worked for evil, just as Volumnia is one in which it has resulted in good. She is disciplined enough to make practical use of all her gifts, though she has not attained perfect self-restraint. Indeed, had she done so she would have been far less dramatic, as it would have smoothed down and pared away those characteristic inequalities which give life to a *rôle*, and by means of which an actor or actress throws light and shade and interest into an author's conception.

Grace Latham, 'Julia, Silvia, Hero and Viola', New Shakspere Society, *Monthly Abstract of Proceedings* (February 1891), 319–50 (read at the 158th Meeting of the Society, Friday, 13 February 1891)

Hero

Discipline is one of Shakspere's favourite subjects, whether it be of life or of education; and we find it especially associated, particularly in certain phases, with his female characters, women being more often subject to it than men, from their subordinate position, far more marked in his day than it is in ours ...

In *Much Ado About Nothing* we find [Shakespeare] has recognized the fact, that to be perfectly successful, discipline must consist of a planting and fostering as well as a weeding out of qualities, and must be carried on with the active co-operation of the will of the subject on which it is exercised. If it be merely, or even chiefly, the work of an external force, more powerful than the nature of the pupil, it acts like iron chains, cramping and weakening, instead of strengthening; just as a scholar may be reduced to a mere machine, with all originality crushed out of him, by an education which is too deep or extensive for his mind to digest.

It is among certain of Shakspere's women that we must look for this aspect of discipline, not among his men; for the reason that it is much more rare to find a boy who has been crushed in this way, their frames and nervous systems being tougher, and their early life and education freer and less monotonous than their sister's [*sic*].

With Hero, in *Much Ado About Nothing*, discipline has been an exterior tyranny, not the lesson of self-government. Father and uncle have busily led their darling in the way in which she should go, forgetting that she must one day shape her course alone; and that to do this with safety, the weak points in her character should have been strengthened. The superior energy of Beatrice, joined to her sarcastic tongue, have thrust her dearly-loved cousin still farther into the background. Hero is too sweet-natured to resent this, and she never tries to gain her ends by unworthy means. Obedience and submission are duties to her, and have been instilled into her until they have become an instinctive habit. Gentle, modest, and unassuming, she plays her part in society, with a quietness which is only saved from insipidity by its grace and good-breeding. This short, brown, pretty creature is the ideal young lady of parents and teachers, and in truth she is as perfect as her education will allow her to be; kind, loving, humble without servility, and bearing grave wrong without personal re-sentment or desire for vengeance ...

But, alas! Hero has lost any small power of self-assertion, or of inde-pendent action that she may ever have had. She can only open her lips when there is no fear of contradiction; a slave does not tell her desires lest they should be thwarted.

Viola

Viola is the ideal woman that almost every great writer has attempted to pourtray [*sic*] under various names and in different circumstances; but only Shakspere has been able to perceive the qualities which compose it, the springs which move it, and to reproduce the exquisite charm of Viola's perfect womanhood, which affects us like a sweet harmony or a delicate perfume.

Dramatically it is a *tour de force*. Its leading characteristics are essentially undramatic, and yet it holds successfully the place of a heroine of comedy. It is full of pitfalls for reader and actress; for the former, whose temptation it is to give undue prominence to its poetic side; for the latter, who feels the necessity of lifting the part to a comedy level, and runs the risk of vulgarizing it in the attempt. To steer clear between these extremes, and indeed to understand the part at all, we must draw a hard-and-fast line between Viola the woman and Cesario the page, the real and the assumed character. The dramatic qualifications of the first belong to a heroine of sentiment and romance, and are its poetry, tenderness and passion; those of the second are the comic affectations and insolences of a spoilt and fashionable young gentleman; not the joyous youngster with his mouth full of witticisms of Rosalind, or the capable, budding professional of Portia, but the character that the Lady of Belmont sketched but never carried out ...

We next see Viola at Court in her page's dress. Unlike her predecessors, Portia and Rosalind, she has no pleasure in it; she is too modest, too intensely feminine to look on it as an escape from conventionality; the restraints which hedge round and guard a woman are dear to her; besides, she is, and feels herself to be, alone; she has no faithful Nerissa or loving Celia by her side. The dress seems to make her more instead of less womanly, and she wears it with gentle dignity and reserve. She can pretend to be insolent for a short space of time, but she has not sufficiently high spirits to flash out in brilliant repartee, or self-assertion enough to be imposing; still she has all the refinement of a high-bred woman, the tact and ease of manner belonging to those who live much in public, and she is as quietly at home here as among the sailors ...

Sent again to Olivia, Viola once more becomes the fantastic young gentleman; but this time she is cold, reserved, and humbly courteous, greatly to the chagrin of the lady, whose wooing she receives with a serious dignity, that takes the edge off a somewhat absurd situation. That she feel it so is evident, and she is indignant with the woman, who forgets herself so far as to press her love on one who does not want it; but it was no part of Shakspere's plan to make his heroines ridiculous, as it would have lowered them in the eyes of the audience, and the scene is presented to us more from the point of view of Olivia than Viola.

M. Leigh-Noel (later Mrs. M. L. Elliott), active 1884–1885

Little is known of M. Leigh-Noel aside from her two books on Shakespeare, *Lady Macbeth: A Study* (1884) and *Shakspeare's Garden of Girls* (1885), attributed simply to 'the author of *Lady Macbeth: A Study*'. She does not appear to have published any other books or periodical articles, and she is not included in contemporary or twentieth-century biographical dictionaries of nineteenth-century authors.

Lady Macbeth: A Study is an extended essay published in a small, handy octavo volume. It capitalised on contemporary interest in Lady Macbeth – a key figure for many women writers on Shakespeare in the nineteenth century, particularly following the powerful and popular performances of Adelaide Ristori and Ellen Terry in the role – by promoting her as a self-sacrificing wife with powerful maternal instincts. In 1884 Leigh-Noel gave a series of talks to the New Shakspere Society on Shakespeare's heroines, in which she pointed out 'the absence, with Shakspere's girls, of maternal relations' and attempted a typology of Shakespeare's female characters – constructing categories such as 'hardy blossoms' and 'hothouse flowers' (1884: 109). The talks were published the following year as *Shakspeare's Garden of Girls* (1885), although Leigh-Noel dropped 'any attempt at systematic classification' (1), focusing instead upon how 'the sisterhood of Shakspeare's heroines' are 'real flesh and blood, creatures we can believe in … Juliet, Imogen, Desdemona, Ophelia, Rosalind and the rest are women we know. They have their counterparts all around us. How [Shakespeare] attained to such familiarity with the feminine nature it is impossible to say' (iii). The volume was dedicated to Mary Anderson, 'America's Girl-flower, in warm recognition of the appreciation her nation has ever manifested for SHAKSPEARE'; an engraving of Mary Anderson as Juliet provides the frontispiece for the book, while on the title-page and in the preface Leigh-Noel quotes Charles Cowden Clarke: 'Shakspeare is the writer of all others whom the women of England should most take to their hearts; for I believe it to be mainly through his intellectual influence that their claims in the scale of society were acknowledged in England, when throughout what is denominated the civilised world, their position was

not greatly elevated above that of the drudges in modern low life'
(*Shakespeare's Characters*, 1863). The volume (sometimes catalogued
under the name of Mrs Elliott) consists of separate chapters on Juliet,
Imogen, Ophelia, Desdemona, Rosalind, Portia, Isabella, Mariana, Julia,
Beatrice, Hero, Viola, Cordelia, Helena, Miranda, Perdita, Jessica, Kath-
erine, Hermia and Helena, waiting women and country girls.

M. Leigh-Noel, *Lady Macbeth: A Study*. London: Wyman & Sons, 1884

Almost all commentators and exponents of Shakspeare have agreed in
their scathing denunciations of the character of Lady Macbeth, and seem
to have taken no trouble to discover any extenuating circumstances that
might modify the enormity of her crime or account for much of the odium
that attaches to her name. Strange that, in an age that has witnessed the
reversal of so many social verdicts upon historical and mythical persons,
no one has been found to champion the cause of one who, with all her
crimes, was a true woman; for I believe it requires only a little care and
patience to discover in Lady Macbeth many true womanly traits and even
endearing qualities. I imagine that the prevalent estimate of her character
is formed, not so much from Shakspeare's portraiture, as from the representation of it by Mrs. Siddons, – a representation that the great actress
herself acknowledged was conceived to suit her own physical gifts and
qualities, rather than the ideal of the poet ...
   We must remember that the age in which the action of the play takes
place is far removed from our scrupulous times; that human life was by
no means as sacred as it is now; and that violence was the common resort
of both mean and noble in their efforts to gain the desire of their souls, –
whether it was the throne of an empire or the purse of a traveller. In those
unruly times, Lady Macbeth seems to have been the solitary inmate of
her lord's castle, cheered only by occasional and fitful visits from her
husband ... She had been a mother, nor was she so far advanced in years
but that she might be again, and, of all pathetic yearnings those of a
childless mother are the most touching. To have had her nature thrilled
with the young life of her babe, and to live only on the remembrance of
the bittersweet joys of maternity, to wake up and miss the magnetic
pressure of infant fingers, to hunger in vain for the feeble cry, and the
touch of the tender lips on her breasts, can only be realised by those who
have passed through such suffering. And her sorrow was the keener in
that she must shut it up in her own bosom and give no utterance to her
anguished moan. If Lady Macbeth had passed through this solitude of
suffering, would not her heart-strings, so rudely torn, have clung the more
tenaciously to her husband? For him she would dream dreams and see

visions; for him she would keep watch in her lonely castle and follow the roar of battle afar off; all her thoughts, all her ambitions, that might have been shared between father and son, were henceforth exclusively devoted to her lord, and her love would become almost maternal in its character, till Macbeth came to lean upon her will and judgment with that unreasoning selfishness that even heroic men sometimes show in their home relations. Brave enough abroad, under the domestic roof their natures seem to yield themselves to helpless dependence on their wives, who, in all matters relating to home rule, are necessarily the stronger ...

It was a terrible price that she had to pay to gratify her husband's ambition. Macbeth had the stronger wishes, she had the stronger will; and, as it is will, not wishes, that prevails in the world, on her fell the heavier burden and the harder work. Had Macbeth been the man he so proudly proclaimed himself, he would have found some other way of achieving his desires than that which evoked such devilish genius in his wife ...

Macbeth did not ask her counsel now but he made her the recipient of all his lamentings, unheedful of her growing agony. He closed his eyes to the fact that her participation in his crime meant any remorse on her side. He suffered, and, manlike, he added the burden of his own futile regrets to the one under which her frail flesh was daily sinking.

Does it not speak for her unselfish womanliness that not a murmur escapes her; but, with infinite patience, she tries on all occasions to allay his fears, and to soothe the grief that, in her own case, is consuming her spirit? Not once does she hint at her own suffering; hence some have concluded she was callous.

Women there are who suffer in silence and alone. They have a dual existence: one of mental and spiritual unrest, and another of apparent calm, which is the only one palpable to their nearest and dearest. If it is their lot to be born with sensitive, delicately-strung nerves, with higher reflective and argumentative powers, they are not content to receive all their tenets of belief second-hand; and, when once embarked upon the field of independent speculation and abstruse theories, where will not a woman's mind wander? ...

Macbeth's love for his wife was now merged in his ambitions, hopes, and fears, amply proving the truth of the aphorism that a man's love is but an incident, – one might almost say an accident, – in his life, whilst a woman's love is her whole life and being. Lacking her husband's confidence, the salt and season of her life were gone ... Oh, for a child to have nestled to her iron heart – to have unbound the frozen milk of her congealed breasts! She could have sobbed out the bitter disappointment, remorse, and horror, had she but been touched with the talisman of infant fingers ... I can imagine her keeping in some locked cabinet – the sole mementos of her maternal joys, – some faded, tiny garment, a little toy, with locks of fluffy, golden hair. How it would contrast the stainless past with the blood-bedewed present! and one pities her as she hurriedly locks up her treasures, unable to bear the agony of the retrospection! Her throat would contract as the tears, scalding and resistless, would spring to her eyes, though she dashes them away lest they should leave their tokens on her face. Haunted with a perpetual fear of betraying herself, again and again she would pace her chamber, crushing her hands together with an unavailing regret for crime.

Shakspeare's Garden of Girls. By the author of 'Lady Macbeth: A Study'. London: Remington & Co., 1885

Juliet

Old Capulet had married a young wife, and Juliet is their only child. It seems to have been a joining of hands rather than hearts. It was doubtless the old man's money and position that was the attraction, for, though a mother at what to us seems an outrageously early age, Lady Capulet lacks the grace and tenderness so dearly associated with that name, and seems in spirit and speech to have more of the nature of the step-mother's [*sic*]. 'Too soon marred are those so early made,' [I.ii.13] most certainly applies to Lady Capulet. She evidently became a mother long before the deeper and truer qualities of womanhood had matured. Her physical development outran her moral growth, and under the chilling influences of great wealth and high rank, the warmer fluids of the soul had thickened and congealed.

It was an ill-assorted match, as extreme youth and gilded age must always be, and the result in the woman's case was apparently an idle, vain, cold, and calculating existence, in which, though still in the heyday of her life, she had acquired a most mercenary spirit, and accumulated a 'little hoard of maxims,' with which to 'preach down a daughter's heart.'

Juliet's father was what a father of his age can scarcely fail to be, incapable of sympathising with his child's feelings or entering into her young life. His dancing days are now a far-off memory, and the festivities he indulges in are attended as functions due to society and not as congenial pastimes. It is his delight to visit the larder, scold the servants, direct the household, and amuse himself with such domestic arrangements as Lady Capulet was too indolent or too superfine to trouble herself with ...

Everything in Capulet's home and style of life contributed to one effect – that of banishing his daughter from her father's society, and driving her to seek amusement and confidence in the company of her nurse. And of what character was she? ... Her garrulity, querulousness,

Drawn by E.C.Wood.   Engraved by F. Bacon.

FIGURE 9. Eleanora C. Wood, *Romeo and Juliet*: Juliet and the Nurse: possibly II.v or III.v (*c.* 1845). Wood (active 1832–56) was a London-based artist who exhibited classical and literary paintings, watercolours and drawings at the British Institution. This domestic and narrative style of illustration is typical of Victorian artists who were addressing a novel-reading public.

and complaints make her out quite an old woman, and it is as such she is generally represented on the stage. She holds a confidential position in the family of the Capulets, and like many old servants, presumes upon her length of service to indulge in familiarities that at any rate show how great an influence she must have had over Juliet's young life and character.

But she had caught the prevailing sin of the house – a mercenary spirit. For gold she is ready to aid a Montagu to wed her master's child ... Then again she is innately vulgar – as her class always have been – and she delights to spice her conversation with indelicate hints and allusions, though, let us hope, the licence she indulged in before Juliet was something new in her intercourse with her, justified perhaps, in her opinion, by the fact that now she was speaking to one who was considered of marriageable age and no longer a child ...

A stranger to her father and mother, her infancy nourished at this rude but kindly woman's breast, it is beyond wonder that Juliet should have escaped all taint of vulgarity, and appear the flower of refinement and gentle breeding that she does. In her character perfect integrity of heart is joined to extreme warmth of imagination, 'sweetness and dignity of manners to passionate intensity of feeling.' She unites the spotless purity of the lily and the voluptuous beauty of the rose ...

Juliet, according to the habits and spirit of that time and country, was at fourteen eligible for marriage. Repugnant as this may be to us, we cannot dispute the fact that under Southern skies the conditions of physical and moral development are vastly different to what they are in the cold North. To represent Juliet on our stage as of the age of Shakspeare makes her would be odious and absurd. It would be ridiculous to the British public to see a mere child in years so precocious in feeling and under-standing. But we are in Italy, and in a far-back period, when society was less conventional and artificial, although romance was let and hindered by the stronger influences of worldly considerations.

In studying the play, however, we soon cease to trouble ourselves by qualms as to Juliet's age. She may be anything from fourteen to four-and-twenty without impairing our conception of the truth and beauty of her character. In the short space of four days she lives a life of many years. She appears before us a child, she leaves us a woman ... the passionate nature of the South works an immediate and wonderful change, trans-forming the child's spirit into the woman's, and in a few hours maturing the whole emotional being. There is in the first view we have of her character a beautiful simplicity and *naïveté* that betoken an utter want of contact with the world, and a charming innocence of the arts of coquetry and conquest, that are only too precociously apparent in many English school-girls of the present enlightened age. But when the sun of love has arisen upon her, and its burning rays touched the bud of passion in her soul, in a moment its closed petals open, and with a blaze of colour, display the glowing heart of the flower that rejoices in its beams, and responds with kindred fervour.

Portia

It is very remarkable how again and again Shakspeare brings into prominence the relations between a father and an only daughter. We have it in Romeo and Juliet, the Tempest, As You Like It, Hamlet; and in the Merchant of Venice, it appears in the two instances of Portia and her lost father, and Shylock and Jessica. But how different is the tie between Portia's father and herself, and Jessica and her father. In the latter case there is an utter want of mutual love, confidence, and loyalty, whilst in the former there is the most steadfast observance of respect to the will of one no longer present to enforce its fulfillment.

Portia's independence of character was in no small degree owing to the position in which, by her mother's death, she found herself placed. She had been from an early age the head of a large household. Upon her shoulders had devolved the care and responsibilities of a great establishment. As a girl she was placed in authority, having servants under her to whom she could say 'go' or 'come' at her pleasure, and who hesitated not to obey. And to these habits of command were added an ease of manner and grace of self-possession acquired by long intercourse with the refined and noble associates of her father's wealthy leisure ...

Morocco's greeting ['Mislike me not for my complexion ...', II.i.1–12] is dignified and gracious ... It was impossible to return any but a kind answer to so earnest and manly a pleading. Portia had no liking for the 'shadow'd livery of the burnish'd sun' [II.i.2]. She much preferred the companionship of one whose skin more nearly approached her own in colour and complexion, but she carefully disguised the repugnance she felt, until the trial was over.

As he persists in hazarding his fortune, she procrastinates. We can imagine the flood of emotion that would beset her. Had she not just been talking of Bassanio, the hero of her girlish dreams, when the arrival of the Moor was announced? ... And now in his place stood the swarthy African, goodly, no doubt, in his proportions as a man, and very probably to the sun kissed virgins of his own land, 'the glass of fashion, and the mould of form' [*Hamlet*, III.i.153]; but there was a great difference between the young Venetian noble and this sable warrior. The contrast between them would rudely shock the sensibilities of the imaginative girl ...

Women, it has been said, love not the man as he is, but the man as they would have him be. They deck him with graces he does not possess, and adorn him with virtues he makes no claim to ... And thus they create an ideal of their own, and fall down and worship the image that they in their fondness have set up.

It was Bassanio's chief merit that he was beloved by a woman like Portia and a man like Antonio. But wise women rarely vindicate their wisdom by their loves. Love is a rock upon which many a reputation for prudence has been wrecked ere now. A woman after giving the most precious part of herself, her heart, scarcely realises that mercenary motives can have any place in her lover's suit. Portia's romance was girlish in those dear old days when prudence was over-stepped by passion. She saw but little of Bassanio's real character and naively overlooked the fact that her fortune was world renowned, and that the young Venetian noble could not fail to have heard how rich a prize the mistress of Belmont would be ... to my mind Bassanio is a type of very many of our day; men to be met with everywhere in good society who attract to themselves the regard of pure women and good men without possessing any positive recommendations, no great principles of action. Bassanio was young, good-looking, and had been rich. His riches he had squandered, not perhaps in riotous living, but in the gratification of expensive tastes, and the generous entertainment of his companions. He had been forced to trespass on the good nature and more carefully husbanded resources of his friends, and now 'having lost one shaft,' he wished to shoot another of the self-same flight, and the self-same way. She was an heiress and a lovely, loveable woman, and he believed himself, or all the world was wrong, the very man to adorn her palace as its lord, and to control her estates as their owner ... And yet we can well believe that in the presence of Portia all meaner motives would die, and that Bassanio would lose sight of everything but her wondrous self. He could not fail to be enthralled by the captivating glamour of the sunny-locked blonde ...

And then what a revelation is made! We have been taught to regard Portia as Shakspeare's type of a strong-minded woman, and very rightly so; but how different his idea is from the popular one current at the present day. Portia is no hard-featured, loud talking, forbidding-looking being in semi-masculine or dowdy attire, but one endowed with all a Juliet's passion, and radiant with a consuming fire. She is indeed polished and sagacious, gifted and well-balanced, distinguished for intellectual excellence and superior common-sense, but she is none the less subject to the overmastering power of the affections ...

In this way Portia has been called the most wonderful of all Shakspeare's feminine creations, for in her he has made clear that the possession of the highest intellectual endowments is compatible in a woman with the age and susceptibilities for tender and romantic love ... But whilst Portia is sincere and thorough in her subjection to the man her heart has chosen as its lord, she assumes the place of partner and not that of servant. There is a dignity in her mien that bespeaks the independence of her nature. When her heart has recovered from the wild throbs of rapture that greeted Bassanio's choice, it beats again with the grave and sweet pulsation that is as natural to it, as a spirit of inference and a capacity for calm logical deduction, united to a playful flow of wit, is natural to her intellect ...

It has been said by an American writer that in Portia, Shakspeare anticipated the intellect of women who can wield gracefully the tools of men, not sacrificing a trait of their essential womanliness. To most the idea of an intellectual woman is associated with the absence of everything that is tender, or, at any rate, romantic. But it is not so with Portia ... Portia is a judge upon the bench, an advocate at the bar, a preacher in the pulpit, a wit in company, a student when alone, a philosopher in thought, a poet in expression, and, above all, a tender and romantic girl growing up into the truest of women and sweetest of wives.

Katherine

In that old home in Padua grew up two girls, Katherine and Bianca. They had everything that wealth could give in the way of comfort and luxury, and Heaven had bestowed upon both more than an average share of beauty, grace, and wit. But whilst Fortune had so richly favoured them in these respects, in another it had been very cruel, for it had taken from them the tender care and gentle overshadowing influence of that richest of all home blessings, a mother's love, that is like the rich tones of an organ which by its music blends together the voices of a congregation, so that what is crude and harsh is lost or hidden to the ear, and harmonises the discordant elements that in greater or less force are found in every family. Deprived of this mellowing influence, the two girls ran into extremes. Katherine, with her restless energy and buoyant spirit, became a termagant; Bianca, with her gentle disposition and intellectual bias, settled down into a bookworm ...

Kate's terror lay in her tongue, where woman's natural weapon of defence is to be found. A man may glory in his brawny arms and the iron bands of his biceps, but a woman's delicate fingers and soft white arms may only coax and caress. With the members a man fights with all she can [do is] merely work and embrace. What then is she to do? ... She could not wear a sword nor assume the doublet and hose. Under provocation she must either scold or sulk, and the lesser evil of the two was to scold.

Her tongue was the only member allowed full liberty. She was rich and was not expected to work, and her spirit was brimming over with energy that could find little or no outlet. She was like the boiler of a steam engine that must have a safety valve or it will explode and scatter wreck and ruin around it. To have closed Kate's mouth would have been like

sitting on a safely valve. What the consequences would have been we dare
not say, for in those days she could not have stumped the country in
favour of woman's suffrage, nor practised in the law courts against Doctor
Bellario, the learned cousin of the Lady of Belmont.

Baptista's home was too monotonous for her energetic spirit. There
was no one for a companion but Bianca, and she was continually poring
over her books, without even 'a word to throw at a dog' [*As You Like It*,
I.iii.3]. How different it might have been if she had had brothers, or if
she had been born in the shires of merry England, where she could have
followed the hounds and matched her temper and spirit against some
refractory steed in her father's stables ...

It is not fair to put all the blame on Kate. It is not always vice that
makes the mare gib. It is as often the stupidity of the groom as the fault
of the horse, and I am therefore inclined to make every excuse for Katherine's vagaries. She was no mere scold. It was not railing for railing she
exchanged, but wit for wit and everything she uttered betokened wonderful intelligence. Flashes of keen wit darted from her tongue, like
lightning from the summer cloud, and in those days, when the only thing
a woman could aspire to was to be married, she had a genuine grievance.
Bianca, the younger, a bookworm, who perhaps could neither cook a
potato, or its equivalent in that age, nor make a petticoat, nor 'say Boh!
to a goose,' was to have a husband, whilst she, who could turn her hands
to anything and manage a household well, husband to boot, was to linger
on the cold shelf of unwilling maidenhood ...

In fact, it is my opinion that in time Katherine would prove to have
tamed Petruchio rather [than] he to have subdued her. We know not how
their married life turned out, but we should think it was a very happy
one, and that Katherine, after all, proved the ruling spirit of the household, having learnt the secret of making her lord imagine that he was
the master, whilst she really directed everything he did. We cannot, however, do better than commit to memory and convert to practice her
concluding words upon the conjugal duty of a true wife [Leigh-Noel
quotes Kate's closing speech, 'A woman moved is like a fountain troubled',
V.ii.141ff.].

Country girls: Audrey, Phoebe, Jaquenetta, Mopsa and Dorcas

There remains to be treated a group of country girls whose charm and
beauty lie in their very homeliness. They are the dog daisies and dandelions
of the Girl Garden, whom it does not do to scan too narrowly for their
aesthetic qualities, however richly they may reward the scrutiny of the
scientist. Shakspeare has not endowed these creatures of his brain with
the ready wit and trenchant tongue that distinguish his rustic clowns. In
the higher ranks of life, on the contrary, it is the women who outvie the

men in these respects, as witness Beatrice and Benedick, Rosalind and
Orlando, Helena and Bertram, Portia and Bassanio ...

But Phoebe and Audrey, Jaquenetta and Mopsa are true to nature in
their bluff honesty and scatty intelligence. They are mental photographs
of the Warwickshire girls of the sixteenth century, when schoolboards
were undreamed of, and skill at the milking pail was the test of merit,
rather than the ordeal of the Inspector's examination ... No one that has
lived in an English farmhouse, away from the influences of large towns
and demoralising railroads, can fail to number amongst his acquaintances
the characters here enumerated. There is Phoebe the flirt, Audrey the
hoyden, Jaquenetta the sprightly, and Mopsa the greedy.

There is little room for romance in any of their bosoms, although
Phoebe is a trifle sentimental. We have met her often. She deems herself
a degree above her fellow villagers on the strength of being able to read
and having once or twice been to town, so she scorns the honest love of
one of her neighbours ... Audrey professes no sentiment and feels none.
Marriage is to her the ultimate goal that every woman has to arrive at. She
does not care to scheme for it. It will come in time. She does not much
desire it except to be like the rest of her sex, but in that respect, to be 'a
woman of the world,' and no longer a mere girl, she gladly welcomes it.
She lays no claim to beauty and she is independent enough to own it ...

Jaquenetta is very different to Audrey. She cannot read, but that is no
blemish in a pretty rustic lass. Indeed it saves her much idle dreaming and
nonsensical and false ideas of life. A little learning is a dangerous thing,
and the style of literature that finds its way into cottage homes is pernicious
and misleading to a degree ... She is a pretty figure in the woodland
landscape, but I fear she came to no good. Between Armado's flatteries
and the clown's importunities she was only too likely to lose her head
and forget her modesty.

Mopsa, in the 'Winter's Tale,' is without either the attractiveness of
Jaquenetta's face or the rough honesty of Audrey, but she is the true
representative of a large class of her sisters, both town and country bred.
She thinks only of herself, and like the daughter of the horseleech, is
continually crying, 'Give, give.' A lover, to her, is merely someone she
can bleed, an instrument to gratify her petty vanity, who as long as he
has money and means is to be cast aside like an old glove.

Helena Faucit, Lady Martin, 1817–1898

Though little remembered today, Helena Faucit was one of the leading English actresses of the mid nineteenth century. She made her London debut in 1836 and was acclaimed for her performances in contemporary drama (playing opposite Macready in Bulwer-Lytton's *The Lady of Lyons* and starring in Robert Browning's plays), and for her portrayal of Shakespeare's heroines – particularly Juliet, Portia, Cordelia and Desdemona: Dinah Maria Craik, the popular nineteenth-century novelist and writer on women, claimed Faucit was 'the best impersonator of Shakespeare's women whom the last generation has ever seen' ('Merely Players', 1886: 417). In 1851 Faucit married the writer Theodore Martin, becoming Lady Martin in 1880 when her husband was knighted; in later life she acted almost entirely for charity, and became a personal friend of Queen Victoria, to whom she dedicated *On Some of Shakespeare's Female Characters: By One Who Has Personated Them* (Edinburgh, 1885).

The volume was originally written in the form of personal 'letters' to her friends: the first to appear, on Ophelia, was written for the novelist Geraldine Jewsbury on her deathbed, who 'had often pressed me to put into writing the substance of what I had said when we talked together of Shakespeare's heroines' (*On Some of Shakespeare's Female Characters*: viii). In 1880 Faucit's letter on Ophelia was printed by *Blackwood's* for private circulation: as Theodore Martin explained in a handwritten note accompanying a presentation copy of *Ophelia*, the letters were 'never meant for publication. But they seemed to me so good that I have had a few copies printed for our immediate friends' (presentation copy of *Ophelia* at the Shakespeare Centre, Stratford-upon-Avon). Letters on Beatrice, Desdemona, Imogen, Juliet, Portia and Rosalind followed; a year later they were serialised in *Blackwood's Edinburgh Magazine* (see the entry for Moira O'Neill (1891) on this periodical), and in 1885 they were collected in a single volume, with chapters on Ophelia, Portia and Desdemona (letters to Geraldine Jewsbury), Juliet (two letters to Mrs S. C. Hall), Imogen (an extended letter to Miss Anna Swanwick), Rosalind (letter to Robert Browning), and Beatrice (letter to John Ruskin).

Faucit explains that Shakespeare figured prominently in her own girl-hood – as an ill child she spent days reading Shakespeare, living 'again and again through the whole childhood and lives of many of Shakespeare's heroines' (1885: 6). 'They became living realities for me', she explains, 'and in impersonating them I learned much, which would not otherwise have been learned, as to the master poet's conception and purpose' (ix). Dinah Maria Craik described the volume as 'essentially a woman's book':

> in a very simple and feminine way, autobiographical without being ego-tistic, she lets us into the secrets of [her] impersonation ... If, in truth, she takes too feminine a view of her poet, if in the minuteness of her criticism she attributes to Shakespeare's women certain nineteenth century qualities which Shakespeare never thought of, and embellishes them with preceding and subsequent episodes wholly imaginary, such as Ophelia's motherless childhood, and Portia's consolatory visit to the dying Shylock, we forgive her, since she has made a contribution to Shakespearian litera-ture quite original of its kind, and which could be done thus by no other person. (1886: 417)

The book was received with acclaim both in England and America: in 1887 the journal *Shakespeariana* (published in Philadelphia) welcomed the swift reprint of 'Lady Martin's excellent and suggestive volume of essays' ('Literary Notes', 1887: 87), while Horace Howard Furness, the Philadelphia-based Shakespeare scholar and editor of the *Variorum Shakespeare* (which collated commentaries by male critics and editors of Shakespeare's works), marked out Faucit's book for particular praise. In 1897 in a letter to his sister Furness writes:

> You speak, dear, of having read Mrs. Jameson. Isn't it delightful, but a far finer book is Lady Martin's *Some of Shakespeare's Female Characters*. Mrs. Jameson looks at the characters as a highly intelligent sympathetic nature would look at them. Lady Martin is the character itself, and interprets to you its every emotion ... In my opinion Lady M's book is the finest that has ever been written on Shakespeare, and outweighs tons of commentaries. (*The Letters of Horace Howard Furness*: I.338–9)

Four editions of Faucit's book appeared within six years of its first publication.

Helena Faucit, Lady Martin, *On Some of Shakespeare's Female Characters: By One Who Has Personated Them*. Edinburgh: Blackwood and Sons, 1885

Ophelia

BRYNTYSILIO, *August* 10, 1880

... My views of Shakespeare's women have been wont to take their shape in the living portraiture of the stage, and not in words. I have, in imagination, lived their lives from the very beginning to the end; and Ophelia, as I have pictured her, is so unlike what I hear and read about her, and have seen represented on the stage, that I can scarcely hope to make any one think of her as I do. It hurts me to hear her spoken of, as she often is, as a weak creature, wanting in truthfulness, in purpose, in force of character, and only interesting, when she loses the little wits she had ...

I look on Ophelia as one of the strongest proofs our great master has left us of his belief in the actor's art (his own), and of his trust in the power possessed, at least by sympathetic natures, of filling up his outlines, and giving full and vivid life to the creatures of his brain. Without this belief, could he have written as he did, when boys and beardless youths were the only representatives of his women on the stage? Yes, he must have looked beyond 'the ignorant present,' and known that a time would come when women, true and worthy, should find it a glory to throw the best part of their natures into these ideal types which he has left to testify to his faith in womanhood, and to make them living realities for thousands to whom they would else have been unknown. Think of a boy as Juliet! as 'heavenly Rosalind!' as 'divine Imogen!' or the gracious lady of Belmont, 'richly left,' ... as the bright Beatrice, and so on, through all the wondrous gallery! How could any youth, however gifted and specially trained, even faintly suggest these fair and noble women to an audience? Woman's words coming from a man's lips, a man's heart – it is monstrous to think of! One quite pities Shakespeare, who had to put up with seeing his brightest creations thus marred, misrepresented, spoiled.

The baby Ophelia was left, as I fancy, to the kindly but thoroughly unsympathetic tending of country-folk, who knew little of 'inland nurture.' Think of her, sweet, fond, sensitive, tender-hearted, the offspring of a delicate dead mother, cared for only by roughly-mannered and uncultured natures! One can see the lonely child, lonely from choice, with no playmates of her kind, wandering by the streams, plucking flowers, making wreaths and coronals, learning the names of all the wild flowers in glade and dingle, having many favourites, listening with eager ears when amused or lulled to sleep at night by the country songs, whose words (in true country fashion, not too refined) come back again vividly to her memory, with the fitting melodies, only, as such things strangely but surely do, when her wits have flown. Thus it is that, when she has been 'blasted with ecstasy,' [III.i.160] all the country customs return to her mind: the manner of burying the dead, the strewing the grave with flowers, 'at his head, a grass green turf; at his heels, a stone,' [IV.v.31–2] – with all the other country ceremonies. I think it important to keep in view this part of her supposed life, because it puts to flight all the coarse suggestions which unimaginative critics have sometimes made, to explain how Ophelia came to utter snatches of such ballads as never ought to issue from a young and cultured woman's lips ...

Only 'when they shall meet at compt' [*Othello*, V.ii.273] will even Hamlet know the grief he has brought upon, the wrong he has done to, this deep and guileless spirit. So far as we see, he has indeed blotted her from his mind as a 'trivial fond record' [I.v.99]. He is so self-centred, so wrapped up in his own suffering, that he has no thought to waste on the delicate girl whom he had wooed with such a 'fire of love,' and had taught to listen to his most honeyed vows. He casts her from him like a worthless weed, without a word of explanation or a quiver of remorse. Let us hope that when he sees her grave, his conscience stings him; but beyond ranting louder than Laertes about what he would do for her sake – and she *dead*! – there is not much sign of his love being worthy, at any time, of the sweet life lost for it ... Now, whatever his own troubles, perplexities, heart-breaks, might be, it is hard to find an apology for such usage of one whose heart he could not but know that he had won. He is even tenderer, more considerate, to his mother, whom he thinks so wanton and so guilty, than to this young girl, whom he has 'importuned with love,' and 'given countenance to his speech with almost all the holy vows of heaven.'

I cannot, therefore, think that Hamlet comes out well in his relations with Ophelia ...

Yours always affectionately,
HELENA FAUCIT MARTIN.

To Miss GERALDINE E. JEWSBURY

Portia

BRYNTYSILIO, NEAR LLANGOLLEN,
September 1, 1880.

'In Belmont is a lady richly left.'

It is such a pleasure to me, dear friend, to do anything to beguile your thoughts from the pain and weariness of your sick-bed, that I will try at once to carry out your wish, and put on paper some of the ideas which have guided me in representing Portia. Your letter tells me that she is 'one of your great heroines,' and that you desire to hear about her most of all.

I am very glad to know you hold her to be a 'real, typical, great lady and woman.' ... I have always looked upon her as a perfect piece of Nature's handiwork. Her character combines all the graces of the richest womanhood with the strength of purpose, the wise helpfulness, and sustained power of the noblest manhood. Indeed, in this instance, Shakespeare shows us that it is the woman's keener wit and insight which see into and overcome the difficulty which has perplexed the wisest heads in Venice. For, without a doubt, as it seems to me at least, it is to her cultivated and bright intelligence, and not alone to the learned Bellario, her cousin, that Bassanio is indebted for the release of his friend Antonio ...

Grave and anxious must have been her thoughts as she crossed the lagoons by 'the common ferry that trades to Venice' [III.iv.53–4]. Hers was not a mind, however, to shrink before difficulty; and, confirmed as she has been by the opinion of the great doctor of laws, she feels sure of success, if she can but be true to herself, and 'forget she is a woman' [*Cymbeline*, III.iv.154] ... Nothing but her deep love, and grateful happy heart, could sustain her through such a trial. To cease to be a woman for the time is not so hard, perhaps, to one who has all her life been accustomed to a position of command and importance; but, in the peculiar circumstances of this case, the effort must have been one of extreme difficulty.

How skilfully, firmly, and gently she begins her task! We may believe that she had some sympathy with Shylock ... She feels for the race that has been proscribed, insulted, execrated, from generation to generation. She finds some excuse for the deep hereditary hate which the Jew has for his Christian oppressor, and for his desire of vengeance in the name and for the sake of his persecuted tribe. She would have understood his yearning for the death of the man who had 'disgraced and hindered him of half a million' [III.i.54–5]; but not that he himself should desire to be the cruel executioner ...

Portia, as a last resource, tries to bring before [Shylock's] mind's eye the horror of the deed – the gash, the quivering flesh, which is to be 'cut off nearest the merchant's heart' [IV.i.232–3] ... and bids him at least have by a surgeon to stop the wounds, 'lest he do bleed to death' [IV.i.258]. No, not even that. 'Tis not in the bond.' He will not do even 'thus much for charity' [IV.i.261]. Now all is clear.

At this point, I have always felt in the acting that my desire to find extenuations for Shylock's race and for himself leaves me, and my heart grows almost as stony as his own. I see his fiendish nature fully revealed. I have seen the knife sharpened to cut quickly through the flesh; the scales brought forward to weigh it; have watched the cruel, eager eyes, all strained and yearning to see the gushing blood welling from the side 'nearest the heart,' and gloating over the fancied agonies and death-pangs of his bitter foe. This man-monster, this pitiless savage nature, is beyond the pale of

humanity: it must be made powerless to hurt. I have felt that with him
the wrongs of his race are really as nothing compared with his own
remorseless hate. He is no longer the wronged and suffering man; and I
longed to pour down on his head the 'justice' he has clamoured for, and
will exact without pity ...

But I could never leave my characters when the curtain fell and the
audience departed. As I had lived with them through their early lives, so
I also lived into their future ... I do not believe that such a woman as I
conceive [Portia] to have been would leave the despised, deserted Jew to
his fate. When she finds that even Antonio's 'mercy' is not of the kind
to satisfy her woman's heart, she vows to herself that, out of her own
great happiness, and in abounding gratitude for it, she will devote herself
to the all but impossible task of converting this 'inexorable Jew.' She goes
alone to his wretched, lonely home, to which he has been accompanied
only by the execrations of the mob. These still ring in his sick ears as he
lies there stunned, bewildered, defeated, deserted. But sharper, more harrowing than all, are his self-upbraidings that he should have left a loophole
in the bond by which the hated Christian merchant has escaped. In his
rage, in his bitter self-accusations, he lashes himself into a state of frenzy.
If left alone much longer to these wild, mad moods, he might destroy
himself. But, before he has time for this, comes to his door, and will not
be denied, this noble lady. He knows her not, roughly enough forbids
her entrance; but with gentle force, and with the charm of her winning
manners and noble and gracious presence, she contrives to gain an entrance. It is little she can do in her first visits. Still she repeats them,
bringing wine and oil and nourishment for the sick body, and sacred
ointment for the bruised mind. The reviled, despised Jew finds himself
for the first time (for, oh, so long!) tended, thought for, cared for. Why
should this be? Never has this been since his early days, – since his beloved
Leah left him, perhaps in his early manhood, when the grief at her loss
hardened his heart. Her gentle presence by his side through life might
have softened down his worst passions, which were only aggravated by
the blow sustained in her loss ... The Jew would find in Portia a likeness
to his beautiful Leah; would, in his weakness, fancy the tender sympathetic
eyes, looking so gently on him, were hers ...

Then on the Jew's side would come a looking forward to [Portia's
visits]; then a hoping, wishing for them, until gradually she had drawn
from him from time to time the story of his life, of his woes, of his own
wrongs, of the wrongs of his race, of his sweet lost wife; of his ungrateful
daughter, who in her flight took not only his ducats, his jewels, but the
ring given him by Leah, 'when he was a bachelor' [III.i.121]. We can
imagine what a sympathising ear was lent to all his tale; how she gave
him 'a world of sighs' [*Othello*, I.iii.146] – this man who had through life

chiefly met with curses, and execrations ... he would begin to feel that, had he gained his cruel will, and his 'deeds been on his head' [IV.i.206] – had he been let to *use* that hungry knife, – there would have been 'the smell o' the blood' [*Macbeth*, V.i.50] under his nostrils day and night; and that same blood would have been upon his soul for ever. Not even the rites of his fathers could have washed it away!

These are his *own* reflections; not forced upon him by Portia. He will recognise her life of self-denial. He will know that with every luxury, every happiness around her, she leaves them all continually to sit with, and comfort, and console his sick body and broken spirit. How can he show that he is grateful? He will do as she wishes; will see the daughter on whom he has poured his curse; will put his blessing in the place of it; will even look upon her Christian husband.

But I have imagined both daughter and husband much altered, purified. Lorenzo, on reflection, has been ashamed, not perhaps of stealing the Jew's daughter, but of accepting the stolen ducats and jewels which she brought with her, and would be longing, if he dared, to make restitution and confess his meanness. Jessica, under the roof of Portia, and within the sphere of her noble influence, could not fail to grow better and purer ... she will reflect upon the graceless step she took in leaving her old, lonely father, whatever might have been his faults, and in robbing him, too. How can she look for happiness in her wedded life, she who has commenced it so unworthily? Oh that she could make reparation! ... And so some day, permission being obtained by Portia, she may be seen at the feet of the old man, there sobbing out her grief and her contrition; and he will remember that he made her 'home a hell,' [II.iii.2] and look gently upon her. Will this be for him the first taste of the blessedness of mercy? 'It blesseth him that gives and him that takes' [IV.i.187].

I think that the Jew will not live long. His body and mind have been too sorely bruised and shaken. But Portia's spell will be upon him to the end. His last looks will be upon the eyes which have opened his, and shown him the 'light to lighten his darkness'; and he who was despised, reviled, and himself at war with all men, will now have felt the happiness of bestowing forgiveness, and the blessed hope of being himself forgiven ...

Ever affectionately yours,
HELENA F. MARTIN.

To Miss GERALDINE E. JEWSBURY

(One or two of my friends, who have seen this letter when printed only for private circulation, and on whose opinion I place a high value, have objected to my 'dream' about Portia's conduct toward Shylock, after the curtain drops, as being conceived too much in the feeling of the present

century. I have, therefore, reconsidered the matter, but cannot give up
my first impression.)

Desdemona

BRYNTYSILIO, NEAR LLANGOLLEN, NORTH WALES,
September 10, 1880.

... In the gallery of heroes and heroines which my young imagination
had fitted up for my daily and nightly reveries, Desdemona filled a
prominent place. How could it be otherwise? A being so bright, so pure,
so unselfish, generous, courageous – so devoted in her love, so unconquerable in her allegiance to her 'kind lord,' even while dying by his hand ...
Of course I did not know in those days that Desdemona is usually
considered a merely amiable, simple, yielding creature, and is also generally
so represented on the stage. This is the last idea that would have entered
my head ...

As in the case of Ophelia and Portia, so also in [Desdemona's]; her
mother had obviously been long dead before Shakespeare takes up the
story ... Like Portia, Desdemona was a noble Venetian lady, but there
was a whole world of difference between their homes and their bringing
up. No proud indulgent father watched the training of Desdemona's
youth, and studied the progress of her heart and mind. Absorbed in state
affairs, he seems to have been at no pains to read his daughter's nature,
to engage her affections or her confidence. Thus, a creature, loving, generous, imaginative, was thrown back upon herself, and left to dream over
characters more noble, and lives more checkered with adventure, than any
she could see or hear of in her father's luxurious home. Making so small
a part of her father's life, and missing the love, or the display of it, which
would have been so precious to her, she finds her happiness in dreams of
worth more exalted than any she has seen, but which she has heard and
read of in the poets and romancers of her own and other times ...

The rapt attention – the eager, tender eyes, often suffused with tears –
when Othello spoke of 'being taken by the insolent foe, and sold to
slavery' [I.iii.137–8] – the parted lips and shortened breath, – if these were
noted by Brabantio, it would seem he held them as of no more moment
than if they had been called forth by some skilled *improvisatore*. The idea
that his daughter's being could be moved, her heart touched, by this
stranger to her race and country ... whose complexion was like 'the
shadowed livery of the burnished sun' [*Merchant of Venice*, II.i.2] had
never crossed his mind. He would as soon have thought of her being
attracted by her torch-bearer or her gondolier, as by one whom he classes
with 'bond slaves and pagans' [*Othello*, I.ii.99].

This wide difference of feeling could not have existed, had there been
any living sympathy between the father and his child. He would have

foreseen the danger of exposing a girl dawning into womanhood, and of sensibilities so deep, to such an unusual fascination, and she would have turned to him when she found herself in danger of being overmastered by a feeling, the indulgence in which might wreck his peace or her own. But the father, who is only the 'lord of duty,' [I.iii.184] has established no claim upon her heart; and that heart, hitherto untouched, is stolen from her during these long interviews, insensibly but for ever.

We are not to think that all this happens suddenly. The father is not surprised into losing his child. If he has been deceived, it is by himself and not by her ...

Ever affectionately yours,
HELENA FAUCIT MARTIN.

To Miss GERALDINE E. JEWSBURY

Imogen

October 1882.

MY DEAR ANNA SWANWICK, –

You wonder, I daresay, at my long delay in yielding to your urgent request that I should write of Imogen – your chief favourite, as you tell me, among all Shakespeare's women. You would not wonder, could I make you feel how, by long brooding over her character, and by living through all her emotions and trials on the stage till she seemed to become 'my very life of life,' I find it next to impossible to put her so far away from me that I can look at her as a being to be scanned, and measured, and written about ... Imogen has always occupied the largest place in my heart ... Can you wonder, then, that I approach my 'woman of women' with fear and trembling? ...

What a picture Imogen presents as we see her next [III. vi] – alone, among the wild hills, in a strange dress, in a strange world – wandering along unknown paths, still far away from Milford-Haven! Oh, that name, Milford-Haven! ... When I read of the great harbour and docks which are now there, I cannot help wishing that one little corner could be found to christen as 'Imogen's Haven.' Never did heroine or woman better deserve to have her name thus consecrated and remembered ... She complains but little. The tender nursling of the Court learns, by the roughest lessons, what goes on in that outer world of which she has seen nothing. 'I see,' she says, 'a man's life is a tedious one' [III.vi.1]. Still, with the patient nobility of her nature, her 'resolution helps her' [III.6.4]. She has set herself a task, and she will carry it through. In her heart, despite what she has said to Pisanio, there is still a corner in which he 'that was the riches of it' continues to hold a place [III.iv.70–1] – for her love is of the

FIGURE 10. Mary Ellen Edwards, *Cymbeline*, I.i.121: 'For my sake wear this' (c. 1890). Edwards (1839–1908) was a prolific painter, engraver and book illustrator who exhibited successfully at the Royal Academy from 1862 onwards, sometimes under her married names: Mrs John Freer (1866–9) and Mrs John Staples (1872–86).

kind that alters not 'where it alteration finds' [Sonnet 116]; and she had learned thoroughly love's first and greatest lesson – fidelity.

It was this scene, and those at the cave which immediately follow, that, as I have said, laid the strongest hold on my young imagination … How delightful a relief after the overwhelming pathos of the previous scene is the accident which brings these noble spirits into contact with a being, like Imogen, in whom all that makes a woman most winning to unspoiled manly natures is unconsciously felt through the boyish disguise! And she – how well prepared she is to take comfort in the gentle, loving thoughtfulness shown to her by these 'kind creatures'! [IV.ii.32] …

How long Imogen remains their guest we are not told – some days it must have been, else all the things they speak of could not have happened. For the first time, their cave is felt to be a home. On their return from their day's sport, a fresh smell of newly strewn rushes, we may think, pervades it. Where the light best finds its way into the cavern are seen such dainty wild-flowers as she has found in her solitary rambles. Fresh water from the brook is there. The vegetables are washed, and cut into quaint shapes to garnish the dishes; a savoury odour of herbs comes from the stewing broth, and a smile, sweet beyond all other sweetness in their eyes, salutes them as they hurry in, each vying with the other who first shall catch it. When the meal is ready, they wait upon Fidele, trying with the daintiest morsels to tempt her small appetite; and, when it is over, and she is couched upon their warmest skins, they lay themselves at her feet, while she sings to them, or tells them tales of 'high emprise and chivalry,' as becomes a king's daughter. Even the old Belarius feels the subtle charm, and wonders, yet not grudgingly, to see how this stranger takes a place in the hearts of his two boys even before himself …

You know how, in my letter on Portia, I said that I never left my characters when the scene closed in upon them, but always dreamed them over in my mind until the end. So it was with Imogen. Her sufferings are over. The 'father cruel,' made so by the 'step-dame false,' [I.vi.1] has returned to his old love and pride in her, – the love made doubly tender by remembrance of all that he has caused her to suffer. The husband – ah, what can measure his penitence, his self-abasement! That *he* had dared to doubt her purity, her honour, – he who had known her inmost thoughts almost from childhood!

But Imogen – can she think of him as before? Yes! She is truly named the 'divine Imogen' [II.i.57]; at least, she has so much of the divine 'quality of mercy' in her, that she can blot from her memory all his doubts, all his want of faith, as if they had never been. Her love is infinite – 'beyond beyond' [III.ii.56]. Hers is not a nature to do things by halves. She has forgotten as well as forgiven. But can Posthumus forgive himself? No! I believe, never. The more angel she proves herself in her loving self-forgetfulness, the blacker his temporary delusion will look in his own eyes. Imogen may surmise at times the thorn which pricks his conscience so sharply. Then she will quietly double the tender ways in which she delights to show her love and pride in him. But no spoken words will tell of this heart-secret between them ...

Happiness hides for a time injuries which are past healing. The blow which was inflicted by the first sentence in that cruel letter went to the heart with a too fatal force. Then followed, on this crushing blow, the wandering, hopeless days and nights, without shelter, without food even up to the point of famine. Was this delicately nurtured creature one to go through her terrible ordeal unscathed? We see that when food and shelter came, they came too late. The heart-sickness is upon her: 'I am sick still – heart-sick' [IV.ii.37]. Upon this follows the fearful sight of, as she supposes, her husband's headless body. Well may she say that she is 'nothing; or if not, nothing to be were better' [IV.ii.367–8]. When happiness, even such as she had never known before, comes to her, it comes, like the food and shelter, too late.

Tremblingly, gradually, and oh, how reluctantly! the hearts to whom that life is so precious will see the sweet smile which greets them grow fainter, will hear the loved voice grow feebler! The wise physician Cornelius will tax his utmost skill, but he will find the hurt is too deep for mortal leech-craft. The 'piece of tender air' [V.iv.140 and V.v.437] very gently, but very surely, will fade out like an exhalation of the dawn. Her loved ones will watch it with straining eyes, until it

> Melts from
> The smallness of a gnat to air; and then
> Will turn their eyes and weep.
>
> [I.iii.20–3]

And when, as the years go by, their grief grows calm, that lovely soul will be to them

> Like a star
> Beaconing from the abodes where the Immortals are
> [cf. Shelley, *Adonais*]

inspiring to worthy lives, and sustaining them with the hope that where she is, they may, in God's good time, become fit to be. Something of this the 'divine Imogen' is to us also. Is it not so?

This was my vision of Imogen when I acted her; this is my vision of her still. –

Ever, my dear friend, affectionately yours,
HELENA FAUCIT MARTIN.
BRYNTYSILIO, LLANGOLLEN, NORTH WALES, *Oct.* 1882.

Elizabeth Wormeley Latimer (née Wormeley), 1822–1904

Born in London to an Admiral and daughter of a Boston East-India merchant, Elizabeth Wormeley Latimer enjoyed a cosmopolitan childhood, growing up in England, Paris, Boston and Virginia. While in Boston in 1842 she met George Ticknor, William H. Prescott and Julia Ward Howe, who encouraged her to write; in 1848, when the Wormeley family settled in New England, Elizabeth published several novels: best remembered today is *Our Cousin Veronica: or, Scenes and Adventures over the Blue Ridge* (1856), in which the female narrator looks forward to the emancipation of slaves. In 1856 Elizabeth Wormeley married and moved to Maryland, where she spent twenty years bringing up her children and, during the Civil War, caring for wounded soldiers. After 1880 she published prolifically: novels, periodical articles, translations from French and Italian (including *The Love letters of Victor Hugo, 1820–1822*, 1901), and popular histories of Europe, Africa and the Middle East, such as *Europe in Africa in the Nineteenth Century* (1895).

Familiar Talks on Shakspeare's Comedies (Boston, 1886) originated as 'Parlor Lectures' given in Baltimore (Maryland) 'to a large and appreciative class of ladies' (v). Women's study clubs had a long pedigree in America – as early as 1635 the colonist Anne Hutchinson opened her Boston home twice a week to women friends to debate theology – but it was not until the late nineteenth century that women's clubs proliferated throughout the United States. In 1890 the establishment of the General Federation of Women's Clubs provided club-women with wider links to the woman suffrage movement, while at a local level the club offered women an opportunity for self-education and mutual support. As one member of Sorosis, a pioneering New York City women's club, explained, 'instead of censure, women who seek to be and do something in the world now find within the club encouragement and generous sympathy' (Martin, 1987: 131).

In the 1880s and 1890s women's literary clubs flourished, many of which were devoted to reading Shakespeare – such as the Stratford Club of Concord (New Hampshire), the Mary Arden Shakespeare Club (New York City), and the Sisters' Shakespeare Society (New Jersey). The programmes of study clubs were varied but often included a reading of a Shakespeare play by club members, individual research, question and answer sessions, general discussion and lectures. In 1887, for instance, the Stratford Club of Concord consisted of as many ladies 'as one parlor will comfortably accommodate when all want good light on their books'. Each member took turns to hold the 'arduous and responsible' office of Critic, who cast the play for reading aloud and prepared a short critical and historical sketch of the play; at the end of each scene questions were asked and notes read. 'We make no pretensions to profound learning', remarked club member Frances Abbott, 'nor frown because some in-quiring member disturbs the dramatic effect by asking for information' (1887: 327–30). The informal and supportive ethos of such clubs allowed women to develop their critical self-confidence – as Adelaide Wood, President of the Friends in Council Shakespeare Class of Topeka (Kan-sas), explained. After studying Anna B. McMahan's course on 'the mysteries of Hamlet's complex nature' and 'the nature of his regard for Ophelia, and the *sweetness and lightness* of that fair maid ... we were allowed the privilege of walking in company with grown-up critics, dramatic and literary, who themselves seldom escaped minor criticism from us, our senses having been sharpened under such a healthful regime' (1887: 326).

With the growth of women's colleges of higher education in the late nineteenth century, more clubs were established to cater for women as 'grown-up critics'. The Shakespeare Society of Wellesley College, for instance, was founded in 1877 exclusively for 'upper undergraduate stu-dents of the college, or specialists who take rank equal to theirs'. It adopted a thematic approach to Shakespeare study with lectures, recita-tions, group discussion, and careful comparison of folio and quarto readings, and was 'constantly in communication' with the New Shakspere Society based at University College, London, 'with whom it has inter-changed valuable papers' (including those by Grace Latham published in the *Monthly Abstracts* and *Transactions of the New Shakspere Society*). In 1886–7 Society members at Wellesley followed a two-year programme studying women in Shakespeare, jointly analysing topics such as 'Women as Daughters' and contributing individual readings towards a series on 'Shakespeare's Women' (Maryette Goodwin, 1887: 73–4). By the 1890s women began to publish courses and questions for study clubs, often in periodicals: Anna Randall-Diehl, for instance, included a 'Study Depart-ment' in *The American Shakespeare Magazine* (the journal of the Fortnightly Shakespeare Club of New York City run largely by women; see the entry for Jessie F. O'Donnell (1897) for more details). Charlotte Porter's and Helen A. Clarke's course of 'Shakespeare Studies' in *Poet-*

Lore (which they jointly edited) included 'topics' for study that inter-
rogate patriarchal values in Shakespeare's play: on *A Midsummer Night's
Dream*, for instance, they ask 'did the service of Diana offer women a
respite from masculine dictation?', and 'why is the choice of Hermia's
father for her no longer supported by the Duke? Does this imply a
criticism on the inconsistency of allowing men their choice, and their
brides none, with which Shakespeare was in sympathy, or is this only
apparent to some modern minds?'. (1904: 100–3). Several women's papers
given at study clubs were later published: in this anthology we have
included further examples from the Countess of Charlemont (1876),
Grace Latham (active 1888–93), M. Leigh-Noel (1884), Kate Richmond-
West (1890), Julia Wedgwood (1890), and Mrs Lauch Macluarin (1897).

Elizabeth Wormeley Latimer's *Familiar Talks on Shakspeare's Comedies* sought to provide a basic introduction to Shakespeare's plays for
the non-specialist. In preparing for the volume Latimer consulted women
writers included in this anthology: 'Mrs. Jameson's most excellent "Characteristics of Women;" Lady Martin's recent letters on some of
Shakspeare's female characters; and a series of papers, still incomplete,
in the English 'Monthly Packet' (edited by Miss Yonge), called 'Shakespeare talks with Uncritical People,' by Constance O'Brian [*sic*]' (v).
Latimer remarks (vi) upon the lack of general studies readily available
to the non-specialist reader:

> a great deal of fugitive Shakspearian Criticism – of the kind I wanted –
> can be found in magazines, inaccessible for the most part to the general
> reader. To all these I acknowledge the greatest obligations, in trying to
> do for each play as a whole what Mrs. Jameson and Lady Martin have
> done for its heroine. To the erudite who write for University men, I leave
> all points of what is called Shakspearian criticism. I have attempted nothing
> but to bring out obvious points of dramatic interest, and to enable those
> whom I addressed to get a clear view of the story and the characters.

Familiar Talks on Shakspeare's Comedies contains 'Parlor Lectures' on
The Winter's Tale, *The Tempest*, *A Midsummer Night's Dream*, *The
Taming of the Shrew*, *Much Ado About Nothing*, *As You Like It*, *Twelfth
Night; or, What you Will*, *The Merchant of Venice*, and *Cymbeline*; the
volume was reprinted in Boston in 1897.

Elizabeth Wormeley Latimer, *Familiar Talks on Some of Shakspeare's Comedies*. Boston: Roberts Brothers, 1886

The Winter's Tale

Hermione, in glad spirits, well pleased with her own success and at the evident admiration of the two men, goes on to be more charming and more gracious to Polixenes than it is wise to have been, – all the time thinking that she is gratifying her husband. She even gives her hand to Polixenes; seeing which, the very fiend of jealousy enters into Leontes, and he breaks out into a speech vulgar, abusive, coarse, such as only a man with a tainted mind, I think, would have thought of.

I conceive of Leontes as *le mari difficile*. It seems to me that Hermione is under the constant fear of offending him; that he is a man whose behavior is guided not by principles but moods, – the hardest of all men to deal with, because a wife never knows 'where to find' such a husband. When Hermione has succeeded, as she thinks, in pleasing him, a weight is lifted off her heart; she has stepped into sunshine, – the last and only gleam of sunshine in the rest of her sad life; for it is a 'Winter's Tale' so far as Hermione is concerned. All pretty graces and sweet coquetries peep out, and she is charming with Polixenes to her own destruction.

Then Leontes, baser and baser, 'beset with doubts and fears, and entangled more and more' in the labyrinth of thorns he has created for himself, turns to his boy. He wishes to make sure, he says, that he is like him – his father. The likeness is too unmistakable for jealousy itself to deny. The whole address to the child – to whom happily its insinuations must have been incomprehensible – is disgusting ...

Some people have wondered why Hermione, who is still alive, should have excluded herself all these years from her husband. Surely, patient Grizzel or Enid might have felt all wifely allegiance to Leontes dissolved by his behavior. Hermione was a queen and mother, as well as a wife. As queen, she had borne degradation; as mother, one child had died through the tyranny of her husband, the other had been cast away. To have condoned all this would have been to lower the character of Hermione. She cannot properly forgive Leontes till one child is restored to her. Remember that if Desdemona – if Imogen – could forgive, they could, through all their wrongs, respect their husbands. The murder of no children lay at Othello's or Posthumus' doors. Hermione as a wife has been repeatedly and publicly insulted. He to whom she gave herself has stooped to baseness and cruelty inconceivable. She knows the inmost nature of the man. Even if she could bring herself to return to him as his wife, it is doubtful whether she could possibly make him happy. She had failed in the pride of her youth, her beauty, her unsmirched purity; since he has dissolved the bands that bound her to him, she accepts her release, – and in my opinion justly. As to repentance – she has known him repent a hundred times. Nothing, it seems to me, need constrain her again to take on his yoke, but the welfare of her child.

A Midsummer Night's Dream

[I.ii] is one of Shakspeare's most inimitable comic scenes and on it the whole play turns. Shakspeare's vulgar folk have none of the exaggeration of those of Dickens; they are like Hardy's or George Eliot's, – comic because they are simply themselves. Shakspeare was no lover of mobs, nor of 'mechanicals,' – he was not imbued with our modern spirit of democracy; but the English vulgar now, and still more in Shakspeare's time, were not like the great body of the American working classes, with whom stupidity is not the danger, but such a keen sense of class interests as will make them easy to be led by demagogues or bosses, while all the time they flatter themselves *they* rule. It is a crude intelligence, combined with self-will and a little knowledge (just enough to mislead the judgment), that is the danger with our working-classes. In Shakspeare's day (and with the ordinary English mob) the danger lay in brutishness, and a sort of impassive stupidity ...

There is a double satire in these scenes with the play-acting mechanics. First, they are satirized as a class, and secondly, there is a satire on the goings-on in a dramatic company.

Observe how Bottom – Bully Bottom – takes everything that he can out of Quince's hands ... His forthputting is exactly what might be expected from a man of his station, accustomed to be looked up to by his fellows. 'Humility,' said old Bishop Griswold of Massachusetts [Alexander Viets Griswold, Bishop of Eastern Diocese, Rhode Island, 1810–48], 'is a virtue I have seen occasionally among the rich, but have never observed among the poor.' ...

Demetrius is as little like a gentleman in his conduct to the poor girl [Helena] as he can well be. He is harsh, rude, cruel. She repels us by the want of self-respect she shows, and her lack of modesty. With this want of modesty, even Demetrius reproaches her, – a lesson out of Shakspeare to any girl whom any young man, rightly or wrongly supposes to be 'running after him.' And yet Helena can theorize well enough upon this subject. Perhaps her own sad experience had taught her that 'we should be wooed, and were not made to woo' [II.i.242] ... Somebody has said that to spare a lover the pleasure of pursuit is to defraud him of one of his masculine privileges; for men were meant for hunters ...

It gives me a bewildering conception of Shakspeare's mighty power of creation when I think that the same hand that made Portia, Imogen, Perdita, and Miranda, fashioned these two commonplace excitable girls [Helena and Hermia]. Yet, ill as they behave, neither quite loses our sympathy, and un-ladylike as much of their conduct is, we do not lose all sense of their being ladies. Very little comment, so far as I know, has been bestowed on Hermia and Helena. To me the skill that wove their flimsiness seems wonderful. Many writers seem to look on Helena as the most wronged, and the most worthy; in which estimate of their characters I cannot myself agree. Helena from the first was mean, cowardly, treacherous, and lacking in modesty. In the end, Hermia, aggravated and excited, turns upon her, and when both have lost their tempers and their dignity there is little to choose between them.

The Taming of the Shrew

It seems to me this introduction [the induction] is as much as to say to the audience, the reader, or posterity, that the play it introduces does not 'hold the mirror up to nature;' it is a farce ...

Old Baptista is a miserable old selfish father; no wonder he bred Katharine to scorn him, and Bianca to deceive him. He is talking to the gentlemen, who are both suitors for Bianca, and, – without a thought for Bianca's happiness or Katharine's honor, but solely because he wants to get rid of a troublesome daughter, – he refuses them Bianca, and throws Katharine at their heads. In spite of her high spirit, the girl, who can scarcely believe her own ears, turns quietly to her father, and asks, can he really mean what he says? The two men, in spite of her father's presence, – that father in whom Katharine finds no protector, – openly scoff at her, and at her reputation. She turns upon them, coarsely and rudely, it is true, but with an instinct of self-defence. A woman left to fight her own battles, with even those of her own household against her, can hardly fail to be rough and rude.

Common opinion, we see, admires the stage heroine Bianca; Lucentio at first falls in love with her; and yet half a dozen Biancas are not worth that shrewish Katharine ... Poor Katharine! brought up amongst such a set as those who surround her, – Baptista, 'the affable and courteous gentleman' as Hortensio calls him, who is in reality, caculating, selfish, unfatherly, and indelicate; the sly Bianca; the fortune-hunting suitors, – universally unpopular, and mistrusted, – no wonder she is a grown-up spoilt child, and she thoroughly acts up to her reputation. She – so far more highly endowed intellectually and in heart than these artificial, selfish, commonplace people – is yet conscious of having won their scorn by her want of self-control; and they are rather pleased to find themselves on some points her superiors, and are ready enough to thrust the conviction home upon her ...

I think [Petruchio] is beginning to feel sorry for Kate, surrounded as she is by a set of fools. 'I know,' he says, 'she is an irksome, brawling scold; if that be all, masters, I hear no harm' [I.ii.188]. And indeed,

Petruchio is right; there are worse faults by far than a quick temper. Then, too, he is pleased to think there is a task before him, – and he feels equal to it. Imagination has a great deal to do with a man's love, and Petruchio is beginning to think fair Kate 'a foeman worthy of his steel.' [Sir Walter Scott, *The Lady of the Lake*, V.10] ...

Grumio is the kind of old servant we have all seen in the Uncle Remus days on southern plantations, – an inveterate grumbler, but absolutely identified with his master and all his master's interests, except when those interests interfere with Grumio's own notions of what is due to himself. [Uncle Remus, a fictional character, was a slave who became a trusted family servant, entertaining children with verses and traditional tales from African-American culture; see Joel Chandler Harris, *Uncle Remus: His Songs and His Sayings*, 1881.] Kate, being his master's wife, is now a part of his master, and as such is entitled to all reasonable consideration. Grumio never complains of *her*, and doubtless all his life Katharine was faithful to him, and he loyal to his mistress. Nevertheless, it is she who will have to put up with his sulks and his tantrums, not he with hers.

Adelaide Ristori, 1821–1906

Born in Friuli (Italy) into a theatrical family, Adelaide Ristori was an internationally acclaimed actress, particularly for her performance in tragedy. At the age of fifteen she joined the Compagnia Reala Sarda, becoming its leading actress within a few years; in the 1840s she was the leading lady of Domeniconi's company, playing opposite the renowned Shakespearean actor Tommaso Salvini (whose performance as King Lear was reviewed by Emma Lazarus and Charlotte Porter, 1883–4). After her marriage to an Italian nobleman in 1847 Ristori retired from the stage for several years, but in 1855–6 she made a successful come-back in Paris with a repertoire of tragic roles that included Schiller's Maria Stuart, Alfieri's Mirra, Legouve's Medea, and Lady Macbeth.

Ristori appeared for the first time in London in 1857, winning acclaim for her powerful performance of Lady Macbeth in the sleep-walking scene, which she acted in Italian. 'Ignorant of English,' reported Kate Field, 'with no knowledge of *Macbeth* but what she has obtained from an inferior translation [by Giulio Carcano], Ristori has made the part of Lady Macbeth her own. It is the interpretation of Shakespeare's soul' (Field, 1867: 54). 'So fully did I enter into the spirit of the part,' Ristori recalls in her *Studies and Memoirs*, 'that during the whole of the act my pupils remained immovable in their sockets, until the tears came into my eyes. And it is from this forced immobility that I date the commencement of my weakened eye-sight' (1887: 57). In the following decade Ristori performed the sleep-walking scene in Italian throughout Britain and Europe (Mary Cowden Clarke went to see her on two occasions; *My Long Life*: 151); Ristori first performed the scene in English in 1873, and in 1884–5 she acted the whole part in English, playing opposite Edwin Booth's Macbeth in the last of four successful American tours.

Ristori's notes on 'Lady Macbeth' form a chapter of her autobiography, *Studies and Memoirs*, which was reissued over seven times by 1907, and published in London, New York, Turin and Paris.

Adelaide Ristori, *Studies and Memoirs.* London: W. H. Allen, 1888

Lady Macbeth

The study of this character presented the greatest difficulties to me. For I saw in Lady Macbeth, not merely a woman actuated by low passions and vulgar instincts, but rather a gigantic conception of perfidy, dissimulation, and hypocrisy, combined by the master hand of Shakespeare into a form of such magnitude that it might well dismay any actress of great dramatic power.

Long and close examination led me to conclude that Lady Macbeth was animated less by affection for her husband than by excessive ambition to share the throne which seemed within his reach. She was well aware of his mental inferiority to herself, of his innate weakness of character and indolence of disposition, that was not to be stimulated into action, even by the thirst for power which was consuming him, and she therefore made use of him as a means for attaining her own ends, and took advantage of the unbounded influence her strong masculine nature and extraordinary personal fascination enabled her to exercise over him, to instill [*sic*] into his mind the first idea of crime in the most natural way, and with the most persuasive arguments ...

It would have seemed easier to credit Lady Macbeth with some feelings of personal tenderness for her husband, had it not been that she was to share the power and dignity with him; but this being so, I maintain that it was not merely ambition and love for her consort which led her to instigate him to evil, but also her desire to mount the throne. It is Lady Macbeth all through who lures on her hesitating husband to commit the deed from which his more cowardly nature shrinks. It is she who tauntingly reminds him of his oath, who reproaches him with pusillanimity; and when he still hesitates, it is she who declares she would drag her infant from her breast, and dash its brains out, sooner than break her plighted word. It is difficult to credit a woman of this kind with any of the feelings of ordinary humanity ...

The terrible soliloquy in this scene ['Come, you spirits / That tend on mortal thoughts, unsex me here', I.v.40–54] ... reveals all the perfidy and cruelty of this woman, who was neither more nor less than a monster in human shape, and shows with what supernatural powers she arms herself in order to succeed in leading her husband to become the instrument of her ambition. In one word, she is henceforth Macbeth's evil genius. With him it is still a question of 'I will,' or 'I will not.' This woman, this serpent, masters him, holds him fast in her coils, and no human power will come to rescue him from them. In consequence I uttered the first words of this monologue in a hollow voice, with bloodthirsty eyes, and with the accent of a spirit speaking from out of some abyss, and, as I continued, my voice

FIGURE 11. Pamela Coleman Smith, *Macbeth*, I.vi: Lady Macbeth greets Duncan (watercolour, 1898). The quotation below, 'The service and the loyalty I owe, In doing it pays itself', is actually Macbeth speaking in I.iv.22–3. Smith (c. 1877– c. 1950) was an American watercolourist and book illustrator who also did stage and costume design. She was working in New York in the 1890s but subsequently lived in England and Jamaica. The original watercolour is very vividly coloured.

grew louder and more resonant, until it changed into an exaggerated cry of joy at the sight of my husband ...

Lady Macbeth has only one short scene in the fifth act, but it is one of Shakespeare's most magnificent conceptions, and tries the powers of an actress to the uttermost. This woman, this colossus of physical and moral force, who, by a word, had the power of conceiving and bringing into execution plots hatched with such infernal power that only an assembly of demons could have succeeded with them – behold her! reduced to the ghost of her former self by the effects of that remorse which gnawed like a vulture at her heart, her reason disturbed until she became so unconscious of herself as to reveal their tremendous secret in her sleep. *Sleep*, did I say? It is rather a fever which mounts to her brain, which makes her drowsy, and only the physical suffering overmastering her spirit with the record of the evil of which it is the cause, controls and regulates her movements, and turns all her ideas astray ...

It cost me long and most anxious study to represent this artificial and duplex manifestation, melting the effects one into the other without falling into exaggeration at every change of manner, voice, or expression of my face. I came upon the scene looking like an automaton, and dragging my feet after me as though they were weighted with lead; mechanically I placed my lamp upon the table, taking care that all my movements should be slow and deliberate, and thus indicate the numbness of my nerve power. My eyes were wide open, but fixed and glassy. They looked, and yet they saw nothing. I breathed hard and with difficulty. My whole appearance, in fact, showed a state of extreme nervous agitation produced by the disorganization of my brain. I endeavoured by these distinct and visible effects to make the change in Lady Macbeth patent to all eyes, and to show that she was suffering from a mental rather than a physical malady, which had a terrible yet all-sufficient cause ...

> Here's the smell of the blood still; all the perfumes of Arabia will not sweeten this little hand. Oh! Oh! Oh! [V.i.50–1]

These exclamations were wrung from me as though a grasp of iron were laid upon my heart which would hardly allow me utterance, and I remained with my head thrown back, breathing with difficulty, as if overcome by a profound lethargy.

During the short dialogue between the lady-in-waiting and the doctor, I feigned that I was transported in my delirium to the scene of the murder of Duncan, and, as though the cause of my change of expression might be the sight of the King's apartment, I advanced cautiously, with my body bent forward towards the right-hand side of the stage, where, as I imagined, the assassination had taken place. I fancied I heard the hasty steps of my husband, and I stood in an attitude of expectation, and with straining eyes, apparently waiting his arrival to assure me that the dreadful deed was accomplished.

Throughout this scene I was careful not to forget that I was a woman speaking in her disturbed sleep; therefore, between each sentence I uttered, I drew my breath in long, half-stifled gasps, and when I came to the words –

> To bed, to bed! there's knocking at the gate. Come, come, come! Give me your hand. What's done cannot be undone. To bed, to bed, to bed! [V.i.66–8]

I changed to a more coaxing and persuasive tone of voice, as though I would obtain ready compliance. Then, terrified by the knocking I fancied I heard at the castle gate, and fearful of a surprise, I showed a violent emotion, a sudden dismay. I imagined it was necessary to conceal ourselves promptly in our apartment, and turned towards it, inviting Macbeth to accompany me, speaking the last two words 'Come, come!' in imperative and furious tones; after which, feigning to seize his hand, I showed that I would place him in safety in spite of himself, and, urging him on with great difficulty, I disappeared from the view of the audience saying in a choking voice:-

To bed, to bed, to bed! [V.i.68]

Here I end my analysis of a character which is one of the most remarkable that has ever been conceived by a human mind, and the study of which is rendered all the more difficult by the singular situations in which the imagination of the poet places Lady Macbeth.

But, as I am assured in my own mind that I have done the best that in me lay, to enter into the true character of this strange personage, I confide this analysis of my interpretation of it to the judgment of the critics, who, it seems to me, should at least appreciate the labour and study I have brought to bear upon it.

Fredericka Raymond Beardsley Gilchrist (née Beardsley), 1846–1950

Described as a 'literary critic' in the 1905 edition of *The Woman's Who's Who of America*, Fredericka Beardsley Gilchrist was born and educated in Oswego, New York State, and settled in New Jersey. An episcopalian, she was involved in philanthropic and civic activities, and belonged to several societies, including the Daughters of Founders and Patriots, and the Woman's Branch of the New Jersey Historical Society. In 1865 she married Robert Gilchrist, later attorney-general of New Jersey (whose interpretation of the Fifteenth Amendment secured the right of suffrage to men of colour in New Jersey). Fredericka Gilchrist apparently published only one volume of literary criticism, *The True Story of Hamlet and Ophelia* (1889), in which she argues that the key to understanding *Hamlet* lies in Hamlet's relationship with women – above all, his well-founded fear that Ophelia will prove as 'pliant under temptation' as his mother (19), revealed by the line Gilchrist reads as 'And shall I couple? Hell!' [I.v.93]. Interpreting the play as primarily the tragedy of 'an unhappy lover' (20), Gilchrist proceeds, scene-by-scene, to elucidate the central relationship between Hamlet and the 'sensuous' Ophelia.

Fredericka Beardsley Gilchrist, *The True Story of Hamlet and Ophelia*. Boston: Little, Brown and Co., 1889

From a father who entertains such broad ideas as to what would dishonor his son, Ophelia has received her moral training. She has grown to womanhood without a mother's tender care and guidance, and never has been taught either to control her impulses, or to know the danger that would result from the indulgence of them ...

[Polonius and Laertes] fear that [Hamlet] may tempt the maiden, and *they fear that she will not resist.* Polonius speaks much warmth, telling Ophelia that people have observed her lack of maidenly reserve, and have cautioned him in reference to the danger there might be to her in such close intimacy with Hamlet ... Do they fear Ophelia will melt in her own fire? At any rate they doubt the ability of her virtue to resist assault, and 'others' have conceived the same doubts ... In Hamlet's presence, and with him, she delights to tread 'the primrose path of dalliance' [I.iii.50]. This Hamlet knows, and the knowledge leads him afterward to condemn her for a fault that he, and he only, had tempted her to commit.

All our sympathies enwrap Ophelia when we see her repudiated and disowned by a lover whom she does not know that she has ever offended ... [But] from Hamlet's point of view we agree with him, and justify him in his decision to renounce his love. We admit, when he reminds us of it, that by a maiden's behavior before marriage we can fortell and determine her demeanor after it; we agree in thinking that reserve and self-control are necessary qualities in a girl who is to make a faithful, self-respecting wife ...

Poor girl! She had no mother to teach her the beauty of reticence or maidenly reserve, and now she pays the penalty of her unconscious fault. We must accept Hamlet's judgment as to the possible frailty of Ophelia. May we not believe that he had seen some sensitiveness, some susceptibility, some riot in her blood, which, pondered on, led to his final judgment of her character, and drove him to the bitter conclusion that he dared not entrust the guardianship of his honor to her? ...

But we must inquire why Shakespeare, when he shows us Ophelia in her madness, presents her exactly as he does. We should be glad if the recollection of her incoherent words might be a little different.

This representation of Ophelia is a justification of Hamlet. Without it, lookers-on at the theater might not agree with him, and might feel that his decision to renounce a loving, meek, obedient maid had proved, as no other of his actions could, the possession of a mind diseased. But Hamlet, early in the play, has had many interviews with Ophelia at which we were not present; he has given many private hours to her; he has recollections that we know not of, which have helped him in his judgment ...

In [IV.v] the presence of Claudius and Gertrude, who were so closely connected with Hamlet, awakens in [Ophelia's] unsettled brain a longing for his love and his caresses, and this she expresses in her songs.

Critics who have not seen the need for Ophelia's self-disclosure have wondered why Shakespeare should put such loose songs upon her lips. They have justified them by saying that she had heard them in her childhood from her nurse, and that, when reason and recollection were destroyed, her earliest impressions ruled her mind, and she now, with no recognition of their impropriety, sang the songs that had lain voiceless in her memory so many years. This is probably true, but Shakespeare undoubtedly meant ... that we should see the natural bent and disposition of her senses, in order that we might justify Hamlet in his decision ... Ophelia had heard other songs in her youth, songs from the *Pious Chanson* maybe [cf. *Hamlet*, II.ii.415], but she did not give them entertainment in her mind.

If we be shown two maids, both crazed by the same combination of circumstances, one of whom sings spiritual songs and turns her thoughts toward Heaven, and the other of whom expresses her grief as Ophelia did, shall we not inevitably decide that they differ in disposition, and that the latter is subject to some insubordination of her senses which may in time lead them to mutiny against her virtue? Shakespeare thought so, and he had faith to believe that with this revelation our judgment would confirm Hamlet's, and free him from too much censure for his rejection of the maiden. We must not forget that Shakespeare *chose* these songs, as calculated to reveal Ophelia's disposition. He could have selected others, had he wished to do so.

It is so ungracious a task to speak of Ophelia in any but words of unqualified admiration, that I feel forced to defend myself for setting down about her what I believe Shakespeare meant to convey; and the prejudices of Ophelia-lovers are so strong, that unless I explain exactly how much I mean to say, they will conceive that more is meant than I express. I believe that Shakespeare meant to portray, in Ophelia, a maiden who was pure in thought and act, but whose disposition, inclination, natural tendency was sensuous. She was the sensuous Northern maiden, as Juliet was the sensuous Southern type, and she was absolutely as continent and chaste as Juliet – but not more so; and I have no doubt that she was also as free and unrestrained in the expression of her love to Hamlet as Juliet was to Romeo ...

Every word which Shakespeare employs for the portrayal of Ophelia's character strengthens this view of it. The subject is so delicate that only light touches can be used in her delineation, but these strokes all lead to the completion of a picture of a maiden who was innocent because she had not been tempted, but who had no backbone of principle or precept to keep her so; – a maiden whose own sensuous nature was the traitor that might deliver the treasures in its charge to an invading libertine, had such an one desired to make conquest of them. It is clear to me that Hamlet believed this, and that Shakespeare meant that we too should recognize it ...

The first time we see her we are shown that father and brother know her disposition, and strongly fear, that, if tempted, she will indulge it. On her next appearance she tells her father of Hamlet's visit to her chamber early in the morning. This visit was an unpardonable liberty. His recklessness did not arise from madness, but from the freedom of his association with Ophelia along 'the primrose path of dalliance' [I.iii.50]. His doubts were torturing him, and he desired to resolve them, and knew that she would excuse a visit that a sane man would not have dared to pay to a lady-love whose maidenly reserve had commanded his respect ...

After all this which looks like censure, shall I be excused if I say I think

Hamlet was wrong in rejecting the maiden? If I say that, had he married her, he would have bounded her horizon, and she would have been as absolutely faithful to him as were Imogen or Desdemona to their husbands? I believe that Hamlet's fidelity to his ideal, which separated him from Ophelia, entailed an unnecessary sacrifice, – a sacrifice to which both were innocent victims. Ophelia's love had root, not in her fancy alone but in the very fibre of her heart; her reason was destroyed by her efforts to conceive of and support life without Hamlet. Such a love could blossom only once, and would have bloomed for Hamlet only.

This conception of Ophelia does not, in my opinion, dethrone or degrade her: it defines her character with strong lines and enhances the beauty and pathos of the play.

(Frances Snow) Julia Wedgwood, 1833–1913

A novelist and critic, Julia Wedgwood is perhaps best remembered for her intimate friendship with Robert Browning following the death of his wife Elizabeth Barrett. Julia Wedgwood was the grand-daughter of the potter Josiah Wedgwood and niece to Charles Darwin; she grew up in a large, well-staffed house in Regent's Park (London) visited by an eminent circle of literary friends and acquaintances, including Wordsworth, Coleridge, Maria Edgeworth, Thackeray and Carlyle. She was educated at Harriet Martineau's school (like Martineau, Julia Wedgwood suffered from congenital deafness), and then Cheltenham Ladies' College; she later attended classes at Bedford and Queen's College. In 1856 she became secretary to Elizabeth Gaskell in Manchester, and in 1858 Wedgwood published her first novel, *Framleigh Hall* under the pseudonym Florence Dawson, followed in 1859 by a second novel, *An Old Debt*. Thereafter Wedgwood published non-fiction: books on Wesley, anti-vivisection, comparative cultural histories of morality, Darwin's *Origin of Species* ('I think that you understand my book perfectly', Darwin commented; Curle, 1937: 7), and for forty years contributed articles to contemporary periodicals, including the *Spectator*, the *Contemporary Review* and *Macmillan's Magazine*. E. M. Forster, who became Wedgwood's secretary, remembered her as 'formidable' on account of her deafness, but 'polite and cordial, extremely modest about her work, and decidedly gay. Her support of the Woman's Movement, like her contributions to the *Spectator* under Hutton, has of course been forgotten: the world hasn't the time' ('"Snow" Wedgwood', 1951: 207). Since 1869 Wedgwood had argued for the 'enlargement of the sphere of Woman' ('Female suffrage': 277), and wrote several articles on women and gender difference. 'I question and criticize', Wedgwood wrote, 'I am not feminine, they say. Well, it is true for good as well as for evil' (letter to Browning, 1864; Curle: 40).

Julia Wedgwood corresponded with men and women such as Harriet Martineau, Elizabeth Gaskell, Thomas Hardy, George Eliot, and Josephine Butler, but only her letters to Robert Browning have been reprinted. The friendship began in 1863 after Browning, twenty years Julia's senior, visited the Wedgwood household; their letters are powerfully intimate, but within two years Wedgwood broke off the friendship, fearing both the 'interpretation put upon it that I ought not to allow' (cited by Ward, 1969: 26) and her own emotional involvement with Browning.

The Contemporary Review, which published Wedgwood's Shakespeare criticism, was a journal with a decidedly religious tone and a circulation of four thousand by 1870; its readers were upper- to middle-class, well educated, often Evangelical and predominantly Liberal in politics. *The Contemporary Review* carried articles on the Bible, current philosophy, science, art and music; in the 1870s it attracted contributions from the likes of Matthew Arnold, Gladstone and Ruskin. By the 1880s the journal had adopted an 'open platform' on religious affairs and a more activist tone, with essays on social reform and political liberalism.

Wedgwood's article on *Julius Caesar* for the *Contemporary Review* originated as a paper given at the St Andrew's Club for Women (Scotland). British club-women had been reading and disseminating Shakespeare since the eighteenth century; in 1736 the Shakespeare Ladies Club was founded to support the proposal for a monument to Shakespeare in Westminster Abbey and to petition theatre managers to put on revivals of Shakespeare's plays, paving the way for Garrick's success in the 1740s. One of its members, Mary Cowper (an elder cousin of the poet William Cowper), wrote a poem pointing out that it was women, not men, who were responsible for the revival of Shakespeare in the eighteenth century: 'In vain to *Pope Minerva* lifts her *Eyes* ... At last the Goddess *her own Sex* inspires ... the softer Sex redeems the Land / And *Shakespear* lives again by their *Command*' ('On the Revival of Shakespear's Plays by the Ladies in 1738', cited by Dobson: 154). By 1756, when Frances Brooke came to review Barry's *King Lear* (reprinted in *Shakespeare: The Critical Heritage*, vol. 4), the opportunities for women to see Shakespeare on stage had increased considerably.

But it was not until the late nineteenth century that women began to study Shakespeare in large numbers in literary societies, whether as members of all-women clubs (such as the St Andrew's Club for Women) or mixed societies, like the Clifton Shakspere Society of Bristol (England). With a membership of 'seven Ladies and eighteen Gentlemen', the Clifton Shakspere Society met fortnightly to read and criticise Shakespeare's plays: women members read papers on Shakespeare to the Society and took responsibility for 'critical departments' examining topics in the plays such as Biblical and Religious Allusions, Puns and Jests, and Tradition and Folk-lore; they also took on the burden of the Society's secretarial work (L. M. Griffiths, 1889: 3). Even the entrenched Royal Shakespearean Club of Stratford-upon-Avon admitted ladies 'for the discussion of any

Shakespearean subject' in 1894, and within five years women were invited to give papers at the Club in place of men (Royal Shakspearean Club Minute Book, 1845–1900: 155 and 218). By the end of the century large numbers of British women were reading, criticising and writing on Shakespeare through their involvement with literary clubs; they also organised lectures, readings and recitals of Shakespeare, such as the reading of *Hamlet* by Forbes-Robertson presented by the Ladies Association of the Hampstead Hospital (London) in 1900 (Folger Library, Program Inventory; on women in the New Shakspere Society, see the entry for Grace Latham (1884); on American women's clubs, see the entries for Elizabeth Wormeley Latimer (1886), Kate Richmond-West (1890) and Jessie O'Donnell (1897)).

Julia Wedgwood, 'The "Midsummer Night's Dream"', *Contemporary Review* (April 1890), 580–7

Was there ever a less interesting quartette than Helena and Hermia, Lysander and Demetrius? Whether they scold, or whether they woo, they leave us equally unmoved; here and there a gem is spared them from the poet's treasury, but for the most part he seems hardly to attend to his pen as it discourses of them. Theseus and his court have more life, and so have the clodhoppers who appear in masquerade before him; but the true interest of the piece lies in fairyland. Its queen is the central figure, and it is interesting to watch her grow in Shakespeare's imagination, from 'that very Mab' of Mercutio [*Romeo and Juliet*, I.iv.88] ... to the Titania beloved by Theseus, and jealous of Hippolyta, who seems as much of a goddess as of a fairy, and whose quarrel with her spouse might come straight from Homer. She has, in the change, grown as much in outward form as in character; instead of the midge-like Mab, appears a stately queen, for whom a human child is a fitting page ... She is full of human preference, human jealousy; she cherishes her page from the recollection of his mother, her faithfulness to whom puts to scorn the fitful friendship of Helena and Hermia ...

    In the attitude of Theseus towards the supernatural, there is something essentially modern. It is very much in the manner of Scott, or rather there is something in it that reminds one of Scott himself. We see, wherever our great novelist enters the world of magic and legend, that he regards it through the medium of a cool, shrewd, eighteenth-century scepticism ... It seems to us that [this] eighteenth-century element is exactly what is given in the well-known speech of Theseus: –

        Tis strange, my Theseus, that these lovers tell of,
                                                              [V.i.1]

says Hippolyta; and he replies: –

> More strange than true, I never may believe
> These antique fables, nor these fairy toys.
> Lovers and madmen have such seething brains,
> Such shaping fantasies, that apprehend
> More than cool reason ever comprehends ...
>
> [V.i.2–6]

Perhaps Shakespeare was much nearer an actual belief in the fairy mythology he has half created than seems possible to a spectator of the nineteenth century. And yet Theseus expresses exactly the denial of the modern world. And we feel at once how the introduction of such an element enhances the power of the earlier views; the courteous, kindly, man-of-the-world scepticism somehow brings out the sphere of magic against which it sets the shadow of its demand. The belief of the peasant is emphasised and defined, while it is also intensified, by what we feel the inadequate confutation of the prince.

The play of the tradesmen which at first one is apt to regard as a somewhat irrelevant appendix to the rest of the drama, is seen, by a maturer judgment, to be as it were a piece of sombre tapestry, exactly adapted to form a background to the light forms and iridescent colouring of the fairies as they flit before it. But this is not its greatest interest, to our mind. It is most instructive when we watch the proof it gives of Shakespeare's strong interest in his own art. It is one of three occasions in which he introduces a play within a play, and in all three the introduction, without being unnatural, has just that touch of unnecessariness by means of which the productions of art take a biographic tinge, and seem as much a confidence as a creation. How often must Shakespeare have watched some player of a heroic part proclaim his own prosaic personality, like Snug, the joiner, letting his face be seen through the lion's head ... In the speech of Theseus ordering the play, we may surely allow ourselves to believe that we hear not only the music, but the voice of Shakespeare, pleading the cause of patient effort against the scorn of a hard and narrow dilettantism ...

> The best in this kind are but shadows, and the worst are no worse, if imagination mend them. [V.i. 212–13]

Here the poet is speaking to the audience; in *Hamlet*, when he addresses the players, his sympathy naturally takes the form of criticism; what the Athenian prince would excuse the Danish prince would amend. But in both alike we discern the same personal interest in the actor's part, and feel ourselves listening as much to a confidence as to a creation. We learn that the greatest genius who ever lived was the one who could show most sympathy with incompleteness and failure. There is nothing scornful, nothing merely critical in his delineation of the rough clowns who shadow forth the loves of Pyramus and Thisbe. On the contrary, almost every touch has a certain delicacy. With the exception of a single obscure allusion, they utter hardly a word that might not fall from the most refined among the audience. Shakespeare throws himself into the part of the actor. He remembers all the patient effort needed to produce a very mediocre result, he pleads that this result shall be regarded through a medium of sympathy . . .

For Shakespeare's sympathy with the members of his special craft is as a window, whence he looks on life as a whole, and sees in its hurry, its transiency, its strange misfit of capacity to claim, of knowledge to impulse, a repetition of the experience of the player. That truth, which is wrought into the very structure of language, whereby the Latin name for a mask has become the modern *person*, reminding us that there is within each of us that which 'sounds through,' not only our outward surroundings, but much that in the eyes of other men makes up ourselves; this could not but haunt the mind of one who knew the players' part both from within and without. 'All the world's a stage;' every man is in some sense an actor, most often an untrained actor, ill at ease in his part . . .

> We are such stuff as dreams are made of.
>   [*Tempest*, IV.i.156–7]

That line haunts us all through the 'Midsummer Night's Dream.' We feel the adventures of the night no mere play of fancy, but a parable of the confusions, the mistakes, the shifting vicissitudes, the inexplicable changes of human attraction and repulsion.

> The course of true love never did run smooth
>   [*A Midsummer Night's Dream*, I.i.134]

seems a bitter theme for so sweet and fanciful a setting, but it is the theme of the whole play. Theseus and Hippolyta have begun with conflict, they may perhaps have a serene interval before them, but we doubt even so far as to Lysander and Hermia, Demetrius and Helena, Oberon and Titania. Even poor Pyramus and Thisbe, murdered by the clowns, how does their history in its caricature repeat the lesson of misfits, barriers, impediments; and then when these are removed, mistakes and misunderstandings, which have just been set before us in the adventures of the night. Was the whole play an expansion of that compliment to Elizabeth, which naturally links itself with the lament over the course of true love? Did Shakespeare mean to imply that 'the imperial votaress who passed on in maiden meditation, fancy free,' [II.i.163] had chosen the better part?

Julia Wedgwood, 'Shakespere's "Julius Caesar"' (a lecture to the St Andrew's Club for Women), *Contemporary Review* (March 1893), 356–68

The world's greatest statesman and warrior, delineated by the world's greatest dramatist – here surely we shall find a character of unique splendour! Is this what we find in Shakespere's Caesar? ... We are accustomed to clothe Shakespere's Julius Caesar with heroic virtue ... [But] Shakespeare seems to remember nothing of almost the greatest conqueror the world has ever seen except his weaknesses. He occupies the chief part of that small proportion of his work allotted to the utterances of Caesar, in delineating such foibles and weaknesses as we should hardly make room for in anything but an exhaustive biography. Especially note the space he gives to his physical weaknesses, telling us such incidents (sometimes against the traditions of history) as that he was a poor swimmer, that he fainted away in a dirty crowd, that he was impatient in the thirst of fever, and the like. One of the lines he allots to the greatest of statesmen and warriors curiously brings out his determination to force upon us a consideration of his weaknesses. 'Come thou on this side, for that ear is deaf' [I.ii.213]. Why should Shakespere interrupt Caesar's speech to Anthony to tell us that? ... Why has [Shakespeare] taken the greatest name in secular history and associated it with weakness, vanity, and superstition, hiding all the glorious achievements it suggests, and insisting only that all which was noblest in Rome rose up gainst the pretensions in which those achievements culminated? ...

The reason why Shakespere has done so seems to me as clear as it is important. The representation of the world's greatest statesman by the world's greatest poet, which appears so pale and ineffective, is in truth a brilliant revelation as to the meaning of history.

When we compare ancient and modern life, the most salient point of antagonism which attracts our attention is the different place which personality takes in the ancient and in the modern world. The feeling of devotion to a personal leader is to us an object of sympathy and respect quite apart from any estimate of its object. One may have the worst opinion of Napoleon, for instance, and yet feel touched at such an instance of devotion on the part of his soldiers as Byron has commemorated in his fine verses beginning –

> Must thou go, my glorious chief.
> > [Byron, 'From the French', *Poems*, 1816]

It teaches us much of the meaning of history – much of the meaning of what we have learned to call evolution, as it affects the world of mind – to reflect that the sentiment which so much stirs modern sympathy ...

is one with which the men of antiquity had no sympathy whatever. Nay, the expression is inadequate. They were not indifferent to it any more than we are; they regarded it with abhorrence equal to our admiration. The classic world, in this respect, may be regarded as a negative photograph of the modern world. The word king ... is in Greek and Latin a spell to evoke inappeasable hatred and terror. To us the name symbolises orderly government and national unity; to them it sounded as the herald of lawless and self-pleasing caprice. It is a new thing with us, after nearly two millenniums [*sic*] of Christian life, that a nation should exist without a personal head. Possibly this may be the condition of the future, many things seem to show that the era of monarchy is drawing towards a close; but throughout the whole history of Europe, from the date of Christianity, national life and monarchy have been inseparable ... But when we reach that brilliant epoch of ancient life which has arrogated to itself, very unjustly, the title of *ancient history*, we find it an assumption and starting-point of all moral feeling that a personal head to the State is incompatible with freedom ...

Of all the proofs of the greatness of Shakespere's genius none seems to me so remarkable as the fact that he should have reflected perfectly this characteristic sentiment of the classical world. No man had ever less of this anti-monarchic feeling than Shakespere himself. Note with what sympathy he paints the devotion to a king in his plays from English history, or, indeed, whenever such a feeling is possible. Remember 'Henry V.' or 'Henry VIII.', and then turn to the speech of Cassius, and observe how the idea of kingly rule seems prefigured and repudiated:

> ... I was born free as Caesar; so were you.
> ... Ye gods, it doth amaze me
> A man of such a feeble temper should
> So get the start of the majestic world
> And bear the palm alone ...
>
>   [I.ii.97–131]

That speech, and every speech of importance which is given him, is a passionate deprecation of the feeling that we know as loyalty ...

Cassius shows us the ignoble form of the recoil from a possible loyalty; its noble form is given in the antagonism of Brutus. We feel in him all the glow of a possible loyalty to Caesar, but some other element is present which turns that glow to resolute opposition. His is not the vulgar passion for equality which we feel in every word from Cassius. He feels, not that he and his brethren are dwarfed by the pre-eminence of one whom he recognises as eminently great, but that the majesty of the invisible state is threatened by the majesty of the visible man ...

He truly declares the principle of his action to the citizens: 'Not that

I loved Caesar less, but that I loved Rome more' [III.ii.21–2] ... We are taken back to the spirit of an age which could not regard any one who aspired to monarchy, even at a time when the alternative of monarchy was a tyranny as cruel, as selfish, and as corrupt as the world has ever seen, without gross injustice. We are reminded that the dawn of personal loyalty was, to the ancient world, as the light of a conflagration.

The change by which individual life took a new sanctity as the old world gave place to the new, is not surprising to those who believe that humanity was at that time flooded with a new influence. The perilous height from which Athens and Rome had hurled every aspirant would naturally cease to appear unfitted for the sons of men, when it was seen that the true Son of Man was also the Son of God. But the change is one that may be recognised by those who have no belief in Christianity. They, of course, will invert cause and effect in describing it. They will say that a legend was created by a change in general feeling corresponding to a certain stage in the spiritual evolution of our race. But both sides must join in the belief, that at a certain stage in the world's history, personality, either for good or for evil, took a new importance ...

Shakespere keeps the living Caesar poor and pale that the dead Caesar may blaze forth in unrivalled splendour. It is an invisible presence which gives the play its meaning. While Caesar is visible we are allowed to see nothing of him but his weaknesses. When he has passed into the Unseen we are reminded that he came at a crisis of the world's history when an old order of things was passing away and all things were made new. We are called on to discern in him one worthy to embody the coming age, we have to recognise – it is but another way of expressing the same truth – that his work did not cease when he ceased to be visible among men, but then entered on its most important and most effective stage. It is the noblest of his enemies who, in his dying exclamation, confesses that the deadly blow has been struck in vain, and that the true Caesar is immortal ...

It is a great thought that the new unity which was to become Christianity had its secular and pagan forerunner, that it was heralded by one whom Shakespere has here represented to us as mighty in the invisible world. It stirs many thoughts of the possibly unsuspected vocation of any life. To me it seems such a warning against opposite political dangers as makes our fitting conclusion – a warning, first, against that distortion of our reverence for the past which refuses to welcome the future; which considers evolution a truth only for the ages which preceded Christianity, and fails to realise that we are living in the great week of creation, and that each of its secular days has its own work, which all are called on to recognise and welcome. And then, too – and this warning seems to me more needed, especially by the young – it should guard us against the readiness to receive any reformer unless he comes 'not to destroy, but to fulfil.' The Past is fulfilled in forms most utterly dissimilar from itself, but by none which repudiate their affiliation with it. But above all, the warning bids us wait to judge the work of a great man till we see it as a whole. It is surely such a lesson in what we mean by Faith as elsewhere we find only on the page of Scripture. By Faith, I mean the trust in character rather than in any results by which we can test the influence of character – the belief elsewhere so perfectly expressed by our great poet that –

> Spirits are not finely touched but to fine issues –
>   [*Measure for Measure*, I.i.35–6]

that these issues transcend our narrow vision, and that when all that we can see of a man's working is ended, his work has but entered on a stage where its results are deeper, wider, every way larger, and nearer to the realm of the Eternal.

Moira O'Neill (pseudonym), active 1891–1934

Little is known of Moira O'Neill aside from her publications: *The Elf-Errant* (1895), *Songs of the Glens of Antrim* (1911), a volume of her *Collected Poems* (1934) and one work of literary criticism – 'Macbeth as the Celtic Type'. *Blackwood's Edinburgh Magazine* in which O'Neill's article appears was a leading monthly journal established by William Blackwood in 1817 to rival the popular Whig periodical *The Edinburgh Review* by appealing to an audience of politically conservative Scottish Tories. 'With a rare consistency', remarked *The Review of Reviews* in 1891, *Blackwood's* 'has contrived to appear for over threescore years and ten as the spirited and defiant advocate of all those who are at least five years behind their time' (*Wellesley Index*, vol. 1: 9). *Blackwood's* published poetry, humour and fiction, and by 1870 had gained a circulation of seven thousand; the journal's prestige and influence drew many authors, while its policy of anonymity appealed to eminent contributors who preferred not to risk their reputations by signing articles.

Moira O'Neill, 'Macbeth as the Celtic Type', *Blackwood's Edinburgh Magazine* (September 1891), 376–83

> I do not propose, within the limits of this article, to discuss the grand motive of the tragedy of 'Macbeth,' or the all-important relation and contrast of his character with his wife's. I am not concerned with Macbeth's character from a psychological point of view. But I would ask attention to a single idea, a very simple one, which occurred to me while listening to a lecture on Macbeth, given by Mr Moulton in Torquay. As the lecturer, after dwelling particularly on such points as Macbeth's superstition, his trust in the supernatural, and his extraordinary impatience of suspense, proceeded to describe the murder-scene, – realising, with faithfully imaginative skill, the heavy night, the gathering tempest, the exultation of the murderer, the instant revulsion of feeling and final collapse of all his power caused by a single moment's *suspense* in the murder-chamber, – suddenly there flashed into my mind the meaning of these strange impulses and quick revulsions of feeling. The murderer was a Celt ...

Undoubtedly it is a mistaken acuteness that discovers national peculiarities in every play where the scene happens to be laid outside of England. The attempt lands us in some very odd predicaments; as when, for example, we are constrained to adduce the national characteristics of a people inhabiting that mysterious portion of the globe, maritime Bohemia! But, though the majority of Shakespeare's characters are – primarily of course, human, but secondarily – English men and women, he has also given us some equally unmistakable types of foreign nations: of the ancient Greek in Ulysses; of the ancient Roman in Coriolanus and Brutus; of the modern Italian in Romeo and Proteus, and the modern Frenchman in Lafeu and Parolles – that is, a nobler and a baser type of the the two nations last named; with sundry minor French, Welsh, and Irish men, kindly but comically drawn. There is therefore no inherent improbability of Shakespeare's having chosen to draw for us a firm and finished likeness of the Celt; such a likeness as I believe he has drawn, with full insight and deep sympathy, in Macbeth.

And indeed, when we remember the unfortunate prominence of Irish affairs, and the activity of certain great chieftains over the water during Elizabeth's reign, we may easily suppose that the attention of Shakespeare and the rest of England was more than once directed to Celtic peculiarities as exhibited by Desmond, the O'Donnell, the Macwilliam, and Somhairle Buoidhe; while the great O'Neills, Shane and Hugh, during their residence in England, must have afforded Shakespeare an opportunity of studying the Celtic type at first hand, from living and striking examples.

This probability granted, the next step is to denote the principal features of that most difficult and deeply contested type of character; and to observe their agreement of difference with the type of character presented to our contemplation in Macbeth.

We will instance, as decisive and indubitably Celtic characteristics, these: –

1. Vital imagination.

2. Mutability.

3. Treachery.

4. Sympathy with Nature.

5. Eloquence.

6. Superstition.

These points, named, it is hoped with some impartiality, the good beside the evil, will not be denied, even by the unsympathetic Saxon, to afford materials capable of grandly various combination and development. Is it hard to imagine that they should have attracted Shakespeare to combine and develop them into a human type of supreme import and beauty? ...

Now to examine these characteristics in Macbeth.

1. *Vital imagination.* – By this I mean a power of realising the unseen, strong enough not only to present to the mind's eye sights and scenes of the past or future, – such is the ordinary function of an ordinarily repro- ductive imagination, – but to make the unseen and the absent *overcome* the visible and present, attaining by mere force of stronger realisation a more absolute existence in the mind of the percipient; such an imagination as sways its possessor with irresistible mastery, so that it may rather be said to possess him than her it ... The susceptibility, or imaginativeness, whichever it may be called, is not, from a moral point of view, more praiseworthy than any other constitutional or hereditary trait. It gives an undeniable charm to the Celtic character; a refining touch to all that is good in it, and a refining force to the appeal of every temptation assailing it. When a man like Macbeth is lost to the power of conscience ... he must remain more or less at the mercy of this terribly vivid imagination. It takes the place of conscience to him ...

2. *Mutability.* – There is not much need of demonstration here. The Celtic mind is mutable. Saxons say we are fickle, which is untrue; fickleness being a defect of the heart, not of the mind, and one not commonly incident to the Celtic heart. Macbeth is a very extreme instance of Celtic mutability; but then, I should like to point out that he is a curiously unattached character, with no strong attraction either to good or evil for its own sake. (Witness the analysis of his character given by his wife in soliloquy, too well known to be quoted here [I.v.15–30], and its confir- mation by Hecate.) ...

3. *Treachery.* – We cannot deny that treachery is a dreadful stain on the Celtic character. It is our national disgrace. Macbeth is therefore made to embody the national sin in an act of the worst treachery of which a Celt can conceive – namely, against a kinsman, a liege lord, and a guest. He is perfectly aware of the heinousness of his offence, at least in the eyes of his countrymen: no shame is reflected on it from his own conscience; because, as before stated, he is devoid of conscience, in the ordinary sense of that term ...

4. *Sympathy with Nature.* – I almost despair of rendering a connected, reasonable, or in any way persuasive account of this most important characteristic, which is perhaps the less surprising, as it has nothing in particular to do with reason, and very little connection with anything else in my limited experience.

The Celtic sympathy with nature is an instinct; the Saxon sympathy with nature is an attachment, more or less profound. They have the advantage of us in possessing poets to notify their love: we have the advantage of them in requiring no poets, while we have eyes and a heart. The Celt is a child of nature: his love is instinctive. The Saxon is, doubtless, a far superior being: his moral feeling is cultivated, his character is high; but his most reckless enemy will not accuse him of being a child of nature. Such a child was Macbeth ...

5. *Eloquence*. – There needs no eloquence to convince us that Macbeth is eloquent! He combines the quick perception of the Celt with the deep susceptibility, the imaginativeness, the sense of beauty, the sense of power, the sense of pathos, and that last, most curious of Celtic gifts, the magnetic *power of appeal* ... To the very end Macbeth retains the same strange beauty of thought and expression, – the result of his Celtic imagination and eloquence, – and to the very end constrains our sympathies ... This power of expression, with its kindred power of ennobling a subject by lifting it into the imaginative region, is the natural heritage of the Celt. Moreover, if you desire to hear of motives higher than you have ever dared conceive, go to the accomplished Celtic villain: and, – unless his native poetry has been overlaid with a superficial utilitarianism, derived from half-Americanised relatives, – you will not be disappointed.

6. *Superstition*. – Macbeth's superstition, instinctive, hereditary, indomitable as it is, is at once the strongest outcome of his nature, the strongest evidence of his nationality, and the strongest support of our claim to Macbeth as pre-eminently the Shakespearian Celtic type. For me, it would be as difficult to dissociate his peculiar superstitious tendency from the rest of his Celtic nature, as it would be to dissociate the peculiar pride of Coriolanus from the Roman's love of ascendancy, and inherited pride of race. But there is the less need to enlarge on this point of superstition, because, being all-important to the comprehension of Macbeth's character, it is made perfectly self-evident from first to last: so much so, indeed, that Macbeth is the acknowledged type of the superstitious in literature ...

People who read plays often acquire a false security of judgment. Because they know 'how it will all end' in every case, they commonly fancy that there must be one inevitable ending for every case, which nothing could have averted. Speaking imaginatively, this is a great mistake. In the case in question, Lady Macbeth might have averted the catastrophe; and very nearly did so. If she had not possessed a superstitious Celt for a husband, there is no saying how the play of 'Macbeth' might have ended. Certainly she understood her husband, as far as one mortal may understand another; but she made the irretrievable mistake of thinking she could reckon with his instability – a mistake almost impossible for a consistent person to avoid, who has experienced some success in dealing with an inconsistent person. A Celt is, at any time, an unsafe thing to reckon with. But a Celt with a dash of genius is absolutely incalculable.

Katharine Lee Bates, 1859–1929

Best remembered today as the author of the patriotic poem 'America the Beautiful' (1895), Katharine Lee Bates was a prominent figure in the woman's intellectual movement in late nineteenth-century America. Born in New England, she entered the newly established Wellesley College in 1876; after fifteen months of graduate study at Oxford she received her Master's degree in 1891, and in the same year was made full professor of English at Wellesley, where she remained until 1925. Bates played a lively role in a flourishing community of women scholars at Wellesley, helping to make an academic career a viable and respected option for women to pursue. She wrote on American literature, English religious drama and Shakespeare, edited the work of Coleridge, Keats, Tennyson, Ruskin, Hawthorne and Thomas Heywood, and invited W. B. Yeats and Robert Frost to Wellesley; she also contributed her own poems to periodicals such as *Contemporary Verse* and *Lippincott's*. 'The chief value of the study of literature', wrote Bates in the preface to her edition of *The Merchant of Venice* (1894), 'is the ennoblement of life ... In this main study Shakespeare is the teacher. The student who has once come under his potent spell will learn – what in all education is best worth learning – to think and feel' (v). Bates was one of the first American women to edit Shakespeare's plays; she was an early member of the Shakespeare Association of America, contributed to the Shakespeare Society of Wellesley College (on this society see the entry for Elizabeth Wormeley Latimer, 1886), ran seminars on 'English Drama Through Shakespeare' in her own home, and called her dog Hamlet.

Bates's edition of *A Midsummer Night's Dream*, from which this extract is taken, was one of three editions she prepared in the 1890s of Shakespeare's comedies for use in the school 'classroom' for *The Students' Series of English Classics*.

Katharine Lee Bates, ed., *Shakespeare's Comedy of A
Midsummer-Night's Dream: The Students' Series of English Classics.*
Boston, New York and Chicago: Leach, Shewell and Sanborn, 1895

Introduction: Structure

From one point of view *A Midsummer Night's Dream* is a triumph of
construction. The most heterogeneous fowl, – a classical hero, a Teutonic
goblin, an Amazonian queen, grotesque English artisans, two brace of
Athenian lovers, and the daintiest woodland fairies that ever sang lullaby
with Philomel, are caught together in a moonshine net of poetry spangled
with allusions to mythical demigods, mediaeval nuns, Warwickshire may-
ers [*sic*], London actors, Indian kings, French coins, Centaurs, sixpences,
the Man in the Moon, Bacchanals, heraldry, Jack and Jill, mermaids, magic
herbs, swords, guns, Tartars, and the Antipodes ... It ought to be all a
jumble, and it is an artistic harmony.

But how? What, in this that looks so helter-skelter, is the unifying
truth? Here the scholars are at variance. The play is a twist of gold cord
and rainbow silks, homespun yarn and shimmering moonbeams. The royal
gold, it is generally agreed, binds the rest together, but does not make a
part of the actual comedy-knot ...

If a diagram may be allowed, it becomes clear that the encompassing
action is that of Theseus and Hippolyta, the human sovereigns. With the
fairy element these never come into contact. The clown action touches
both, and so does the action of the Athenian lovers. All the perplexities

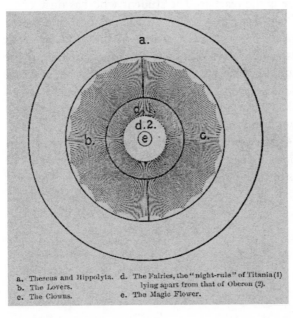

a. Theseus and Hippolyta.   d. The Fairies, the "night-rule" of Titania (1)
b. The Lovers.   lying apart from that of Oberon (2).
c. The Clowns.   e. The Magic Flower.

FIGURE 12.
Original diagram from
Katharine Lee Bates, *A
Midsummer Night's
Dream*
a. Theseus and
Hippolyta
b. The Lovers
c. The Clowns
d. The Fairies, the
'night-rule' of Titania
(1) lying apart from
that of Oberon (2)
e. The Magic Flower.

of the plot proceed from the fairies, save the cross in the loves of Helena and Demetrius, which is resolved by the fairies. The elves are thus at the centre of the comedy, although Titania has so far withdrawn herself from her wee lord, – as bent on maintaining masculine supremacy in fairyland as Theseus is in Athens, – that she, too, undergoes the witchery of the magic juice. The web of enchantment that overspreads the play radiates from the mischievous little flower love-in-idleness, and its ready agents, the 'king of shadows' and 'sweet Puck' [II.i.40].

The contrasted features here are the waking world, the world of day-light, scepticism, reality, and the dream-world, the world of moonshine, charm, illusion. These two worlds must forever lie apart. So long as the poet observes this verity, what matter if Athens and London are shaken up together, and the classic ages masquerade in feudal dress? ...

The drama opens in the realm of reality. Theseus and Hippolyta, in the briefest of conversations, unconsciously strike the keynotes of moon-light, dream, and love ... The second act introduces us to quite another world. We live with spirits for our company; and although once the moonlight glades are crossed by the fleeting figures of Demetrius and Helena, and again the fragrant turf is pressed by the weary forms of Lysander and Hermia, the human world they represent has already waxed more unreal than fairyland ... The fifth act, like the first, opens in the realm, not of Oberon, but of Theseus – yet with a difference. The literalism of the players parodies the realistic theories of the duke, the 'very tragical mirth' [V.i.57] of the interlude mocks the forest adventures of the lovers, and possibly Bottom himself vaguely suspects derision in the plaudits. The world of fact is never so stable and serious again after a midsummer night in fairyland. And when, at last,

> The iron tongue of midnight hath told twelve
>
> [V.i.363]

and the palace is hushed and dim, frolic trippings and warbled notes and glimmering sprites bless the bridal chambers, sweeping away the impurities of life's toilsome hours, and purging man's mortal grossness yet once more with the mysteries of moonlight, dreams, and love.

Mary Anderson (later Madame de Navarro), 1859–1940

A leading American actress of the late nineteenth century, Mary Anderson was renowned for her performances in contemporary drama and Shakespeare. She grew up in Louisville, Kentucky, and began reading Shakespeare at the age of twelve; two years later, after seeing the famous American Shakespearan actor Edwin Booth, Mary made the controversial decision to leave her 'unbearable' school (a Catholic academy for girls) and 'clandestinely' pursue an acting career (*A Few Memories*: 30). She set up a study for herself at home – furnished with a photograph of Booth and a bust of Shakespeare – and undertook a course of ten acting lessons, making her debut as Juliet at the age of sixteen in Louisville, November 1875, to great acclaim. The following year she toured American theatres, playing in New York in 1877, and in 1878, aged nineteen, she began her first European tour. In the 1880s Anderson undertook a gruelling schedule of touring on both sides of the Atlantic; after visiting Verona she produced *Romeo and Juliet* at the Lyceum Theatre, London, and in 1887 she produced *The Winter's Tale*, 'my pet play' (249), with Forbes-Robertson playing Leontes opposite Anderson's Hermione and Perdita – the first time the parts of mother and daughter were doubled. She became acquainted with Edwin Booth, General Sherman, Victor Hugo and Wilkie Collins, and met and discussed Shakespeare with other leading Shakespearian actresses – including Charlotte Cushman, Sarah Bernhardt, Adelaide Ristori and Helena Faucit. In 1889 Anderson became seriously ill, and collapsed after playing Hermione in Washington, DC. It was her last performance: in June 1890 she married Antonio F. de Navarro in London, and the following year she sold all her stage dresses, theatrical scenery and stage props, and moved with her husband to Worcestershire (England). Anderson explains that the life of a leading, touring actress had become increasingly difficult for her; she was longing to enjoy 'that privacy which is so dear to most women' (129).

Her autobiography, *A Few Memories* (1896) was written 'more for young girls (who may have the same ambitions that I had) than for any one else: to show them that the glitter of the stage is not all gold' (1). In the volume she records her experiences of playing Shakespeare's heroines and producing his plays, and her discussions with performers, critics and enthusiasts of Shakespeare.

Mary Anderson (Mme. de Navarro), *A Few Memories*. London: Osgood, McIlvaine and Co., 1896

At the age of twelve, I first heard the name of him who was to awaken the serious side of my nature, and eventually shape my later career. One night, Dr. Griffin [Anderson's step-father], who had in his youth prided himself on his acting as an amateur, took down from the bookshelf, a large, well-worn, red and gold volume.

'This,' he said, 'contains all the plays of William Shakespeare, and I mean to read to you the great master's masterpiece, Hamlet.' Though I understood nothing of the subtle thought and beauty of the tragedy, the mere story, characters, and above all that wonderful though nameless atmosphere that pervades all of Shakespeare's dramatic works, delighted and thrilled me. For days I could think of nothing but the pale face and inky cloak of the melancholy prince. The old red volume had suddenly become like a casket filled with jewels, whose flames and flashes, I thought, might glorify a life. I often stopped to look at it with longing eyes, and one day could not resist climbing up to take it from its shelf. From that time most of my play hours were spent poring over it ...

We were blest with but little of this world's goods at the time, and my help in the household being needed, I was taught the culinary art. In a few months I could cook an excellent dinner when called upon. I remember sitting by the stove with a basting spoon (to be used on a turkey) in one hand, and Charles Reade's 'Put Yourself in his Place' in the other. 'The Winter's Tale,' 'Julius Caesar,' and 'Richard the Third' were also read as I sat by the kitchen-fire baking bread. The theory that it is impossible to do two things at once, did not appeal to me. I felt certain that no one could enjoy the poet's inspiration more than I, and at the same time turn out a better loaf. Thankful I have always been for the knowledge of these useful arts – which I think every girl should master – as they are wholesome both for mind and body ...

In the South most of the servants were negroes. Among ours was a little mulatto girl ('nut-brown maid,' she called herself), whose chief attraction to me was her enthusiasm for the theatre. One night in desperation I went to her while she was washing dishes in the kitchen, and there unfolded all my hopes. It was to her I first acted, and it was she who gave me my first applause. The clapping of those soapy, steaming hands seemed to me a veritable triumph. Believing that a tragic manner alone would sufficiently impress the situation on the 'nut-brown maid,'

I began with a hollow voice and much furrowing of the brow, 'Juli, wilt thou follow and assist me when I quit my childhood's home to walk in the path of Siddons, Kemble, and Booth?' 'Oh, Miss Manie, you kin count on dis pusson, fo' de Lor' you kin! Why, my stars, what a boss actor you is! But you mus' 'low me to call your maw'; and in a trice she was gone ... After that evening in the kitchen, I read scenes or acted them nightly to our small household, usually from 'Hamlet,' 'Richard,' or Schiller's 'Maid of Orleans.' ...

[Mary Anderson makes her debut playing Juliet at Louisville, Kentucky, November 1875:] I became feverishly anxious to begin. It was hard to stand still while waiting for the word. At last it came: 'What, ladybird! God forbid! where's the girl? what, Juliet,' [I.iii.3–4] and in a flash I was on the stage, conscious only of a wall of yellow light before me, and a burst of prolonged applause. Curiosity had crowded the house. 'Why, it's little Mamie Anderson. How strange! it's only a few months ago since I saw her rolling a hoop!' &c. &c., were some of the many remarks which, I was afterwards told, ran through the audience.

The early, lighter scenes, being uncongenial, I hurried through as quickly as possible. Even these were well received by the indulgent audience. But there was enthusiasm in the house when the tragic parts were reached. Flowers and recalls were the order of the evening. While things were so smiling before, they were less satisfactory behind the curtain. The artist who had acted in the play before my birth, forgot his words, and I had to prompt him in two important scenes. In the last act, the lamp that hangs above Juliet, as she lies in the tomb, fell, and burned my hands and dress badly, and to make matters worse, Romeo forgot the dagger with which Juliet was to kill herself, and that unfortunate young person had, in desperation, to despatch herself with a hairpin. But, in spite of much disillusion, a burnt hand and arm, and several other accidents, the night was full of success, and I knew that my stage career had begun in earnest ...

To make oneself acquainted with a character, the chief difficulty lies, not in memorising the lines, but in determining by the closest study how different characters act in situations common to all. Rosalind may be madly in love with Orlando; yet she can jest, be merry, and have a mock marriage; while the gentle Imogen, under the same conditions, would droop and fade away. Desdemona may be separated from her love; yet she does not fret nor mourn at his absence. Absence to Juliet is death. Queen Constance goes mad, raves, and tears her hair at the loss of her son. Hermione, on hearing of the death of Mamilius, swoons like one dead, revives, and after living for sixteen years away from those she loves best, suddenly comes back into their midst without any outward sign of great emotion. These are all noble women, to whom their love is their life; and yet how differently each expresses what she feels! Fortunately,

Shakespeare always gives a keynote to the nature of most of his characters. For instance, Hermione, when accused by her husband, bears herself with quiet dignity, though wounded irreparably in her deepest affection ...

> I must be patient till the heavens look
> With an aspect more favourable.
>
> [II.i.106–7]

This speech shows Hermione to be a woman of great self-control and dignity, even in the most terrible situation conceivable, and was my clue to her character. Such a creature would be incapable of unbridled excitement or violently expressed emotion even under the greatest pressure. Many, I believe, did not sympathise with my outward calmness in the accusation scene; but I resolved not to give up my conception of the master's text for any stage effect. The common belief that Juliet is merely a sentimental love-lorn maiden seems to me fallacious. From the moment she loves Romeo, Juliet becomes, in my humble opinion, a woman capable of heroic action in all that concerns her love ...

, Of course some natures are inconsistent, and must be dealt with accordingly. The development of these various types, with their natural personality, mannerisms, &c., is a most engrossing study. How would such a man or woman weep under given circumstances? Would he or she weep at all? And so in joy as well as sorrow, under the influence of every emotion, they have their individual way of doing everything. The art is to make the character harmonious from beginning to end; and the greatest actor is he who loses his own personality in that of his *role*.

Emily Perkins Bissell (pseudonym Priscilla Leonard), 1861–1948

Social welfare worker, anti-suffragist and initiator of the anti-tuberculosis Christmas seal in America in 1907, Emily Perkins Bissell was born and lived for most of her life in Wilmington, Delaware. After attending Miss Charlier's private school in New York City, Bissell visited homes of the poor in Wilmington and began her charitable work by founding in 1889 the West End Reading Room, which sponsored the city's first free kindergarten and the first public playground in Delaware. She was an active club-member, belonging to the Anti-Saloon League (rejecting the officially suffragist Woman's Christian Temperance Union), holding the post of President of the Delaware Anti-Tuberculosis Society for forty years (1908–48), and serving for eight years as chairman of social services for the Delaware State Federation of Women's Clubs. In 1914 she helped to secure Delaware's first child labour law and maximum-hour law for women in industry, but Bissell was an active opponent of women's suffrage, maintaining that the vote would add to women's burdens, lead to family discord, and double the Negro and immigrant vote. In the 1890s she began to publish articles (many attacking women's suffrage), short stories and poems under the pseudonym Priscilla Leonard in contemporary periodicals, including *The Century Magazine*, *Outlook* and *Harper's Bazaar*.

Bissell's entertaining article on 'The Mistaken Vocation of Shakespeare's Heroines' was written under the pseudonym of Priscilla Leonard for the humorous section of *The Century Magazine*, 'In Lighter Vein'. Bissell gives a tongue-in-cheek account of a paper delivered by a woman 'lecturer' to her 'sisters' in an unidentified 'Twentieth Century Woman's Club' (by the late nineteenth and early twentieth centuries women's 'Twentieth Century Clubs' could be found across the United States, including Buffalo, Detroit, Chicago, Minnesota, Oklahoma, and Wyoming). *The Century Magazine* was noted for its conservatism on women's issues by the turn of the century; Bissell's parody would have appealed to the journal's anti-suffragist readers – but it also aroused the interest of *The American Shakespeare Magazine*, which reprinted the article in

1897 (for more on *The Century Magazine* see the entry for Emma Lazarus, 1883).

Priscilla Leonard, 'The Mistaken Vocation of Shakespeare's Heroines', *The Century Magazine*, LIII:2 (new series vol. XXXI) Christmas number (December 1896), 319–20 [reprinted in *The American Shakespeare Magazine*, 3 (December 1897), 369–72]

'My subject,' said the lecturer, as she stepped gracefully upon the platform of the Twentieth-Century Woman's Club, 'will commend itself to you, my sisters, as one which women alone can fully appreciate. I have chosen it because the world needs to hear a loud and convincing protest from the progressive Womanhood of this new era against Shakespeare's attitude with respect to his heroines. Doubtless you have been taught in youth, as I was, to consider him as an unsurpassed delineator of female character; doubtless Rosalind and Juliet, Portia and Cordelia, Ophelia and Imogen, Viola and Beatrice, have been held up before you as the ideals of a perfect Womanhood. Doubtless, also, you have believed it all, and never stopped to think that Shakespeare himself was but a man, and that his commentators have been men without being Shakespeares. The masculine conception of feminine character has thus been forced upon us. Shall we submit? (Cries of "No!" "No!") Or shall we test the poet by the higher criticism of advanced Womanly thought? (Cries of "Yes!" "Yes!" and enthusiastic applause.)

'Let us, then, examine the pretensions of Shakespeare. I do not deny that he shows in many cases a remarkable appreciation of the superlative qualities of woman. I will go further: I will admit that many of his heroines, in themselves, are ideally conceived. But – partly in deference to the opinions of his benighted age, now happily far behind us (Cheers), and partly through his own ignorance and his own prejudices – I charge him, before the tribunal of cultivated modern Womanhood, with criminal injustice in placing his heroines in every play at a disadvantage. Hampered by a tyrannical plot, and bound to uncongenial or overbearing heroes, their energies are fettered and their true sphere closed against them. I am prepared to give convincing examples of what I assert (Cries of "Hear!" "Hear!") – examples which will show you that the whole structure of Shakespeare's dramas rests upon the disfranchisement of those heroines whom he is falsely supposed to idealize. (Great excitement.)

'I will begin with the four great tragedies, so-called, "Hamlet," "Macbeth," "Othello," and "Lear." The tragedy is not, as some have falsely asserted, in the nature of the heroes of these plays, but in the misplacement of the heroines. Take, for instance, the gentle, obedient

Ophelia. What cruelty to place her in such an unsuitable position as she is unjustly forced to occupy! The woman for Hamlet, ladies, was Lady Macbeth! (Wild applause.) His weak irresolution would have vanished with that intrepid counselor by his side. "Hie thee hither," she would have said,

> That I may pour my spirits in thine ear,
> And Chastise with the valour of my tongue
> All that impedes thee! ...
> > [*Macbeth*, I.v.26–8]

It is sixteen to one, my sisters, that Hamlet would have killed the king half an hour after Lady Macbeth came to court. (Cheers.) Yet the only use that Shakespeare makes of this heroic woman is to urge forward a hesitating criminal to his doom. (Groans and hisses.) Macbeth was not a bad man – only a weak one. He needed a woman like Portia to manage him. If those celebrated remarks,

> The quality of mercy is not strained,
> It droppeth as the gentle rain from heaven
> Upon the place beneath; it is twice blessed, etc.,
> > [*Merchant of Venice*, IV.i.184–6]

had been made to him by the lady of Belmont, he would have let Duncan go unharmed, and probably been an ornament to the highest circles of Scottish society until the end of his days. And Portia certainly would have been much more in her element ruling the Highland clans, and laying the law as the thane's lady, than as the wife of an ordinary Venetian citizen who had to borrow money from his friend to get married on! (A voice, "Down with Bassanio!") Or, going further, if we study Othello's character, we find that either Beatrice or Juliet would have had no trouble whatever with him. Juliet would have convinced him beyond the possibility of a doubt as to her single-hearted and boundless affection for him alone:

> My bounty is as boundless as the sea,
> My love as deep; the more I give to thee,
> The more I have, for both are infinite;
> > [*Romeo and Juliet*, II.ii.133–5]

while Beatrice, by her quick wit, would have dispersed his jealousies like a summer cloud, laughed away his suspicions, and teased him out of his authority. "Would it not grieve a woman to be overmastered with a piece of valiant dust? to make an account of her life to a clod of wayward marl?" she would have protested saucily; and she would have exposed Iago mercilessly with the help of her keen eye and clever tongue. (Great applause.) As for Lear, Rosalind in Cordelia's place would have had far more tact than needlessly to offend her choleric old father.

> If with myself I hold intelligence,
> Or have acquaintance with my own desires ...
> Never so much as in a thought unborn
> Did I offend your highness,
> [*As You Like It*, I.iii.47–52]

she would have protested tenderly; and I venture to say that she would have been more than a match afterward, single-handed, for Regan and Goneril combined. In a word, ladies, with these heroines in their appropriate places, there would have been no tragedies at all among Shakespeare's works! (Prolonged applause.)

'And what holds good with the great dramas, my hearers, I repeat with regard to the lesser ones. If Miranda or Ophelia had been in Juliet's place, they would never have disobeyed their fathers for a moment, or dreamed of falling in love against orders. Paris would have been accepted without a murmur, and, on the whole, would probably have made a much better husband for either of them than Romeo, who was notoriously fickle. Julius Caesar, if he had had Brutus's Portia, or even Isabella, to wife, instead of that submissive Calpurnia, would in all likelihood have obeyed her warning and stayed at home that day, and there would have been no fatality to mark the ides of March; while a wife like Imogen or Cordelia, frank, yet tenderly loyal, would have cured Timon of Athens of his foolish misanthropy, and made a good citizen out of him in no time. ("Hear!" "Hear!")

'In view of these plain facts, my sisters, can we longer accept William Shakespeare as an authority? (Cries of "No!" "No!") Shall we keep him upon our bookshelves, and read him to our girls? (A voice, "Never!") Shall we not regard him, rather, as well-meaning, but inadequate – blind to the true powers of Woman and the illimitable wideness of her sphere?' Here the lecture concluded amid continued feminine applause, and cries of 'Down with Shakespeare!'

Louise Rossi and Elvina Mary Corbould, active 1874–1909

Little is known of Louise Rossi and Elvina Mary Corbould aside from their publications: Louise Rossi wrote a novel (*An Unconventional Girl*, 1896) a fairy story (*The Disappearance of Anthea*, 1901), and dramatised Tennyson's *The Princess* for schools. Elvina Mary Corbould was a prolific writer of best-selling knitting and sewing books (published under her initials, E. M. C.); she also wrote a story for children, *Sweet Little Rogues* (London, 1876). *Side-Lights on Shakspere* seems to be Rossi's and Corbould's only work of literary criticism. The volume was designed 'to supply the information required by students preparing for examination' but also sought to appeal to 'the general reader'; in 1900 it was reprinted in a 'cheap edition', presumably in order to capitalise on the student market for Shakespeare criticism. Louise Rossi contributed chapters on 'Shakspere and his Sonnets', *As You Like It*, *Julius Caesar*, *Macbeth* and *King Henry VIII*; E. M. Corbould wrote on *A Midsummer Night's Dream*, *King Richard II*, *The Merchant of Venice*, *King Henry V* and *Hamlet*.

L. Rossi and E. M. Corbould, *Side-Lights on Shakspere*. London: Swan Sonnerschein, 1897

L. Rossi: 'Shakspere and his Sonnets'

To facilitate the study of Shakspere's works, the leading authorities have agreed to divide his career of authorship into Four Periods, fancifully named by Prof. Dowden: 1st, 'In the Workshop'; 2nd, 'In the World'; 3rd, 'Out of the Depths'; and 4th, 'On the Heights'. It is of infinite assistance to consider the plays in the chronological order of their production, and thus trace their connection with each other, and with the mind of the author ...

[After 1597] trouble came to Shakspere, although the tide of his worldly prosperity never turned. A shadow fell upon his spirit, which darkened until all his laughter died away, and 'Out of the Depths' welled up solemn thoughts of life and death, and the 'undiscovered bourn' beyond – of sin and suffering – of crime and despair. We have no external evidence of the sorrows of Shakspere's life; the little that we know of them we hear from his own lips, in the broken whispers of the sonnets.

The first thing that strikes the student in the sonnets is the lack of sequence and order in their arrangement. They were published in the year 1609, that is, after the series of tragedies, at the beginning of his Fourth Period, just as he reached 'The Heights'.

Now we have proof that many of the plays were published without the sanction of Shakspere. In the preface to the First Folio, written by his friends Hemynge and Condell, they state that the public had been 'abused with divers stolen and surreptitious copies, *maimed and deformed by the frauds and stealths* of injurious imposters that exposed them' ['To the great Variety of Readers', *First Folio*, 1623: A3] ... Supposing, then, that the sonnets were stolen, it is probable that the malice of the publisher showed itself in two ways: by transposing the order of their arrangement, so that the advantage of context should be lost, and by including in the collection some that were never intended for publication at all. The two last, Nos. 153 and 154, have no connection with the rest, being evidently studies belonging to the 'Venus and Adonis' period. No. 145 is not a sonnet at all, for it consists of octosyllabic instead of decasyllabic lines, and is possibly by another writer. Of the remaining sonnets, 126 have reference to a man and 25 to a woman. The man to whom the sonnets were addressed has been identified as William Herbert, Earl of Pembroke, a lad of not more than nineteen when he was grappled to Shakspere's soul with 'hooks of steel': the woman as Mary Fitton, Maid of Honour to Queen Elizabeth; but on evidence which is not conclusive.

It is hard to think without some tenderness of the woman whom Shakspere loved, but it seems that there is not much good to be said of her. She was false – so false that she could not be true to any one, not even to Shakspere, and she forsook him for his friend. This is the story told in the sonnets, and with it the record of Shakspere's suffering, and how he rose above it, and at last forgave his boy friend. But the scars remained. He speaks of himself as being old before his time: –

> My glass shows me myself indeed,
> Beaten and chopp'd with tann'd antiquity.
>
> (No. 62.)

And again in 138: –

> She knows my days are past the best,

when he could not have been more than thirty-five! There is at Stratford a strong impression, or tradition, that when Shakspere returned to settle there for good, he was literally worn out ...

The interpretation of the sonnets presents one of the greatest difficulties in the whole range of Shaksperian criticism. The mistake seems to lie in considering them as a whole, instead of taking them singly, and remembering that their present arrangement was made without the authority of Shakspere. Most of them are autobiographical, according to the opinion of such competent authorities as Coleridge, Wordsworth, Swinburne and Dowden; and it would seem as though they were written in the manner of a diary, forming thus a context or accompaniment to the plays of their period ...

It is certain that through the sonnets we may approach more nearly to the man Shakspere than by any of the plays. He lays bare the deepest feelings of his passionate heart, and shows a side of his character unrevealed to any friend. Who could have supposed that the man who carved his way from rustic obscurity to triumphant success had in him such a capacity for a feminine depth of devotion? or that a man who had so keen an interest in property could plead so piteously for love? (No. 23).

E. M. Corbould: 'The Life of King Henry V. (1599)'

Shakspere has given us pictures of several kings of England, but incomparably the finest is the portrait of Henry V. This kingly character is one that would appeal very strongly, both to Shakspere's own nature, and to the spirit of the age in which he lived.

Another reason for the subject matter of the play of 'Henry V.' being especially congenial to the bent of Shakspere's mind, is the opportunities it affords for strong situations, varied action, and for free scope to the ardent patriotism which burnt with so clear and brilliant a light among the unforgotten great who made Elizabeth's reign so memorable an epoch in English history ... Shakspere's love of his country seems to have made the production of this especial play a task of peculiar pleasure to him.

'Henry V.' bears the clear stamp of the age in which it was written; a very manly age. To be great – to do great things – seems to have been part of the very being of so many of the distinguished men in Elizabeth's reign. With all their faults or mistakes, a certain stately simplicity and majestic common-sense marks them out, and puts them on a different level from both their predecessors and their successors ...

With respect to the king's early life, and the difference between Prince Hal and King Henry V., Shakspere does not exactly follow the popular tradition of a sudden and miraculous alteration in the whole being and disposition of the monarch. On the contrary, he represents the change in his character as wrought in natural fashion, by the transition from careless irresponsible boyhood to manhood, and the solemn conscientiousness which the newly awakened sense of responsibility would inevitably create in one who felt within himself the power to become a ruler of men.

Allusions to the wildness of Prince Hal's early days, irresistibly remind us of the rumoured vagaries of Shakspere's own youth! Many of his biographers have endeavoured to soften and explain away all that offends their sense of what a great man's youth should have been. But why should we wish this done? Men are moulded out of their faults, as well as developed from their early promise of virtue. An ardent undisciplined youth, full of energy, vigour and health, is like an unbroken colt running wild for want of training. It is only natural that a thoughtless young fellow, endowed with super-abundant life and energy, and love of frolic, should be attracted to the society of other equally daring spirits. And that, without the faintest trace of real vice, he should yet (out of pure love of fun) be led into all manner of scrapes and rash adventures. Yes, in the category of those over whom old men shake their heads and predict a bad end, we may number the two untamed eager spirits who developed into William Shakspere, poet, and Henry V., victor of Agincourt.

In the best imaginative works, the writer never obtrudes his own personality; yet when he is describing a character that he evidently loves, we may be sure that it is in some respects his own; consciously, or unconsciously, he is, to a certain extent, describing himself. Henry's adaptability to all occasions, his enjoyment of jesting, and yet his fitness for war, his vehemence and yet his power of self-command, his ease in all classes of society, reflect Shakspere's own many-sided nature. All through his delineation of Henry V's character, we can clearly trace his own conviction of how life's race ought to be run; we have a distinct view of what he himself would have striven after, had his own disposition been of exactly similar cast, had there existed in his being no complexity of 'Hamlet,' had there been no deep spiritual problems for the profound thinker to solve, and no imaginative fervour to exhaust in the great tragedies of the soul and of life.

Jessie Fremont O'Donnell, 1860–1897

Jessie O'Donnell was born in Lowville, New York State, daughter of the Senator of the State of New York, John O'Donnell. She contributed poems, short stories, sketches and essays to periodicals; her first volume of poetry, *Heart Lyrics*, was published in New York in 1887, followed in 1892 by a novel, *A Soul from Pudge's Corner* (New York). She died at the age of thirty-seven: Anna Randall-Diehl, editor of *The American Shakespeare Magazine* in which O'Donnell's essay on Ophelia appeared, remembered her as 'a young woman of rare attainments as a scholar; a writer who had won her way to merited recognition', and who 'had many engagements to give original readings upon lecture platforms' ('Miss Jessie F. O'Donnell', 1897: 146–7).

The *American Shakespeare Magazine*, founded in 1894, was published in New York 'in the interest of Shakespearean Students throughout the World, and especially in the interest of the Fortnightly Shakespeare Club of New York City', to which O'Donnell belonged. The Fortnightly Shakespeare Club was started by Anna Randall-Diehl and run largely by women: 'few organizations', wrote Margherita Arlina Hamm in 1897, 'have had a more tangible effect upon the literary and club life of American women' ('The Fortnightly Shakespeare Club of New York': 318; on women's Shakespeare study clubs in America, see the entries for Elizabeth Wormeley Latimer (1886) and Kate Richmond-West (1890)). The club encouraged and promoted women as critics of Shakespeare: in February 1897, for instance, three women gave papers at the club-meeting announced as 'Ophelia Night', and eight other women read 'digests upon the character of Ophelia, not exceeding fifty words' ('Ophelia Night', 1887: 92). The Club's journal, *The American Shakespeare Magazine*, published the work of many women writers, and carried essays, critical extracts (such as Anna Jameson's *Characteristics of Women*), book and theatre reviews, news, poetry, notes on Shakespeare clubs and societies, a 'Shakespearian Bureau' advertising women readers, teachers, and lecturers on Shakespeare, and a 'study department' written by Anna Randall-Diehl; by 1897 it was sent to 'every State and Territory, to Canada, the West Indies, England, France and other countries' (December 1897: Editorial Page).

Jessie F. O'Donnell, 'Ophelia', *The American Shakespeare Magazine*, 3 (March 1897), 70–6

O broken lily! how shall one rightly treat of her loveliness, her gentleness, and the awful pathos of her fate? Who shall dare to hint that she was not altogether faultless? One feels as if wantonly crushing some frail blossom in criticising so beautiful a creation, yet such is my thankless task.

To my mind, Ophelia has been much over-rated by writers on this play of 'Hamlet,' and when stripped of the glamor of Shakespeare's magic verse and the lenient tenderness we give always to the dead ... she will be found a simple shallow girl, pure and delicate as a snowflake, but utterly unfit to mate with that marvellous intellect of Hamlet's, or to become the ruler of a kingdom ... She appears but seldom on the stage, and the words she utters are brief and few, yet she occupies in the reader's thought a place quite disproportionate to her actual presence in the play ...

My conception of Ophelia is a young, motherless girl, who had been kept by her father carefully shut away from all knowledge of the world, perhaps secluded in a convent, until a very recent introduction at Court. Mrs. Jameson rightly says in this connection, 'Polonius was just the man to send his son into the world to learn of good and evil, and keep his daughter from every taint' [1832: 188].

Ophelia, then, fresh from a life of privacy, enters the magnificent Court ... meets the young Lord Hamlet, a prince well loved of the people, and possessing every attraction apt to win a susceptible, not over-clever girl, quick to respond to the first words of love whispered to her maiden ear ... Can we wonder that Hamlet seemed to her like a prince from the fairy tales she had scarcely outgrown, that she

> Sucked the honey of his music vows.
>
> [III.i.164]

and that when he sought her love, he did not sue long or vainly? In this early stage of their courtship, there appears to have been no restraint placed upon their intercourse. Ophelia had taken Hamlet's gifts and listened to his tender vows, doubtless whispering hers in return, and when Laertes' warning and Polonius' interdict came, the mischief was already done.

Yet we do not find Ophelia confessing this. This fact has been cited as an illustration of her exquisite sensibility and delicacy; to me, it is the reverse. For while not once confessing her love for Hamlet, or admitting that she has encouraged him, she calmly relates his passion for her; from an exaggerated sense of filial obedience she brings Polonius the letter which Hamlet has written in a despairing moment, a letter which should have been sacred from all eyes but hers, though she chose not to reply to it. Later, she allows herself to be stationed where Hamlet may make love to her, though she knows they are surrounded by spies who will hear and report, perhaps jeer at, every word he utters.

A being of the exquisite delicacy portrayed by Mrs. Jameson could not have done this. A woman who loved Hamlet could not have thus subjected him to the contempt and indifference of outsiders, even as a test of his sanity.

So we come to another question. *Did* Ophelia love Hamlet? Yes, at first, as much as a shallow nature like hers could love. As we have seen, the girl-heart went out to him from the first, not because he was the one man in the universe to her, but, as many girls love, because he was, presumably, the first attractive one who had crossed her path. Then came Polonius' chidings and commands.

Ophelia had never been taught to think for herself; she had doubtless all her life looked up to her father as her guide and guardian; she was as ignorant of his true character as she was of that of Hamlet; she loved and revered him, and, accustomed to implicit obedience, meekly yielded to his commands.

A braver woman might have given as ready obedience, but she would have said: 'I love Lord Hamlet, and though I give him up as you demand, I will be as true to him as to you. He shall not think me inconstant, but know that I deny his suit at your commands.'

But Ophelia was weak and timid, and dare not to her 'own self be true,' [I.iii.78] and thus it happened that when Hamlet most needed a friend – most needed *her* – she miserably failed him.

Mrs Lauch Macluarin, active 1897

Very little is known of Mrs Lauch Macluarin: she is not listed in contemporary or twentieth-century biographical dictionaries, and 'The Woman whom Shakespere did not Contemplate' appears to be her only published work. Macluarin's entertaining article on the lack of business-women among Shakespeare's female characters was apparently read to the Dallas Federation of Literary Clubs under the auspices of 'the Sheakespeare [*sic*] Club of Dallas' in 1897 (the Dallas Shakespeare Club of Texas was open to both men and women members, and reported its activities in *Shakespeariana*). Macluarin's article was printed in *The American Shakespeare Magazine*, the journal of the Fortnightly Shakespeare Club of New York run largely by women, and edited by Anna Randall-Diehl (see the entry on Jessie F. O'Donnell (1897)).

Mrs Lauch Macluarin, 'The Woman whom Shakespeare did not Contemplate', *The American Shakespeare Magazine*, 3 (November 1897), 331–5 (read at the reception given to the board, of the State Federation of Literary Clubs, by the Sheakespeare [*sic*] Club of Dallas, 28 October 1897)

The noble orthodoxy of this club is that Shakespeare has told us everything, about everything, that is, and was, and is to come.

This immensity of message should naturally include the business woman, and Portia is the rudimentary specimen with which we have bolstered up our theory ...

Did Portia make all, or any, of the money which brought adventurers in from every coast? We confess she did not make it; her father left it to her.

Did she become seized and possessed of Belmont through purchase, or foreclosure of mortgage? She did not; her father left it to her.

Was she independent in the choice of a husband? We wish she had been, but admit that fate and her father saw to that matter, too.

Did she spend her money like a business woman? Well – hardly.

Did she have any reason to suppose that Bassanio had a business mind? None that she has stated.

Did he not have a habit of shooting arrows to locate his business ventures? Reluctantly we say, he did.

Was this calculated to inspire the business world with confidence? We think not.

Would Mrs. Hettie Green have bought up his paper at anything below 99 per cent. discount on the face value? We are American, and here we answer firmly, she would not. [Henrietta Green, 1834–1916, was a financier at the US Stock Exchange with holdings in railroad, government and municipal bonds, and a wealthy heiress; she was reputed to be the richest woman in the United States in the late nineteenth century.]

Now for that trip to Venice.

Did Portia proceed in regular business way? Did she say: 'Let me think! Ah, I have it! You know, Nerissa, that it was my some time habit to entertain my mind with legal problems, and to that end I made some books, which those of lesser learning have accepted for authorities. Look me up my work on Bailments, and bring it me. I shall refresh myself with it. You, meanwhile, make ready my best clothes. We must away to Venice.' Did she do and say any of these things? We are sorry, but she did not.

Did she not borrow her argument as well as her cap and gown from one Bellario of Padua? To the best of our information and belief, she did.

Was it not pity for Antonio and love for Bassanio that suggested the stratagem? We think so, and are reminded that business propositions do not originate in the heart, but in the head ...

Business ability is brain convertible into coin ... It does not depend on sentiment and culture, though it is not inconsistent with both. To weep over the honest woman at the corner and tell her to depart, be clothed and fed, notwithstanding ye give her not, may be sentiment, but it is not business. To pity her, to take her home with you (you need a servant, she a situation), put her at some employment (out of reach of the valuables), pay her four dollars per week when you have paid five, and you have a popular combination – sentiment and business ...

I know the business woman takes risks, but she knows something about the maturity of chance, whether she has studied Proctor or not, and that there is such a thing as ratio between risk and profit. She does not make a brilliant rush at nothing and expect to get her hands full.

Another characteristic of the business woman is her thoroughness. She may be elementary, but she is never superficial. She is not all hypothesis, but a fact. She is not the woman who could be, but the woman who is ...

Some may hold that Jessica was a business woman, since she had such facility for acquiring property, but her subsequent proceedings do not support the theory. She showed no interest in the money after she got it. There was some commercial talk about Christian converts raising the price of pork, but it originated with the Gobo boy [*sic*; see III.v.35–6], and not with her. She did not even know that she had affected the market, and when Lorenzo came, instead of asking him where he deposited the money, in whose name, and if he took a receipt, she went off talking about music and moonlight like any other nice, sweet girl in love.

And there was the princess, too, who was sent by the king, her father, to Navarre to attend to some business – something about 'the surrender up of Aquitaine' [*Love's Labour's Lost*, I.i.137] ... Here was a good situation and a beginning for the business woman but Shakespeare did not acknowledge her. For that matter, he had plenty of other situations – maidens out of employment, weeping over the country with no way out of distress or dilemma but a husband, whom it is safe to say he always provided. In fact, a matrimonial agency could not have brought about more matches. Alas, poor girls! There was no business for them but lovemaking, and no bargain but the 'world without end' bargain.

That a woman could not go out in the world wearing her own clothes (mark you, Shakespeare always equipped her with doublet and hose and manly tricks for the struggle), but, as I say, wearing her own clothes and manners, and demand her share of purse and prosperity, through her own exertions respecting and respected, was far from his conception. We do not blame him. How could he anticipate her, great man that he was, any more than he could the typewriter and the phonograph and other pleasant and surprising things we have?

For my part, I am satisfied with Portia as just Portia – a beautiful, clever, kind lady of quality in the best sense of the word, meaning just what our great man intended she should.

Laura Stubbs, active 1898–1913

Little is known of Laura Stubbs aside from her publications: *Stevenson's Shrine: The Record of a Pilgrimage* (1903, reissued 1912), and *Myths and Parables: Adapted from Plato* (1913). Her study 'On Shakespeare's Women as Ideals' was serialised in three parts in *The Stratford-upon-Avon Herald*, a weekly regional newspaper.

Laura Stubbs, 'That Shakespeare's Women Are Ideals', *The Stratford-upon-Avon Herald*, 3 parts: 1 July 1898, 22 July 1898, 29 July 1898

There is not one ideal woman in all of Shakespeare's plays. They are one and all too true to humanity, to heredity, to environment for that. And yet inasmuch as he was poet first, man after, in every one of his heroines there is some trait, or attribute, or virtue idealised, consecrated ... Shakespeare's women are ideals, inasmuch as they constitute the element of redemption in the plays; inasmuch as they purify the moral atmosphere and are strong to sanctify by some splendid combination of word and deed. And here I cannot insist too strongly on the fact that in nine cases out of ten the weakness, insincerity, or moral blackness of the man is thrown into relief against the strength, the virtue, or the stainless purity of the woman. If I have any quarrel with the dramatist it is that his women are, as a rule, too prone to forgive, too ready to condone. Else had Claudio lived and died a bachelor and Hermione remained a beautiful statue to the end of the play. That Bertram was utterly unworthy of the fidelity of Helena in 'All's Well that Ends Well' goes without saying. On this point Mr. Ruskin says 'Shakespeare has no heroes; he has only heroines' [*Sesame and Lilies*, 1865: 185]. There is not one entirely heroic figure in all his plays except the slight sketch of Henry V., exaggerated for the purposes of the stage, and the still slighter one of Valentine in 'The Two Gentlemen of Verona.' ... Whereas there is hardly a play that has not a perfect woman in it steadfast in grave hope and errorless purpose. Cordelia, Desdemona, Isabella, Hermione, Imogen, Queen Katharine, Perdita, Sylvia, Rosalind, Helena, and last, and perhaps loveliest, Virgilia, are all faultless, conceived in the highest heroic type of humanity.

If you study the plots of the plays you must notice that the catastrophe is invariably caused by the fault or folly of a man; the redemption, if there be any, by the wisdom or virtue of a woman ... In 'Romeo and Juliet' the wise and brave stratagem of the girl wife is brought to fatal issue by the reckless impatience of her husband. In 'The Winter's Tale' and in 'Cymbeline' the happiness and existence of two princely households, lost through long years and imperilled to the death by the folly and obstinacy of the husbands, are redeemed at last by the queenly patience and wisdom of the wives. In 'Measure for Measure' the foul injustice of the judge and the foul cowardice of the brother are opposed to the victorious truth and adamantine purity of a woman. In 'Coriolanus' the mother's counsel, acted upon in time, would have saved her son from all evil; his momentary forgetfulness of it is his ruin ... Take, again, Portia, the unlessoned girl, who appears among the helplessness, the blindness, and the vindictive passions of men as a gentle angel bringing courage and safety by her presence, and defeating the worst malignities of crime by what women are fancied most to fail in – incision and accuracy of thought. Such in broad light is Shakespeare's testimony to the position and character of women in human life. He represents them as infallibly faithful and wise counsellors, strong always to sanctify even when they cannot save ... I am not unaware that in order to make a book or a play readable you must have the contrast of the sexes, but in Shakespeare that contrast is mainly in favour of the women. It is, as a rule, they who consecrate and lift the situation above the level of the common place ...

Cordelia is the type *par excellence* of absolute sincerity. So true by instinct that she cannot tell a lie, even though a kingdom and a husband be at stake. Contrast her with Rosalind in 'As You Like It.' 'Why talk we of fathers when there is such a man as Orlando,' exclaims the gay, brave-hearted girl. Had Cordelia made such a speech she would have forfeited all further claim on our sympathy or interest ... In [Rosalind's] wooing of Orlando we have the idealisation of coquetry. Were it not so entirely idealised it would be vulgar. As it is we, too, fall in love with the innocent merriment of the girl, who loves but must needs first tantalise the man of her choice. In Celia we have friendship in absolute perfection. It is Celia's love for Rosalind that endears her to us; without it she would be dull company. Celia in love with Oliver is wholly uninteresting. Celia the friend is ideal ...

Miranda in 'The Tempest' is the type of innocence. She says, with all the naivete of a child, 'How beauteous mankind are,' and only her Eve-like purity can justify such a remark as this to a man whom she has only just seen a few hours ... [Professor Moulton] says, and I think justly, only the most delicate and subtle acting can save Miranda from appearing forward and unwomanly. And, indeed, he conceives her as better left to the imagination of the reader than acted on the stage [Richard Green Moulton, *Shakespeare as a Dramatic Artist: A Popular Illustration of the Principles of Scientific Criticism*, 3rd ed., revised and enlarged, Oxford, Clarendon, 1893: 249–50].

Ophelia is the ideal of sensitiveness. She is the victim of a hyper-sensitive nature, and is too highly-strung and too terse to be a fitting complement to Hamlet. She may be summed up in her own words, 'Sweet bells jangled.' It is only in her hour of distraction, when the acutely-sensitive brain has given way under the cruel strain put upon it, that we realise all that she might have been to Hamlet had not her over-sensitiveness to the nature of family ties driven her to a mistaken sense of duty to a time-serving father and exacting brother. This misconception of duty trammels her independence of action, spoils her clear sense of judgment, and eventually leaves her like drift-wood on the sea of life – the veritable sport of destiny. Miranda remonstrates with Prospero on his treatment of her lover, Ferdinand, while Ophelia is dumbly quiescent in regard to Hamlet, until she almost, but I think not quite, justifies Ruskin's hard summing-up of her character as follows: 'Observe that among all the principal figures of Shakespeare's plays there is only one weak woman, Ophelia, and it is because she fails Hamlet in the critical moment, and cannot in her nature be a guide to him when he needs her most, that all the bitter catastrophe follows' [1865: 185–6] ...

To pass all Shakespeare's heroines in review would occupy too much space. I can only indicate a few of the more striking of the types, which are Volumnia of patriotism, Cordelia of absolute sincerity, Rosalind of coquetry, Celia of friendship, Helena of love repulsed yet ever persisting, Hermione of constancy, Miranda of absolute innocence, Ophelia of sensitiveness, Portia of feminine resource, Isabel of virtue, Viola of unselfishness, Juliet of pure passion of love, Beatrice of wit, Hermione and Helena in 'All's Well' of forgiveness, Imogen, Hero, and Desdemona, of injured innocence, and, finally, Lady Macbeth of the supremacy of the will power ...

If you dispute the fact that Shakespeare's women are the saviours of the situation, if you deny them the power to idealise the plays in any special sense, if you refuse to regard them as types of virtues, still there remains the fact that duly with his historical women Shakespeare has idealised the existing conception ... Read for yourselves the Chronicle Histories of the times and the sources whence he took his plays. Compare the earlier King John of 1591 with his masterpiece written only a few years later, and almost an adaptation of the same. Contrast the two Constances, possibly the earlier one was truer to actual fact, but in the contrast lies the consecration of a mother's love, of a mother's sorrow for a dead child. It is the same with Virgilia, with Calphurnia, with Brutus'

Portia. It is the same with them all. It is especially noticeable in Henry VIII. Here is the story of the wrongs of Queen Catherine [*sic*], saint first, queen after. Shakespeare first compels our admiration, then commands our pity for the injured lady. There was the rough material ready to hand, and out of the unwieldy mass of accumulated facts this poet artist wove his dream of fair women ...

Methinks I can see them yet, this fair garden of girls, lit up by the dream glory of that sacred radiance – glory in the light that never was on sea or land.

Mary Bradford-Whiting, active 1889–1932

Little is known of Mary Bradford-Whiting aside from her publications, the majority of which were of a religious nature, compiled for the Christian Knowledge Society and the Religious Tract Society. Bradford-Whiting also wrote a novel (*The Torchbearers*, 1904) and stories for children (such as *A Thorny Way* for the Nelson's Girls' Library, reprinted twice), and in 1922 she published *Dante and his Poetry*, followed ten years later by *Dante the Man and the Poet* (Cambridge, 1932). The new series of *The Gentleman's Magazine* which published Bradford-Whiting's Shakespeare criticism was a monthly journal carrying fiction, essays, reviews and obituaries. With an estimated circulation of ten thousand in 1870, the journal appealed to an educated middle- to upper-class readership, and by the late nineteenth century regularly printed contributions from women.

Mary Bradford-Whiting, 'Mothers in Shakespeare', *Gentleman's Magazine*, 285:2011 (July 1898), 33–41

Shakespeare is said to have entered into all phases of human experience, and to have depicted all shades of human character, but from his gallery of portraits he has omitted one figure, the absence of which does not seem to have been generally noticed by his critics: the ideal mother, tender, constant, and true, sympathetic alike in the prosperity and adversity of her children.

The 'fathers' of Shakespeare are a well-known and touching group, exhibiting towards their children a tenderness and a display of affection such as we are usually wont to connect with the maternal relationship. Prospero regards the crying infant who impedes his flight not as a burden, but as his best blessing … Lear is mistaken and ill-advised in his affection, and yet it is a warm and tender heart which he pours out upon his daughters … Brabantio's heart is bound up in his 'maid,' so 'tender, fair, and happy,' so that her loss to him … 'engluts and swallows other sorrows' [*Othello*, I.iii.57] …

But the 'mothers' of Shakespeare are singularly few in number. Miranda is motherless, and so are not only Desdemona and Cordelia, but Rosalind,

Celia, Silvia, Hero, Jessica, Imogen, and Helena! Perdita has a mother, it is true; but it is in her relations as a wife, rather than as a mother, that Hermione is represented ... Juliet has a mother, to whose heart of stone she appeals in vain: –

> ... O, sweet my mother, cast me not away! –
>> [*Romeo and Juliet*, III.v.198]

Hamlet has a mother, each remembrance of whom is a pang to his distressed mind, and of whose conduct he can only say: –

> Let me not think on't. Frailty, thy name is woman! –
>> [*Hamlet*, I.ii.146]

... Volumnia is a noble woman; but it is her strength and force of character, and not her tenderness, which are brought before us ...

The play of 'King John' contains a character which has been regarded by many critics as the perfect type of maternal affection. It is solely and entirely as a mother that Constance is represented, and as such she has won a widespread admiration.

But, to the candid reader, it is amply manifest that the passionate grief of Constance is due rather to indignation for her supplanted prince than to love for her 'pretty Arthur' [III.iv.89]. She is a very woman in her want of self-control; as violent as Elinor ... That Constance has been ill-treated there is not a shadow of doubt, but like most women with a grievance she never fails to make the most of it ... with vehement tongue and bitter speech she heaps reproaches upon her mother-in-law, until we feel ... that Elinor had a good deal of justification for her denunciation of Constance as

> An unadvised scold.
>> [II.i.191]

This violence has been excused on the plea that it is only produced by her depth of mother love; but can this theory be proved from the play? Is it not rather true that there is a strain of unreality about her affection for Arthur, finely though she expresses it? A true mother loves best the weakling of her flock, and lavishes most affection on that one which stands most in need of it; but Constance frankly confesses that if her boy had been ugly or deformed she would have experienced very different feelings towards him [III.i.43–50] ... This is not true mother love ...

After studying her character, can we say that [Shakespeare] has here portrayed the perfection of motherhood? Every other phase of woman's life he has entered into with the marvellous sympathy of genius: Cordelia is an ideal daughter, Imogen and Desdemona are ideal wives, Juliet and Miranda are perfect types of 'maiden lovers,' Isabella is an ideal sister,

Celia and Rosalind give the lie to the well-worn sneer at women's friendship; Paulina is a type of the faithful attendant who passes her life in devotion to her mistress ... But where is the ideal mother?

Whether the circumstances of Shakespeare's own life account in any way for his unusual treatment of the maternal character can be now but a matter of conjecture. Of Mary Arden we know too little to determine what she was in herself, or what effect she produced upon her poet son; while, though it is clear that there was a close tie of love between Shakespeare and his daughters, there is nothing to show what terms existed between them and their mother ...

This only we know of certain knowledge, that although Shakespeare has sounded with the plummet of his genius all the depths of woman's love as wife, daughter, sister, servant, and friend, he has left unexplored that mighty power of motherhood which is one of the great elemental forces of the world, and of which, when found in its perfection, it may be truly said that it 'beareth all things, believeth all things, hopeth all things, endureth all things' [1 Corinthians, 13:1].

Bibliography

Primary sources

Abbott, Frances M., The Stratford Club of Concord, *Shakespeariana*, 4 (1887), 327–30.

[Anderson, Mary], *Romeo and Juliet: As Performed by Miss Mary Anderson and Company at the Lyceum Theatre*, London, W. S. Johnson, 1884.

Anderson, Mary Anderson (Madame de Navarro), *A Few Memories* London: Osgood, McIlvaine and Co., 1896.

Anderson, Mary (Madame de Navarro), *A Few More Memories*, London, Hutchinson and Co., 1936.

Miss Mary Anderson as Hermione, anon., *Shakespeariana*, 4 (1887), 283–4.

Appleton, James Morgan, The Delia Bacon Theory, *Appleton's Journal*, 48 (June 1880), 493.

Bacon, Delia Salter, *Tales of the Puritans*, New Haven, A.H. Maltby, and New York, G. C. and H. Cavill, and J. Leavitt, 1831.

Bacon, Delia Salter, *The Philosophy of the Plays of Shakspere Unfolded*, London, Groombridge and Sons, 1857. Reprinted by AMS Press, New York, 1970.

Bacon, Theodore, *Delia Bacon: A Biographical Sketch*, London, S. Low, Marston, Searle and Rivington Ltd., 1888, and New York, Houghton, Mifflin and Co., 1888.

Baillie, Joanna, *A Series of Plays in which it is Attempted to Delineate the Stronger Passions of the Mind* (usually known as *Plays on the Passions*), 3 vols, London, T. Cadell and W. Davies, 1798–1812. Reprinted by Garland Publishers, New York, 1977, and Woodstock Books, New York, 1990.

Baillie, Joanna, *Poems*, Oxford and New York, Woodstock Books, 1994.

Baillie, Joanna, *The Dramatic and Poetical Works of Joanna Baillie*, London, Longman, Brown, Green and Longmans, 1851.

Baillie, Joanna, *The Letters of Joanna Baillie, 1801–1832*, ed. Chester Le Lambertson, 2 vols, Cambridge, MA, 1956.

Balmanno, Mary, *Pen and Pencil*, New York, Appleton and Co., 1858.

Barr, Amelia Edith, *The Young People of Shakespeare's Dramas: For Youthful Readers*, New York, Appleton and Co., 1882.

Barr, Amelia Edith, *All the Days of My Life*, New York and London, Appleton and Co., 1913. Reprinted by Arno Press, New York, 1980.

Bates, Katharine Lee, ed., *Shakespeare's Comedy of The Merchant of Venice*, The Students' Series of English Classics, Boston, New York and Chicago: Leach, Shewell and Sanborn, 1894.

Bates, Katharine Lee, ed., *Shakespeare's Comedy of A Midsummer-Night's Dream*, The Students' Series of English Classics, Boston, New York and Chicago, Leach, Shewell and Sanborn, 1895.

Bates, Katharine Lee, *Shakespeare's Comedy of As You Like It*, The Students' Series of English Classics, Boston, New York and Chicago, Leach, Shewell and Sanborn, 1896.

Bates, Katharine Lee, *The English Religious Drama* [1893], Folcroft, PA, Folcroft Library Editions, 1977.

Bates, Katharine Lee, *Shakespeare: Selective Bibliography and Biographical Notes*, Wellesley, MA, Wellesley College, 1913.

Bates, Katharine Lee, *America the Beautiful, and Other Poems*, [1911], New York, RGA Press, 1969 and Toronto and New York, Maxwell Macmillan International, 1993.

Beale, Dorothea, *Reports Issued by the Schools' Inquiry Commission on the Education of Girls*, London, David Nutt, 1869.

Beale, Dorothea, *King Lear: A Study*, Cheltenham, Thomas Hailing, 1881.

Beale, Dorothea, *Work and Play in Girls' Schools*, London, New York and Bombay, Longmans, Green and Co., 1898.

Beecher, Catharine, *Truth Stranger Than Fiction: A Narrative of Recent Trans-actions, Involving Inquiries in Regard to the Principles of Honor, Truth, and Justice, which Obtain in a Distinguished American University*, New York, privately published by the author, 1850.

Bissell, Emily Perkins, (Priscilla Leonard), The Mistaken Vocation of Shake-speare's Heroines, *The Century Magazine*, LIII:2 (new series vol. XXXI) Christmas number (December 1896), 319–20 [reprinted in *The American Shakespeare Magazine*, 3 (December 1897), 369–72].

Boaden, James, *Memoirs of Mrs. Siddons*, 2 vols, London, Henry Colburn, 1827.

Boaden, James, *Memoirs of Mrs Inchbald: Including her Familiar Correspondence with the Most Distinguished Persons of her Time*, 2 vols, London, R. Bentley, 1833.

Boswell's Life of Johnson, 2 vols, ed. George Birkbeck Norman Hill, Oxford, Clarendon Press, 1964 [2nd ed.].

Bowdler, Henrietta, *The Family Shakespeare*, 4 vols, London, Hatchard, 1807.

Bowdler, John, *Memoir of the late John Bowdler, Esq., to which is Added, Some Account of the late Thomas Bowdler, Esq., Editor of the Family Shakspeare*, London, Longman, 1825.

Brackett, Anna Callender, ed., *The Education of American Girls: Considered in a series of Essays*, New York, C. P. Putnam's Sons, 1874.

Bradford-Whiting, Mary, Mothers in Shakespeare, *Gentleman's Magazine*, 285: 2011 (July 1898), 33–41.

Brooke, Frances (pseud. Mary Singleton), On Barry's *King Lear*, *The Old Maid*, 18 (13 March 1756), 103–6, reprinted in *Shakespeare: The Critical Heritage*, ed. Brian Vickers, Oxford, Clarendon, 1968, vol. 4: 247–9.

Browning, Robert, *New Letters of Robert Browning* eds William Clyde DeVane and K. L. Knickerbocker, New Haven, Yale University Press, 1950.

Campbell, Thomas, *Life of Mrs Siddons*, 2 vols, London, Effingham Wilson, 1834. Reprinted by B. Blom, New York, 1972.

Cavendish, Margaret, Duchess of Newcastle, *CCXI Sociable Letters*, London, William Wilson, 1664. Reprinted by Scolar Press, Menston, 1969 and Garland Publications, New York, 1996.

Churchill, George B., *Shakespeare in America*. Address delivered at the annual meeting of the German Shakespeare Society, 23 April 1906.

Clarke, Charles Cowden, *Shakespeare-Characters: Chiefly Those Subordinate*, London, Elder and Co., 1863.

Clarke, Charles and Mary Victoria Cowden, *Recollections of Writers*, London, Sampson Low and Co., 1878. Reprinted by Centaur Press, Sussex, 1969.

Clarke, Charles and Mary Victoria Cowden, *The Shakespeare Key*, London, Sampson Low, Marston, Searle and Rivington, 1879. Reprinted by F. Ungar Publishing Co., New York, 1961

Clarke, Mary Victoria Cowden, Shakespeare – Studies of Women, *The Ladies Companion*, 1849–54.

Clarke, Mary Victoria Cowden, On Shakspeare's Individuality in his Characters: Shakespeare's Lovers, *Sharpe's London Magazine* (1850), 3 parts: 168–72, 343–8, 138–75.

Clarke, Mary Victoria Cowden, *The Girlhood of Shakespeare's Heroines*, 5 vols, London, W. H. Smith and Son, Simpkin, Marshall and Co., 1850–2. Reprinted by AMS Press, New York, 1974.

Clarke, Mary Victoria Cowden, *The Girlhood of Shakespeare's Heroines; in a Series of Fifteen Tales: A New Edition, Condensed by her Sister, Sabilla Novello*, London, Bickers and Son, 1879.

Clarke, Mary Victoria Cowden, *The Complete Concordance to Shakspere: Being a Verbal Index to all the Passages in the Dramatic Works of the Poet* [1845]. Revised ed., London, W. Kent and Co., and Boston, Little Brown and Co., 1854. Reprinted by AMS Press, New York, 1973.

Clarke, Mary Victoria Cowden, *World-Noted Women: or, Types of Womanly Attributes of all Lands and Ages*, New York, Appleton and Co., 1858. Reprinted by D. Appleton, New York, 1957.

Clarke, Mary Victoria Cowden, Recollections of Mary Lamb, by One Who Knew Her, *National Magazine*, 3 (1858), 360–5.

Clarke, Mary Victoria Cowden, *Shakespeare's Works, Edited, with a Scrupulous Revision of the Text, by Mary Cowden Clarke*, London and New York, Trubner and Appleton and Co., 1860.

Clarke, Mary Victoria Cowden, Helen Kate Furness, *Shakespeariana*, 1 (1883–4), 71.

Clarke, Mary Victoria Cowden, Shakespeare's Self as Revealed in his Writings, *Shakespeariana*, 3 (1886), 145–57.

Clarke, Mary Victoria Cowden, Shakespeare as the Girl's Friend, *Shakespeariana*, 4 (1887), 355–69 [reprinted from *The Girl's Own Paper* (London), June 1887].

Clarke, Mary Victoria Cowden, *My Long Life: An Autobiographical Sketch*,

London, T. Fisher and Unwin, 1896. Reprinted by Scholarly Press, Grosse Point, Michigan, 1968.

Clarke, Mary Victoria Cowden, *Letters to an Enthusiast*, London and Chicago, Kegan Paul, Trench, Trubner and Co., Ltd, and A. C. McClurg and Co., 1904.

Collier, John Payne, *Notes and Emendations to the Text of Shakespere's Plays from Early Manuscript Corrections in a Copy of the Folio, 1632, in the Possession of J. P. Collier*, [1842] 2nd ed., London, Whittaker and Co., 1853.

Craik, Dinah Maria Mullock, Merely Players, *The Nineteenth Century* (September 1886), 416–22.

D., A. R. and K. L. G., A Club of Two, *Shakespeariana*, 4 (1887), 406–7.

Dall, Caroline Wells Healey, *What We Really Know About Shakespeare*, Boston, Roberts Brothers, 1886

[Dall, Caroline], review of Caroline Dall, *What We Really Know About Shakespeare*, Reviews: A New Guide to Shakespeare, anon., *Shakespeariana*, 3 (1886), 141–3.

[Dallas Shakespeare Club], The Dallas Shakespeare Club, *Shakespeariana*, 4 (1887), 325–6.

Doran, John, *A Lady of the Last Century (Mrs. Elizabeth Montagu): Illustrated in her Unpublished Letters; Collected and Arranged, with a Biographical Sketch, and a Chapter on Blue Stockings*, London, 1983. Reprinted by AMS Press, New York, 1973.

Dowden, Edward, *Shakspere: A Critical Study of his Mind and Art*, London, Henry S. King and Co., 1875.

Dowden, Edward, Shakespeare's Portraiture of Women, *Shakespeariana*, 4 (1887) 201–19.

Dox, Julia C., A Grand Shakespearean Festival: The Peoria Women's Club, *American Shakespeare Magazine*, 3 (May 1897).

The Drama, anon., *Shakespeariana*, 3 (1886), 36–42.

[Easton, Miss L. B.], A San Francisco Shakespeare Class, *Shakespeariana*, 3 (1886), 522–3.

Farrar, J. Maurice, *Mary Anderson: The Story of her Life, and Professional Career*, New York, N. L. Munro, 1885.

Faucit, Helena, On Some of Shakespeare's Female Characters, *Blackwood's Edinburgh Magazine*, January 1881 – January 1891.

Faucit, Helena, Lady Martin, *On Some of Shakespeare's Female Characters: By One Who Has Personated Them*, Edinburgh, Blackwood and Sons, 1885. Reprinted by AMS Press, New York, 1970.

Field, Kate, *Adelaide Ristori: A Biography*, New York, John Gray and Green, 1867.

Friends in Council Shakespeare Class of Topeka, The Friends in Council Shakespeare Class of Topeka, Kansas, *Shakespeariana*, 4, 1887, 326.

Furness, Horace Howard, *The Letters of Horace Howard Furness*, ed. Horace Howard Furness Jayne, 2 vols, Boston, Houghton Mifflin, 1922.

Furness, Mrs Horace Howard (Kate), *A Concordance to Shakespeare's Poems*, Philadelphia, J. B. Lippincott and Co., 1875.

Gervinus, Georg Gottfried, *Shakespeare, Commentaries* [1849], trans. F. E. Bunnett, 2 vols, London, Smith, Elder and Co., 1863.

Gilchrist, Anne, *Mary Lamb*, Eminent Women Series, London, W. H. Allen and Co., 1889.

Gilchrist, Fredericka Beardsley, *The True Story of Hamlet and Ophelia*, Boston, Little, Brown and Co., 1889.

Goodwin, Maryette, Shakespeare Society of Wellesley College, *Shakespeariana*, 4 (1887), 73–4.

Griffith, Elizabeth, *The Morality of Shakespeare's Drama Illustrated*, London, Cadell, 1775. Reprinted by Cass, London, and AMS Press, New York, 1971.

Griffiths, L[emeul] M[atthews], The Clifton Shakspere Society, *Shakespeariana*, 1 (1883–84), 159.

Griffiths, L[emeul] M[atthews], *Evenings with Shakspere: A Handbook to the Study of His Works, with Suggestions for the Consideration of Other Elizabethan Literature Containing Special Help for Shakspere Societies*, Bristol, J. W. Arrowsmith, 1889.

Hamilton, Catherine, *Women Writers: Their Works and Ways*, 2nd series, London, Ward, Lock and Bowden Ltd, 1893.

Hamm, Margherita Arlina, The Fortnightly Shakespeare Club of New York, *The American Shakespeare Magazine*, 3 (October 1897), 318–20.

Hampstead Hospital, Ladies Association of, Programme for December 1900, Folger Library Program Inventories (miscellaneous, 2. Lectures, Readings, Recitals).

Handcock, Annette (Countess of Charlemont), Gruach (Lady Macbeth), *Transactions of the New Shakspere Society*, 1st series, 3–5 (1875–8), 194–8.

Hawthorne, Nathaniel, letter to William Davis Ticknor, Liverpool, 16 June 1857, Folger Library MS Y. c. 1363(2).

Hawthorne, Nathaniel, *Our Old Home*, 2 vols, London, 1863. Reprinted by Ohio State University Press, Columbus, Ohio, 1970.

Hazlitt, William, *Characters of Shakespeare's Plays* in *The Round Table: A Collection of Essays*, 2 vols, [1817], reprinted with an introduction by Catherine MacDonald Maclean in Everyman's Library, London, Dent, 1969.

Heard, J., Why Women Should Study Shakespeare, *Manhattan* (June 1884), 620–8.

Holinshed, *Holinshed's Chronicles as used in Shakespeare's Plays*, ed. Allardyce and Josephine Nicoll, London, J. M. Dent and Sons, 1955.

Inchbald, Elizabeth, *The British Theatre*, 25 vols, London, Longman et al., 1806–9. Reprinted by G. Olms, Hildesheim, NY, 1970.

An Indian Imitation of Lamb's Tales from Shakespeare, The Book Table, anon., *The American Shakespeare Magazine*, 3 (March 1897), 94.

Jameson, Anna, *Memoirs of the Loves of the Poets: Biographical Sketches of Women Celebrated in Ancient and Modern Poetry*, [1829], Freeport, NY, Books for Libraries Press, 1972.

Jameson, Anna, *Characteristics of Women, Moral, Poetical, and Historical*, 2 vols, London, Saunders and Otley, 1832. Reprinted as *Shakespeare's Heroines:*

Characteristics of Women, Moral, Poetical and Historical by AMS Press, New York, 1970, Folcroft Library Editions, Folcroft, PA, 1977 and Norwood Editions, Norwood, PA, 1978.

Jameson, Anna, *Characteristics of Women, Moral, Poetical and Historical*, 2nd ed., 'corrected and enlarged', London, Saunders and Otley, 1833.

Jameson, Anna, *Sisters of Charity and the Communion of Labour: Two Lectures on the Social Employments of Women*, [1855] London, Longman, 1859. Reprinted by Hyperion Press, Westport, Conn., 1976.

Jameson, Anna, *Anna Jameson: Letters and Friendships, 1812–1860* ed. Beatrice (Mrs Steuart) Erskine, London, T. Fisher Unwin, 1915.

Jeune, Susan Elizabeth Mary, intr., *Ladies at Work: Papers on Paid Employment for Ladies: By Experts in Severall Branches*, London, A. M. Innes, 1893.

Jones, Chloe Blakeman, *The Lovers' Shakspere*, Chicago, A. C. McClurg and Co., 1897.

Kemble, Frances Anne, *Journal of a Residence on a Georgian Plantation in 1838–1839* [1863], ed. John A. Scott, London, Jonathan Cape, 1961.

Kemble, Fanny, Lady Macbeth, *Macmillan's Magazine*, 17 (February 1868), 354–61.

Kemble, Frances Anne, *Record of a Girlhood*, 3 vols, London, Richard Bentley and Sons, 1878.

[Kemble, Frances Anne], review of Frances Anne Kemble, *Record of a Girlhood*, anon., *Quarterly Review*, 94 (July 1882), 83–123.

Kemble, Frances Anne, *Notes upon Some of Shakespeare's Plays*. London: Richard Bentley & Son, 1882. Reprinted by AMS Press, New York, 1972.

Kemble, Frances Anne, *Further Records, 1848–1883: A Series of Letters*, [1891], New York, B. Blom, 1972.

L., J. V., Shakespeare Societies of America: Their Methods and Work, *Shakespeariana*, 2 (1885), 480–8.

Ladies at Work; see Susan Elizabeth Mary Jeune

Lamb, Mary, pseudonym Sempronia, On Needlework, Letters to the Editor, *British Ladies Magazine* (1815): 257–60.

Lamb, Mary and Charles Lamb, *Tales from Shakespear. Designed for the Use of Young Persons*, 2 vols, London, Godwin's Juvenile Library, 1807.

Lamb, Mary and Charles Lamb, *The Letters of Charles and Mary Anne Lamb*, ed. Edwin W. Marrs, Jr, 3 vols, Ithaca and London, Cornell University Press, 1976.

Lamb, Mary and Charles Lamb, *The Works of Charles and Mary Lamb*, ed. E. V. Lucas, 5 vols, New York, AMS Press, 1968.

Latham, Grace, O Poor Ophelia!, *Transactions of the New Shakspere Society* (1880–5), Pt II, 401–30.

Latham, Grace, On Volumnia, New Shakspere Society, *Monthly Abstract of Proceedings* (February 1887), 69–90.

Latham, Grace, Julia, Silvia, Hero and Viola, New Shakspere Society, *Monthly Abstract of Proceedings* (February 1891), 319–50.

Latimer, Elizabeth Wormeley, *Familiar Talks on Some of Shakspeare's Comedies*, Boston, Roberts Brothers, 1886.

[Latimer, Elizabeth Wormeley], review of Elizabeth Wormeley Latimer, *Familiar Talks on Some of Shakespeare's Comedies*, Literary Notes, anon., *Shakespeariana*, 3 (1886), 579.

Latimer, Elizabeth Wormeley, *Europe in Africa in the Nineteenth Century* [1895], New York, Negro Universities Press, 1969.

Lazarus, Emma, *Songs of a Semite: The Dance to Death, and Other Poems* [1882], Upper Saddles River, NJ, Literature House, 1970.

Lazarus, Emma, Salvini's 'King Lear', *Century Magazine*, 26:10 (May 1883), 89–91.

Lazarus, Emma, *Emma Lazarus: Selections from her Poetry and Prose*, ed. Morris U. Schappes, New York, Emma Lazarus Federation of Jewish Women's Clubs, 1982.

Lee, Jane, On the Authorship of the Second and Third Parts of *Henry VI*, and their Originals, *Transactions of the New Shakspere Society*, 3–5 (1875–8), 3 parts, 219–310.

Leigh-Noel, M., Shakspere's 'Garden of Girls', *New Shakspere Society: Monthly Abstract of Proceedings*, (Oct.–Dec. 1884), 109–12.

Leigh-Noel, M., *Lady Macbeth: A Study*, London, Wyman & Sons, 1884.

Leigh-Noel, M., *Shakspeare's Garden of Girls*, London, Remington & Co., 1885.

Lennox, Charlotte, *Shakespear Illustrated: or the Novels and Histories on which the Plays of Shakespear are Founded, Collected and Translated from the Original Authors*, 3 vols, London, A. Millar, 1753. Reprinted by AMS Press, New York, 1973.

Leonard, Priscilla; see Emily Perkins Bissell

Lewes, Louis, *The Women of Shakespeare*, trans. Helen Zimmern, London, Hodder Brothers, 1894.

Literary Notes, anon., *Shakespeariana*, 4, 1887, 87.

Macauley, Elizabeth Wright, *Tales of the Drama*, Chiswick, London, Sherwood, Neely and Jones, 1822, and Exeter, New Hampshire., Robinson and Towle, 1833.

Macauley, Elizabeth Wright, *The Autobiographical Memoirs of Miss Macauley*, London, privately printed by the author, 1834.

Macauley, E. W., Obituary of, anon., *Gentleman's Magazine*, July 1837, 96.

Macluarin, Mrs Lauch, The Woman whom Shakespeare Did not Contemplate, *The American Shakespeare Magazine*, 3 (November 1897), 331–5.

Marble, Charles C., Some Readers of Shakespeare, *Shakespeariana*, 3 (1886), 385–95.

Martin, Sir Theodore, The Drama in Connexion with the Fine Arts, *Dublin University Magazine*, July 1846, 102–4.

Martin, Sir Theodore, *Helena Faucit (Lady Martin)*, Edinburgh and London, Blackwood and Sons, 1900.

Maxwell, Caroline, *The Juvenile Edition of Shakspeare: Adapted to the Capacities of Youth*, London, Chapple, N. Hailes, Wells and C. H. Williams, 1828.

Mellish, George H., The Fortnightly Shakespeare Club, *The American Shakespeare Magazine*, 3 (March 1897), 92.

Mercier, Anne (Mrs Jerome Mercier), Oedipus and Lear, *Argosy* (November 1879), 368–72.

Montagu, Elizabeth, *An Essay on the Writings and Genius of Shakespear, Compared with the Greek and French Dramatic Poets: With some Remarks upon the Misrepresentations of Mons. de Voltaire*, London, J. Dodsley, 1769. Reprinted by AMS Press, New York, 1966, F. Cass, London, 1970 and A. M. Kelley, New York, 1970.

Montagu, Elizabeth, *The Letters of Mrs Elizabeth Montagu, with Some of the Letters of her Correspondents* [1809–13], 4 vols, New York, AMS Press, 1974

Moulton, Richard Green, *Shakespeare as a Dramatic Artist: A Popular Illustration of the Principles of Scientific Criticism*, 3rd ed., revised and enlarged, Oxford, Clarendon, 1893.

New Books: Delia Bacon on the Philosophy of Shakspere's Plays, anon., *The National Magazine*, July 1859, 149–51.

Novello, Sabilla, ed., Mary Victoria Cowden Clarke, *The Girlhood of Shakespeare's Heroines: in a Series of Fifteen Tales: A New Edition, Condensed by her Sister, Sabilla Novello*, London, Bickers and Son, 1879.

O'Brien, Constance, Shakspere Talks With Uncritical People, *The Monthly Packet*, 1879–91.

O'Donnell, Jessie Fremont, *Heart Lyrics*, London and New York, G. P. Putnam's Sons, 1887.

O'Donnell, Jessie F[remont], Ophelia, *The American Shakespeare Magazine*, 3 (March 1897), 70–6.

Miss Jessie F. O'Donnell, anon., *American Shakespeare Magazine*, 3 (May 1897), 146–7.

O'Neill, Moira, Macbeth as the Celtic Type, *Blackwood's Edinburgh Magazine* (September 1891), 376–83.

Ophelia Night, Shakespeare Clubs and Societies, anon., *Shakespeariana*, 3 (1887), 92.

Palmer, Henrietta Lee, *The Stratford Gallery; or the Shakspeare Sisterhood: Comprising Forty-Five Ideal Portraits*, New York, Appleton and Co., 1859.

Palmer, Henrietta Lee, *Rhode Island Tales: Depicting Social Life During the Colonial, Revolutionary and Post-revolutionary Era*, New York, The Purdy Press, 1928.

The Philadelphia Shakespeare Society, anon., *Shakespeariana*, 4 (1887), 324.

Phipson, Emma, *The Animal-Lore of Shakespeare's Time*, London, Kegan Paul, Trench & Co., 1883.

[Phipson, Emma], review of Emma Phipson, *The Animal-Lore of Shakespeare's Time*, anon., *Shakespeariana*, 1 (1883–4), 62–3.

Porter, Charlotte, An Unprized Maid, *Shakespeariana*, 1 (1883–4), 12–14.

Porter, Charlotte and Helen A. Clarke, Shakespeare Studies: 'A Midsummer Nights Dreame', *Poet-Lore*, 8:8 (1896), reprinted in *Poet-Lore* (1904), 99–106.

Pott, Mrs Henry, *The Promus of Formularies and Elegancies, Being Private Notes circ. 1594, Hitherto Unpublished, by Francis Bacon, Illustrated and Elucidated by Passages from Shakespeare*, London, Longman and Co., 1883.

Preston, Mary, *Studies in Shakspeare: A Book of Essays*, Philadelphia, Claxton, Remsen and Haffelfinger, 1869.

Raikes, Elizabeth, *Dorothea Beale of Cheltenham*, London, Archibald Constable and Co., 1908.

Raymond, Ida; see Mary T. Tardy

Recent Shakspearian Literature, anon., *The Gentleman's Magazine*, n. s. 4 (December 1867), 729–36.

Richmond-West, Kate, *Interpretation of 'A Winter's Tale'*, Chicago, Knight & Leonard Co., 1890. Reprinted in 1890 under the name Kate Richmond-Green.

Ristori, Adelaide, *Studies and Memoirs*, London, W. H. Allen, 1888.

Madame Ristori's English Tour: Opinions of the London Press on Madame Ristori as 'Lady Macbeth' in English, 1882 (Folger Library Collection).

Rolfe, W. J., School Courses in Shakespeare, *Shakespeariana*, 4 (1887), 313–16.

Rossi, L[ouise] and E[lvina] M[ary] Corbould, *Side-Lights on Shakspere*, London, Swan Sonnerschein, 1897.

Royal Shakspearean Club Minute Book, 1845–1900, Stratford Records Office, DR 289/1/1.

Ruskin, John, *Sesame and Lilies* [1865], reprinted in *The Literary Criticism of John Ruskin*, ed. Harold Bloom, New York, Da Capo Press, 1965.

Seymour, Mary, *Shakespeare's Stories Simply Told*, London, T. Nelson and Sons, 1893.

Shakespeare Clubs and Societies, anon., *Shakespeariana*, 3 (1887), 92.

Shakespeare in the Literary Magazines, anon., *Shakespeariana*, 1 (1883–4), 238–9.

The Shakespeare Society of Seneca Falls, anon., *Shakespeariana*, 4 (1887), 179.

Siddons, Sarah, Memoranda: Remarks on the Character of Lady Macbeth, in Thomas Campbell, *Life of Mrs Siddons*, 2 vols, London, Effingham Wilson, 1834.

Siddons, Sarah, Obituary of, anon., *The New Monthly Magazine*, July 1831, 31.

[Sisters' Shakespeare Society], The Sisters' Shakespeare Society, *Shakespeariana*, 1 (1883–4), 159.

Smith, Mary Lilian Rochfort (Teena), *A Memoir, with Three Woodbury-types of her, one each of Robert Browning and F. J. Furnivall, and Memorial Lines by Mary Grace Walker*, London, 1883.

Stowell, Mary B., The Ladies' Literary Club, *Shakespeariana*, 4 (1887), 377.

Stubbs, Laura, That Shakespeare's Women Are Ideals, *The Stratford-upon-Avon Herald*, 3 parts: 1 July 1898, 22 July 1898, 29 July 1898.

Stubbs, Laura, *Stevenson's Shrine: The Record of a Pilgrimage*, Boston, L. C. Page, 1903.

Tardy, Mary T. (pseud. Ida Raymond), *The Living Female Writers of the South*, Philadelphia, 1872.

A Testimonial to Mrs. Mary Cowden Clarke, Author of the Concordance to Shakespeare, New York, privately printed for Subscribers to the Testimonial, 1852.

Theobald, Lewis, *Shakespeare Restored: or, a specimen of the many errors, as well committed, as unamended, by Mr Pope in his late edition of this poet*, London, 1726. Reprinted by AMS Press, New York, 1970.

Thom, William Taylor, Shakespeare Study for American Women, *Shakespeariana*, 1:4 (1884), 97–102.

Tucker, Margaret Isabella, Shakespearian Characters: Constance and Lady Anne, *Shakespeariana*, 1 (1883–4), 229–30 and 305–6.

Wedgwood, Julia, Female Suffrage, Considered Chiefly with Regard to its Indirect Results, *Woman's Work and Woman's Culture: A Series of Essays*, ed. Josephine E. Butler, London, Macmillan and Co., 1869.

Wedgwood, Julia, The 'Midsummer Night's Dream', *Contemporary Review* (April 1890), 580–7.

Wedgwood, Julia, Interview in *The Woman's Herald. The Only Paper Conducted, Written, and Published by Women* (also known as *The Women's Penny Paper*), 4:134 (23 May 1891), 481–2.

Wedgwood, Julia, *Nineteenth Century Teachers and Other Essays*, London, Hodder and Stoughton, 1909.

Wedgwood, Julia, Shakespere's 'Julius Caesar' (A lecture to the St Andrew's Club for Women), *Contemporary Review* (March 1893), 356–68.

Whitman, Walt, Democratic Vistas, in *Collect and Other Prose* [1892], reprinted in *Walt Whitman: Prose Works 1892*, vol. 2, ed. Floyd Stovall, New York, New York University Press, 1964.

Wilson, John, review of Anna Jameson, *Characteristics of Women*, *Blackwood's Edinburgh Magazine*, 33 (January–April 1833), Part I (January 1833) 124–42.

Wilson, John, Mrs Siddons, *Blackwood's Edinburgh Magazine*, 38 (August–September 1834), Parts I and II, 149–72 and 355–72.

Windle, C. F. Ashmead, *Discovery of Lord Verulam's Undoubted Authorship of the 'Shakspere' Works*, San Francisco, J. Winterburn and Co., 1881.

Wood, Adelaide H., Friends in Council Shakespeare Class, Topeka, Kansas, *Shakespeariana*, 4 (1887), 326–7.

Secondary sources

Aaron, Jane. 'Double Singleness': Gender Role Mergence in the Autobiographical Writings of Charles and Mary Lamb' in Susan Gorag Bell, Marilyn Yalom and Lillian Robinson, eds, *Revealing Lives: Autobiography, Biography and Gender*, Albany: State University of New York Press, 1990, 29–41.

Aaron, Jane, Charles and Mary Lamb: The Critical Heritage, *Charles Lamb Bulletin*, 59 (July 1987), 73–85.

Altick, Richard D., *The Cowden Clarkes*, Oxford, Oxford University Press, 1948. Reprinted by Greenwood Press, Westport, Conn., 1973.

Anthony, Katharine Susan, *The Lambs: A Study of Pre-Victorian England*, London, Hammond and Co., 1948.

Argyros, Ellen, 'Intruding Herself into the Chair of Criticism': Elizabetha Griffith and *The Morality of Shakespeare's Drama Illustrated*, in Frederick M. Keener and Susan E. Lorsch (eds), *Eighteenth-Century Women and the Arts*, New York, Greenwood Press, 1988, 283–9.

Ashton, Helen and Katharine Davies, *I Had a Sister: A Study of Mary Lamb, Dorothy Wordsworth, Caroline Herschel, Cassandra Austen*, London, Lovat Dickson Ltd, 1937.

Auerbach, Nina, *Ellen Terry, Player in her Time*, New York, W. W. Norton, 1987.

Auerbach, Nina, Revelations on pages and stages, *Victorian Literature and Culture*, 21 (1993), 1–18.

Auerbach, Nina, Playing Macbeth's Wife: Did the Spirits Come?, seminar paper presented at the Shakespeare Association of America Annual Convention 1994.

Avery, Emmett L., The Shakespeare Ladies Club, *Shakespeare Quarterly*, 7 (1956), 153–8.

Baym, Nina, *American Women Writers and the Work of History, 1790–1860*, New Brunswick, Rutgers, 1995.

Beer, Gillian, Lamb's Women, *Charles Lamb Bulletin*, 6 (1984), 138–43.

Bell, Malcolm, *Major Butler's Legacy: Five Generations of a Slaveholding Family*, Athens and London, University of Georgia Press, 1987.

Blair, Karen J., *The History of American Women's Voluntary Organizations, 1810–1960: A Guide to Sources.* Boston, G. K. Hall and Co., 1989.

Blunt, Reginald (ed.), *Mrs Montagu, 'Queen of the Blues': Her Letters and Friendships from 1762 to 1800*, 2 vols, London, Constable, 1923.

Booth, Michael R., *Three Tragic Actresses: Siddons, Rachel, Ristori*, Cambridge and New York, Cambridge University Press, 1996.

Brady, Marilyn Dell, Kansas Federation of Colored Women's Clubs, 1900–1930, *Kansas History*, 9:1 (spring 1986), 19–30

Carhart, Margaret Sprague, *The Life and Work of Joanna Baillie*, New Haven, Yale University Press, 1923. Reprinted by Archon Books, Hamden, Conn., 1970.

Carlisle, Carole J., The Critics Discover Shakespeare's Women, *Renaissance Papers* (1979), 59–73.

Carlisle, Carole J., Helen Faucit, Lady Martin, *Shakespeare Studies*, 16 (1983), 205–33.

Chielens, Edward E., *American Literary Magazines: The Eighteenth and Nine-teenth Centuries*, London and New York, Greenwood Press, 1986.

Clarke, A. K., *A History of the Cheltenham Ladies' College, 1853–1953*, London, Faber and Faber, 1953.

Craik, T. W., Charles and Mary Lamb: *Tales from Shakespear*, *Charles Lamb Bulletin*, 49 (January 1985), 2–14.

Curle, Richard, ed., *Robert Browning and Julia Wedgwood: A Broken Friend-ship as Revealed in their Letters*, London, John Murray and Jonathan Cape, 1937.

Derrick, Patty S., Rosalind and the Nineteenth-century Woman: Four Stage Interpretations, in *Theatre Survey: The American Journal of Theatre History*, 26 (1985), 143–62.

Desmet, Christy, 'Intercepting the Dew-Drop': Female Readers and Readings in Anna Jameson's Shakespearean Criticism, in Marianne Novy, ed. *Women's*

Re-Visions of Shakespeare, Urbana and Chicago, University of Illinois Press, 1990, 41–57.

Dobson, Michael, *The Making of the National Poet: Shakespeare, Adaptation and Authorship, 1660–1769*, Oxford, Clarendon Press, 1992.

Doody, Margaret Anne, Shakespeare's Novels: Charlotte Lennox Illustrated, *Studies in the Novel*, 19 (1987), 296–310.

Ellegard, Alvar, *The Readership of the Periodical Press in Mid-Victorian Britain*, Goteborg, Elanders Bokryckeri Aktiebolag, 1957.

Erickson, Peter, *Rewriting Shakespeare, Rewriting Ourselves*, Berkeley, University of California Press, 1991.

Fitzmaurice, James, Margaret Cavendish on her Own Writing: Evidence from Revision and Handmade Correction, *Papers of the Bibliographical Society of America*, 85 (1991), 297–307.

Flint, Kate, *The Woman Reader 1837–1914*, Oxford, Clarendon Press, 1993.

Folger Collective on Early Women Critics, ed., *Women Critics 1660–1820*, Bloomington, Indiana, Indiana University Press, 1995.

Forster, E. M., 'Snow' Wedgwood, *Two Cheers for Democracy* [1951], Harmondsworth, Penguin Books Ltd, 1965, 206–7.

Franklin, Colin, *Shakespeare Domesticated. The Eighteenth-Century Editions*, Aldershot, Scolar Press, 1991.

Gallagher, Catherine, *Nobody's Story: The Vanishing Acts of Women Writers in the Marketplace, 1670–1820*, Berkeley, University of California Press, 1994.

Gross, George C., Mary Cowden Clarke: *The Girlhood of Shakespeare's Heroines* and the Sex Education of Victorian Women, *Victorian Studies*, 16 (1976), 37–58.

Gryllis, Rosalie Glynn, *Queen's College 1848–1948*, London, Routledge and Sons, 1948.

Hankey, Julie, Helen Faucit and Shakespeare: Womanly Theater, in Marianne Novy, ed., *Cross-Cultural Performances: Differences in Women's Re-Visions of Shakespeare*, 50–69.

Hankey, Julie, Victorian Portias: Shakespeare's Borderline Heroine, *Shakespeare Quarterly*, 45:4 (winter 1994), 426–48.

Hopkins, Vivian Constance, *Prodigal Puritan: A Life of Delia Bacon*, Cambridge, MA, Belknap Press, 1959.

Jackson, Russell, 'Perfect Types of Womanhood': Rosalind, Beatrice and Viola in Victorian Criticism and Performance, *Shakespeare Survey 32*, (1979), 15–26.

Johnson, Charles F., *Shakespeare and his Critics*, Boston and New York, Riverside Press Cambridge and Houghton Mifflin Co., 1909.

Jones, Kathleen, *A Glorious Fame: The Life of Margaret Cavendish, Duchess of Newcastle, 1623–1673*, London, Bloomsbury, 1988.

Kamm, Josephine, *How Different from Us: A Biography of Miss Buss and Miss Beale*, London, Bodley Head, 1958.

Kennard, A. [Nina H.], *Mrs Siddons*, London, W. H. Allen, 1887.

Lefer, Diane, *Emma Lazarus*, New York, Chelsea House, 1988.

Levine, Lawrence W., *Highbrow/Lowbrow: The Emergence of Cultural*

Hierarchy in America, London and Cambridge, MA, Harvard University Press, 1988.

Levine, Philippa, *Feminist Lives in Victorian England: Private Roles and Public Commitment*, Oxford, Basil Blackwell, 1990.

Mare, Margaret, and Alicia C. Percival, *Victorian Best-seller: The World of Charlotte M. Yonge*, London, George G. Harrap and Co. Ltd., 1947.

Marsden, Jean I. ed., *The Appropriation of Shakespeare*, London, Harvester-Wheatsheaf, 1991.

Martin, Theodora Penny, *The Sound of Our Own Voices: Women's Study Clubs 1860–1910*, Boston, Beacon Press, 1987.

Melchiori, Barbara Arnett, Undercurrents in Victorian Illustrations of Shakespeare, in Werner Habicht, D. J. Palmer and Roger Pringle, eds, *Images of Shakespeare*, London and Toronto, Associated University Press, 1988.

Miller, Betty, *Robert Browning: A Portrait*, London, John Murray, 1952.

Misenheimer, Carolyn, The Pleasures of Early Enlightenment: The Lambs' Tales from Shakespeare, *Charles Lamb Bulletin*, 67 (July 1989), 69–82.

Moers, Ellen, *Literary Women*, London, W. H. Allen, 1977.

Myers, Elisabeth P., *Katharine Lee Bates, Girl Poet*, Indianapolis, Bobbs-Merrill, 1961.

Myers, Sylvia Harcstark, *The Bluestocking Circle: Women, Friendship, and the Life of the Mind in Eighteenth-Century England*, Oxford, Clarendon, 1990.

Newton, Judith, Engendering History for the Middle Class: Sex and Political Economy in the *Edinburgh Review*, in Linda M. Shires, ed., *Rewriting the Victorians: Theory, History and the Politics of Gender*, London and New York, Routledge, 1992.

Novy, Marianne, ed., *Women's Re-Visions of Shakespeare*, Urbana and Chicago, University of Illinois Press, 1990.

Novy, Marianne, ed., *Cross-Cultural Performances: Differences in Women's Re-Visions of Shakespeare*, Urbana and Chicago, University of Illinois Press, 1993.

Novy, Marianne (ed.), *Engaging with Shakespeare: Responses of George Eliot and Other Women Novelists*, Athens, Georgia and London, University of Georgia Press, 1994.

Pares, Martin, *A Pioneer: In Memory of Delia Bacon, February 2nd 1811 to September 2nd 1859*, London, Francis Bacon Society, 1958.

Perrin, Noel, *Dr Bowdler's Legacy*, New York, Atheneum, 1969.

Peterson, Jean, Victorian Secrets: Sexual Knowledge and Shakespearean Daughters in the 19th Century, seminar paper presented at the Shakespeare Association of America Annual Convention 1994.

Reynolds, Myra, *The Learned Lady in England, 1650–1750*, Boston, Houghton Mifflin, 1921.

Robbins, Fred W., Scribner's Monthly, in Edward E. Chielens, ed., *American Literary Magazines: The Eighteenth and Nineteenth centuries*, London and New York, Greenwood Press, 1986, 364–9.

Roberts, Sasha, Shakespeare 'creepes into the womens closets about bedtime': Women Reading in a Room of Their Own, in Gordon McMullan (ed.),

Renaissance Configurations: Gender, Bodies, and Space in Early Modern England, London, Macmillan, forthcoming.

Robinson, Herbert Spencer, *English Shakesperian Criticism in the Eighteenth Century*, New York, H. W. Wilson Co., 1932.

Rogers, Katharine M., Britian's First Woman Drama Critic: Elizabeth Inchbald, in Mary Anne Schofield and Cecilia Macheski (eds), *Curtain Calls: British and American Women and the Theater, 1660–1820*, Athens, Ohio University Press, 1991, 277–90.

Russell, Anne E., 'History and real life': Anna Jameson, *Shakspeare's Heroines* and Victorian Women, *Victorian Review: The Journal of the Victorian Studies Association of Western Canada*, 17:2 (winter 1991), 35–49.

Schwartz, Narda Lacey, *Articles on Women Writers: A Bibliography*, Santa Barbara, ABC-CLIO, 1986.

Sedgwick, Ellery, The Atlantic Monthly, in Edward E. Chielens, ed., *American Literary Magazines: The Eighteenth and Nineteenth Centuries*, London, Greenwood Press, 1986.

Shattock, Joanne and Michael Wolff, *The Victorian Periodical Press: Samplings and Soundings*, Leicester and Toronto, Leicester University Press and University of Toronto Press, 1982.

Shevelow, Kathryn, *Women and Print Culture: The Construction of Femininity in the Early Periodical*, London and New York, Routledge, 1989.

Small, Miriam Rossiter, *Charlotte Ramsay Lennox: An Eighteenth Century Lady of Letters*, New Haven, Yale University Press, 1935.

Steadman, Florence Cecily, *In the Days of Miss Beale*, London, E. J. Burrow, 1931.

Stedman, Jane W., Theatre, in J. Don Vann and Rosemary T. Van Arschel, eds, *Victorian Periodicals and Victorian Society*, Aldershot, Scolar Press, 1994, 162–76.

Taylor, Gary, *Reinventing Shakespeare: A Cultural History from the Restoration to the Present*, New York, Weidenfeld and Nicolson, 1989.

Thomas, Clara, *Love and Work Enough: The Life of Anna Jameson*, London, University of Toronto Press, 1967.

Thompson, Ann, Pre-Feminism or Proto-Feminism?: Early Women Readers of Shakespeare, *Elizabethan Theatre*, 14 (1996), 195–211.

Ward, Masie, *Robert Browning and his World: Two Robert Brownings?*, London, Cassell, 1969.

Wedgwood, Barbara Lee, The Mysterious Disappearance of the Browning–Wedgwood Letters, *Browning Society Notes*, 11:1 (April 1981), 1–7.

Wedgwood, Barbara Lee, *A Critical Study of the Life and Works of Julia Wedgwood*, Ph.D., University of London, 1983.

Westfall, Alfred Van Rensselaer, *American Shakespearean Criticism, 1607–1865*, London and New York, Benjamin Blom, 1968.

Williamson, Marilyn L., *Raising Their Voices: British Women Writers 1650–1750*, Detroit, Wayne State University Press, 1990.

Wise, Winifred Esther, *Fanny Kemble*, New York, Putnam, 1966.

Wolfson, Susan J., Explaining to her Sisters: Mary Lamb's *Tales from Shakespear*, in Marianne Novy, ed., *Women's Re-Visions of Shakespeare*, Urbana and Chicago, University of Illinois Press, 1990, 16–40.

Woof, Pamela, Dorothy Wordsworth and Mary Lamb, Writers, *Charles Lamb Bulletin*, 66–7 (April–July 1989), 82–93.

Woolford, John, Periodicals and the Practice of Literary Criticism, 1855–64, in Joanne Shattock and Michael Wolff, eds, *The Victorian Periodical Press: Samplings and Soundings*, Leicester and Toronto, Leicester University Press and University of Toronto Press, 1982, 109–43.

Young, Bette Roth, *Emma Lazarus in her World: Life and Letters*, Philadelphia, Jewish Publication Society, 1995.

Ziegenrucker, Emil, *Joanna Baillie's 'Plays on the Passions'*, Hamburg–Barmbeck, Druck von F. Starch, 1909.

Ziegler, Georgianna, Accommodating the Virago: Nineteenth-century Representations of Lady Macbeth, seminar paper presented at the Shakespeare Association of America Annual Convention 1994.

Ziegler, Georgianna, Women Artists and the Boydell Shakespeare Gallery: A Brief History, seminar paper presented at the Shakespeare Association of America Annual Convention, 1995.

Ziegler, Georgianna, Suppliant Women and Monumental Maidens: Shakespeare's Heroines in the Boydell Gallery, in Walter Pape and Frederick Burmick, (eds), *Boydell's Shakespeare Gallery*, Bottrop, Verlag Peter Pomp, 1966, 89–102.

Dictionaries

[Allibone's] *A Critical Dictionary of English Literature and British and American Authors, living and deceased*, Allibone, Samuel Austin, Philadelphia and London, J. B. Lippincott and Trubner and Co., [1859] 1877.

American Authors, 1600–1900, Kunitz, S. J. and H. Haycraft, New York, H. W. Wilson Co., 1938.

American Women Writers, Mainiero, Lina, ed., 2 vols, New York, Frederick Ungar, 1980.

American and Theatrical Biography: A Directory, Wearing, J. P., London and Metuchen, N.J., The Scarecrow Press, 1979.

Appleton's Cyclopaedia of American Biography, Wilson, James Grant and John Fiske, 6 vols, New York, Appleton and Co., 1888–9.

A Supplement to Appleton's Cyclopaedia of American Biography, Wilson, James Grant, vol. 7, New York, Appleton and Co., 1901.

A Biographical Dictionary of Women Artists in Europe and America since 1850, Dunford, Penny, London and New York, Harvester Wheatsheaf, 1990.

Biography and Genealogy Master Index: 1981–85 Cumulation, McNeil, Barbara, ed., Detroit, Gale Research Co., 1985.

Biography and Genealogy Master Index. 1986–90 Cumulation, McNeil, Barbara, ed., Detroit, New York, Fort Lauderdale and London, Gale Research Co., 1990.

British Women Writers: A Critical Reference Guide, Todd, Janet, ed., New York, Continuum, 1989.

Bryan's Dictionary of Painters and Engravers, enlarged ed. in 5 vols, London, Bell and Sons, 1904.

The Cambridge Guide to the Theatre, Banham, Martin, ed., Cambridge, Cambridge University Press, 1992.

Dictionary of American Authors, Adams, Oscar Fay, Boston and New York, Houghton, Mifflin and Co., [1897], 4th ed. revised and enlarged, 1904.

Dictionary of American Biography, Johnson, Allen and Dumas Malone, eds, 20 vols, New York, Charles Scribner's Sons, 1928–36.

Dictionary of American Biography, London, Oxford University Press, 1933.

The Dictionary of British Artists, 1880–1940, Johnson, J. and A. Greutzner, Woodbridge, Antique Collectors Club, 1976.

Dictionary of British Eighteenth Century Painters in Oils and Crayons, Waterhouse, Ellis, Woodbridge, Antique Collectors Club, 1981.

Dictionary of Literary Biography. Volume 71: American Literary Critics and Scholars, 1880–1900, Detroit, Bruccoli Clark Layman, 1988.

Dictionary of National Biography, Leslie Stephen, ed., London, Smith, Elder and Co., 1887.

A Dictionary of North American Authors deceased before 1950, Wallace, William Stewart, Toronto, Ryerson Press, 1951.

The Dictionary of Victorian Painters, Wood, Christopher, 2nd ed., Woodbridge, Antique Collectors Club, 1978.

The Feminist Companion to Literature in English, Virginia Blain, Patricia Clements, and Isobel Grundy, eds, London, Batsford, 1990.

Feminist Periodicals, 1855–1984: An Annotated Critical Bibliography of British, Irish, Commonwealth and International Titles, David Doughan and Denise Sanchez, Brighton, Harvester, 1987.

Historical Biographical Dictionaries Master Index, McNeil, Barbara and Miranda C. Herbert, eds, Detroit, Gale Research Co., 1980.

National Cyclopaedia of American Biography, 57 vols, New York and Clifton, NJ, James T. White and Co., 1892–1977.

Notable American Women 1607–1950: A Biographical Dictionary, Boyer, Paul S., Edward T. James, and Janet Wilson James, eds, 3 vols, Cambridge, MA, Belknap Press, 1971.

The Oxford Companion to American Theatre, Bordman, Gerald, New York and Oxford, Oxford University Press, 1984.

The Oxford Companion to Children's Literature, Carpenter, H. and Mari Prichard, eds, Oxford, Oxford University Press, 1984.

The Oxford Companion to the Theatre, Hartnoll, Phyllis, ed., Oxford, Oxford University Press, 1983.

The Oxford Guide to British Women Writers, Shattock, Joanne, Oxford, Oxford University Press, 1993.

The Waterloo Directory of Victorian Periodicals, 1824–1900, Phase I, Wolff, Michael, North, John S. and Deering, Dorothy (eds), Montreal, Wilfred Laurier University Press, n.d.

Wellesley Index to Victorian Periodicals, 1824–1900, ed. Walter E. Houghton, 5 vols, Toronto, University of Toronto Press, 1966–89.

A Woman of the Century: Biographical Sketches, accompanied by Portraits, of Leading American Women, Frances Elizabeth Willard and Mary Ashton Livermore, Buffalo, NY, C. W. Moulton, 1893.

Woman's Who's Who of America, Leonard, John William, New York, American Commonwealth Co., 1915.

Works by Shakespeare

Page numbers in *italics* refer to figures

Index

Page numbers in *italics* refer to figures

Lamb, Charles, 49–50, 81
Lamb, Mary Anne, 2, 6, 46, 49–50, 81; *Letters of Charles and Mary Anne Lamb*, 49; 'On Needlework', 49; *Tales from Shakespear*, 46, 50–3, 62, 81, 103
language, 12–13, 18, 25–8, 33, 43, 47, 56; *see also* characters, female; obscenity
Latham, Grace, 3, 132, 142, 165, 197–8; 'Hero', 170–1; 'O Poor Ophelia', 165–8; 'Viola', 171–2; 'On Volumnia', 168–70
Latimer, Elizabeth Wormeley, 3, 6–7, 132, 142, 160, 196, 214, 225, 240; *Familiar Talks on Some of Shakspeare's Comedies*, 196, 198–201; *Our Cousin Veronica*, 196
Lazarus, Emma, 2, 157, 233; 'Salvini's "King Lear"', 158–9, 161, 203
Lee, Jane, 132
Legouve, 203
Leigh-Noel, M., 3, 5–6, 173, 198; *Lady Macbeth: A Study*, 173–6; *Shakspeare's Garden of Girls*, 132, 146, 173, 176–83
Lennox, Charlotte, 2, 6, 15; *Shakespear Illustrated*, 15–21, 44
Leonard, Priscilla; *see* Emily Perkins Bissell
libraries, 50, 67, 69, 70, 86, 87; Birmingham Shakespeare Library, 83; British Library, 66; Brotherton Collection, Leeds, 96; Shakespeare Centre, Stratford-upon-Avon, 184
Lippincott's, 157, 225
London, 40, 42, 49, 56, 58, 104, 121, 127, 177, 203, 212, 228; Bishop of, 46; *see also* theatres
Longman, Thomas Norton, 42
Lyttelton, Lord George, 22

Macauley, Elizabeth Wright, 58; *Tales of the Drama*, 59–61
Macluarin, Mrs Lauch, 198, 243; 'The Woman whom Shakespeare did not Contemplate', 243–5
McMahan, Anna B., 197
Macmillan's Magazine (U.K.), 116–20, 212
Macready, Charles William, 184
MacWhorter, Alexander, 104
madness, 28, 49, 104; in Shakespeare, 21, 28, 108, 116, 158, 167, 205–7, 209–11, 248
Malcolm II, 133
Malone, 116
Manning, Frederick George, 49, 133
Marmontel, Jean-François, 29
marital relations, 1, 5, 83, 88–9, 99–100, 102, 116; in Shakespeare, 32, 35, 38–9, 56–7, 76, 88–9, 106, 114, 119–20, 133–4, 145, 149, 155, 163–4, 169, 173–6, 182, 194–5, 199–200, 202, 204–5, 207, 211, 214, 224, 234–5, 247
marriage in Shakespeare, 33, 51–3, 56, 99–100, 144, 178, 183, 245
Marshall, Isabel, 132
Martin, Theodore, 184
Martineau, Harriet, 212
masculinity, 75–6, 84–5, 95, 102, 118–20, 137, 144, 175, 180, 200, 238; relations between men, 61, 147, 237; *see also* characters, male; effeminacy; fatherhood
Maxwell, Caroline, 62; *Juvenile Edition of Shakspeare*, 62–5
Medea, 203
Mercier, Anne (Mrs Jerome), 135; 'Oedipus and Lear', 135–7
Middleton, Thomas, 27
Miles, A. H., 116
Milton, John, 27
Mirra, 203
monarchy, 105–9, 140, 158, 218–19, 238; *see also* political relations
Montagu, Elizabeth, 2, 6, 22–3, 30, 39, 47; *An Essay on the Writings and Genius of Shakespear*, 23–8
Montgomery, William, 9
The Monthly Packet, 142, 165, 198
morality, 16, 24, 25, 27, 30–1, 36, 39, 43, 67, 70, 72, 78, 90–1, 101, 139,

Poetry Society of America (New York City), 160; Religious Tract Society (U.K.), 250; Royal Shakespearean Club of Stratford-upon-Avon, 213–14; St Andrew's Club for Women (Scotland), 3, 213, 217; Shakespeare Association of America, 225; Shakespeare Ladies Club (U.K.), 2, 213; Shakespeare Society of New York, 106; Shakespeare Society of Wellesley College (Massachusetts), 197, 225; Sisters' Shakespeare Society (New Jersey); Sorosis (New York City), 196; Stratford Club of Concord (New Hampshire), 196–7; Twentieth Century Woman's Club (U.S.A.), 232–3; West End Reading Room (Delaware), 232; Woman's Christian Temperance Union (U.S.A.), 232

Somerset, Duchess Dowager of, 168

Sophocles, 24, 33, 135–7

Sorbonne, Paris, 160

sources; *see* Shakespeare, use of sources

The Spectator, 212

Staples, Mrs John, 193

Statue of Liberty, U.S.A., 157

Steevens, George, 116

Stevenson, Robert Louis, 116

Stowe, Harriet Beecher, 150

The Stratford-upon-Avon Herald, 246

Stuart, Mary, 203

Stubbs, Laura, 246; 'That Shakespeare's Women are Ideals', 246–9

suffrage, 126–7, 145, 150, 218; Fifteenth Amendment, 208; women's, 6–7, 114, 138, 150, 160, 182, 196, 212, 232–3

Swanwick, Anna, 184, 192

Tacitus, 26

Tardy, Mary T., 110

Tate, Nahum, 44

Taylor, Gary, 9

Tennyson, Lord Alfred, 199, 225, 236

Terry, Ellen, 173

Thackeray, W. M., 212

theatres; Covent Garden, London, 29, 115; Drury Lane, London, 54, 56, 115; King's Head, Worcester, 54; Lyceum, London, 228; Smock Alley Theatre Company, Dublin, 29; Theatre Royal, Dublin, 29

Theobald, Lewis, 1, 116

Thom, William Taylor, 6–7

Thoreau, Henry David, 157

Ticknor, George, 196

Todd, Janet, 46

Trollope, Anthony, 116

Tucker, Margaret Isabella, 163; 'Constance', 163; 'Lady Anne', 164

Twain, Mark, 157

Uncle Remus, 202

United Kingdom, 203; Bristol, 42; Lancashire, 150; Manchester, 54, 212; Norwich, 42; Stratford-upon-Avon, Warwickshire, 159, 183, 246; Suffolk, 42; Torquay, 221; Worcestershire, 228; *see also* England; London

United States of America, 68, 116, 203; Connecticut, 104; Delaware, 232; Georgia, 115; Illinois, 232; Kansas, 154, 197; Kentucky, 228, 230; Louisiana, 130; Maryland, 126, 196; Massachusetts, 116, 126, 130, 160, 196; Michigan, 232; Minnesota, 232; Ohio, 104; Oklahoma, 232; New England, 126, 131, 196, 225; New Hampshire, 58, 196; New Jersey, 104, 196, 208; New York State, 15, 208, 232, 240; Pennsylvania, 160; South, 110, 115, 202, 229; Texas, 150, 243; Virginia, 6, 196; Wyoming, 232; *see also* Baltimore, New York City, Philadelphia

universities; *see named institutions*; education

University College, London, 132, 197

D'Urfey, Thomas, 19